1004899280

D1442200

Strategic Issues in International Retailing

Existing concepts and theories of international business fit uneasily with international retailing. New ideas and approaches are needed to understand the activity of international retailers. *Strategic Issues in International Retailing* illustrates and evaluates the strategies of international retailers, exploring concepts and developing theories that enable an understanding of retailing at an international level.

This accessible and informed text is illustrated with in-depth case studies of international retailers including:

- Inditex-Zara
- Carrefour
- The Boots Group PLC
- Royal Ahold
- Tesco.

Strategic Issues in International Retailing is a significant contribution to the field, and a must-read for all those studying or working in international retail.

John Dawson is Professor of Marketing at the University of Edinburgh, Scotland. He also holds professorial positions at ESADE, Barcelona, Spain, the University of Stirling, Scotland, and the University of Marketing and Distribution Sciences, Kobe, Japan.

Roy Larke is a professor at the University of Marketing and Distribution Sciences, Kobe, Japan where he teaches retailing.

Masao Mukoyama is Professor of Retailing and Dean of the Graduate School of Marketing and Distribution Sciences in Kobe, Japan.

Strategic Issues in International Retailing

Edited by

John Dawson, Roy Larke and Masao Mukoyama

Routledge
Taylor & Francis Group

LONDON AND NEW YORK

LIBRARY
GRANT MacEWAN
COLLEGE

First published 2006
by Routledge
2 Park Square, Milton Park, Abingdon, Oxon OX14 4RN

Simultaneously published in the USA and Canada
by Routledge
270 Madison Ave, New York, NY 10016

Routledge is an imprint of the Taylor & Francis Group, an informa business

© 2006 Edited by John Dawson, Roy Larke and Masao Mukoyama

Typeset in Perpetua and Bell Gothic by
Florence Production Ltd, Stoodleigh, Devon
Printed and bound in Great Britain by
MPG Books Ltd, Bodmin

All rights reserved. No part of this book may be reprinted or
reproduced or utilized in any form or by any electronic, mechanical,
or other means, now known or hereafter invented, including
photocopying and recording, or in any information storage or
retrieval system, without permission in writing from the publishers.

British Library Cataloguing in Publication Data
A catalogue record for this book is available from the British Library

Library of Congress Cataloging in Publication Data
   Strategic issues in international retailing/edited by John Dawson,
   Roy Larke, and Masao Mukoyama.
        p. cm.
   Includes bibliographical references and index.
   1. Retail trade.   2. International trade.   3. Strategic planning.
   I. Dawson, John A.   II. Larke, Roy, 1962–   III. Mukoyama, Masao.
HF5429.S77 2006
658.8'7–dc22   2005030133

ISBN10: 0–415–34370–4 (hbk)
ISBN10: 0–415–34371–2 (pbk)
ISBN10: 0–203–63962–6 (ebk)

ISBN13: 978–0–415–34370–1 (hbk)
ISBN13: 978–0–415–34371–8 (pbk)
ISBN13: 978–0–203–63962–7 (ebk)

Contents

Figures

Tables

TABLES

Notes on contributors

Steve Burt is Professor of Retail Marketing at the Institute for Retail Studies, University of Stirling, Scotland, and a visiting professor at Lund University in Sweden. He is also President of the European Association for Education and Research in Commercial Distribution. His research interests include structural change in retailing, retail branding and retail internationalization, and he has published in journals such as the *British Journal of Management*, *European Journal of Marketing*, *Journal of Marketing Management* and the *International Review of Retail Distribution and Consumer Research*.

Sang Chul Choi is Professor of Marketing and Distribution Systems at the Faculty of Commerce, University of Marketing and Distribution Sciences, Kobe, Japan. He worked as a senior researcher at KIET (the Korea Institute for Industrial Economics and Trade) in Seoul, Korea for several years before moving to Japan where he obtained a Ph.D. in Commerce at Kobe University. His research is in the long-term and continual (*keiretsu*) relationships between manufacturers and retailers in the Japanese market and in comparative research on the distribution system in East Asian countries.

Keri Davies is a senior lecturer in the Department of Marketing at the University of Stirling. His research interests lie in the area of retail internationalization and retail location. Recent work has included a study of the shops run by Scottish community cooperatives and research into the role of the large trading houses or *sogo sosha* in the restructuring of Japanese retailing.

John Dawson is Professor of Marketing at the University of Edinburgh, Scotland. He also holds professorial positions at ESADE, Barcelona, Spain, the University of Stirling, Scotland, and the University of Marketing and Distribution Sciences, Kobe, Japan. He has also held visiting positions elsewhere in Europe,

South Africa, the US, Australia and Japan. He is a fellow of the Royal Society of Edinburgh. His research interests are in international retailing, retail innovation, measurement of performance in retailing and the interrelationships between European and Asian approaches to retail management.

Marc Dupuis is Emeritus Professor at the European School of Management (ESCP-EAP), Paris. He has been a visiting professor at universities in the US, Argentina, Vietnam, Thailand and Japan, and is the author of several books and articles on retailing. As a consultant he remains in close contact with retailers and their suppliers. His research interests are international retailing, innovation in retailing and retail strategies. He is the founder of CERIDICE (the International Research Centre for Retailing and E-Commerce) located in Paris.

Jean Fournioux is a graduate from HEC-Paris, School of Management. After several positions in marketing he was in charge of international development for the French retail chain FNAC. He was responsible for opening stores in Brazil, Taiwan and six countries in Europe. He is now a director of the international wine merchant Castel where his responsibilities include sales and marketing.

Roy Larke is a professor at the University of Marketing and Distribution Sciences, Kobe, Japan where he teaches retailing. He is the author of numerous articles about Japanese retailing, the distribution system and consumer behaviour, and he is currently editor-in-chief of *Japan Consuming* magazine. He is author of *Japanese Retailing*, published by Routledge, 1994, and co-author of *Japan – A modern retail superpower*, published by Palgrave Macmillan, 2005. In addition to academic work, he consults for a wide range of companies, particularly those looking to enter the Japanese market.

Masao Mukoyama is Professor of Retailing and Dean of the Graduate School of Marketing and Distribution Sciences in Kobe, Japan. He is also a chairman of the Society of Asian Retailing and Distribution. He received a Ph.D. in Commerce from Kobe University in 1996. His research interests are in retail internationalization, behaviour of innovative retailers and private brand development in which he has published several books and papers.

Acknowledgements

The editors and contributors wish to acknowledge the support and help given by executives of many retail firms and support agencies who have spent time discussing retailing. We thank them for their forbearance and help in our understanding of the complexities of international retailing. Thanks are also extended to the Ministry of Education, Culture, Sports, Science and Technology of Japan for the financial support provided for the research project that underpins the studies on which this book is based. This book is one of a series of results from this project and would not have been possible without the generous support of the research grant from the Ministry.

Abbreviations

AMS	Associated Marketing Services
BCM	Boots Contract Manufacturing
BHI	Boots Healthcare International
BRI	Boots Retail International
BTC	Boots the Chemist
CAD	computer aided design
CAM	computer aided manufacturing
CWT	Carrefour World Trade
DMG	Direct Marchandises Groupe
ECR	efficient consumer response
EDLP	Every Day Low Prices
EMD	European Marketing Distribution
EVA	Eerstelijns Voorzieningen Almere
FAQ	frequently asked questions
FMCG	fast moving consumer goods
GNX	Global Net Exchange
GRDI	Global Retail Development Index
ICT	information and communication technologies
IRTS	International Retail and Trade Services
ITM	Intermarché
MGB	Metro Group Buying
OLI	ownership, location, internalization
OTC	over the counter
PDA	personal digital assistant
POS	point of sale
ROCE	return on capital employed
SKU	stock keeping units
UNCTAD	United Nations Conference on Trade and Development
WTO	World Trade Organization

Chapter 1

The increase in international activity by retailers

John Dawson and Masao Mukoyama

INTRODUCTION

Retailing is now an international activity. The upsurge, during the last two decades of the twentieth century, in the internationalization of retailing came after several centuries in which international activity by retailers was exceptional. International activity in retailing is evident in many ways: in the sourcing of goods for resale, the operation of shops, the use of foreign labour, the adoption of foreign ideas and the use of foreign capital. In all respects there has been both an increase in the volume of international activity and a widening of the spatial reach of international activity.

Although the most evident aspect of internationalization is the presence of foreign-owned shops in a country it is important to appreciate that retail internationalization as a concept is much wider in scope. The international retailers that are claiming, in the twenty-first century, to be global companies, have a significant international basis to all their functions. It is this condition of internationalization as affecting the total firm that distinguishes international retailing now from the historical piecemeal activity.

While this integration of international concepts into all the activities of retailers is relatively new, such is not the case in the production sector where major firms have had a broadly based international perspective for several decades. There has been a substantial body of research over many years that explored the nature of internationalization within production and manufacturing. The extent to which this stream of research can be related to the retail sector is unclear. There have been calls for research on retailers to borrow from the established research concepts developed to explain the internationalization processes in production (Brown and Burt 1992) but calls have become weaker in recent years as it is unclear to what extent ideas are transferable from production to distribution (Wrigley *et al.* 2005).

With the increased volume and apparent change in nature of internationalization it is appropriate to look at the foundations of the process by which retailers move from being essentially domestic firms with domestic concerns to being firms that look outwards from their domestic markets and seek expansion in foreign markets. The temporal and spatial aspects together with the magnitude of the process of retailer internationalization operate within various cultures and environments and so provide a set of foundations from which analysis of the overall process may proceed.

The aim of this introductory chapter, therefore, is twofold. First, there is consideration of how the major functions of retailing have become more international. Second, contrasts between the internationalization of retailing and manufacturing are explored and how the emergence of a new view of retailing has increased the degree of difference between retailing and manufacturing. By developing these linked issues the foundation is provided for Chapter 2, which considers the nature of the internationalization process in retailing and its measurement. Chapter 3 develops the issues in terms of propositions prior to a series of firm-based analyses of the processes involved in retailer internationalization.

THE INTERNATIONALIZATION OF SOURCING

A major function of retailers is to provide consumers with a range of products for potential purchase. Historically only a small proportion of these products was sourced from foreign countries and even in such cases the goods were usually obtained by intermediary wholesalers or importers who then sold to the retailers. Thus, for example, foreign fruit was rarely purchased from the source directly by the retailer but was obtained through a wholesale market at which import agents and wholesalers managed the flow of products. Similarly with clothing and furnishings, generally one or more importer and merchant wholesaler were involved. Some of the department stores in the nineteenth century were exceptional in sending their buyers abroad to obtain products and then ship them back to the home store but even this changed to involve wholesalers to a greater extent as department stores grew. Such items, nonetheless, constituted a very small proportion of the totality of retail sales. The internationalization of production over the last 30 years, together with the increase in direct buying activities of retailers has resulted in the internationalization of the purchasing function of retailers.

The volume of products directly imported by retailers has increased with the major retailers often operating regional buying offices, notably since 2000 in China, to consolidate this purchasing activity (Gereffi and Korzeniewicz 1994). This direct purchasing encompasses food products, for example Japanese retailers sourcing salmon directly from Chile and Norway, British and German retailers sourcing vegetables directly from Spain (Dolan and Humphrey 2000, 2004),

Canadian retailers sourcing fruit directly from the US and Mexico. Burch and Goss (1999) provide examples from Australia and place the development into an historical context. This activity is not limited to food, with retailers in Europe, North America and Japan dealing directly with manufacturers in East Asian countries supplying clothing (Gereffi 1999), shoes, electrical equipment, furniture, household hardware, sports equipment, etc. (Leslie and Reimer 1999, 2003; Hughes and Reimer 2003). The intercontinental flows of merchandise directly sourced by retailers are now a significant and increasing part of world trade. Retailers, in consequence, have internationalized their direct purchasing and sourcing practices substantially since the mid-1980s.

Activity since 2000 in sourcing from China illustrates the international nature of this retail activity. Table 1.1 shows the structure and magnitude of sourcing activity from China for some of the major international retailers in 2003. Wal-Mart's purchases from China in 2003 amounted to $15 billion; an amount larger than the retail sales of all but the 50 or so largest retailers in the world. Wal-Mart plans to increase this volume by at least $10 billion between 2003 and 2006. To support this, in 2005 it started to build, in Quanzhou City, a dedicated 15,000-square-metre logistics centre for footwear. Initially, the centre will be capable

Table 1.1 *Examples of retailers' sourcing activities from China*

Company	Structure	Sourcing in 2003	Plans
Wal-Mart	4 meetings per year: 2 in Shenzhen, 2 in Dallas	US$15 billion	$25–30 billion in 3 years
Carrefour	Purchasing centres in 11 cities coordinated by 4 regional purchasing offices with delegated responsibility	US$2.1 billion	$2.6 billion in 2004
Home Depot	2 sourcing offices in China	–	Increase to about 10 per cent stores sales
Tesco	1 sourcing centre	US$0.5 billion	$1.5 billion in 3 years
Metro	Import agent GEMEX Trading has partnership with Chinese B2B internet portal Sparkice	–	Unspecified increase
Kingfisher	Via strategic alliance with global sources	US$1 billion	Unspecified increase
GAP	Several sourcing offices	14 per cent of product	Unspecified increase
Aeon	Via strategic alliance with global sources	–	Sourcing centre established 2004

of processing 10 million pairs of shoes per year with a second phase capacity of 30 million pairs. It is forecast by Wal-Mart that a 10 per cent reduction in logistic costs for these items will result from this development. Other major retailers have substantial volumes being sourced from China and similarly plan for growth in this aspect of international activity. The changes in status of China in respect of WTO regulations and the removal of tariffs on clothing in 2004 resulted in a substantial upsurge of directly sourced clothing by European retailers that only became limited subsequent to intervention by European Commission.

The extent of this growth in recent years can be seen from the export data from China for selected products. Table 1.2 shows the position for some product groups where products quickly enter the retail sector. Imports by Japanese clothing retailers, already over US$10 billion in 1997 rose 40 per cent over the following four years. Similarly large import volumes of toys and games in the US rose by over 30 per cent and footwear imports in the US were over $10 billion in 2001. The fastest growing product category of all for retailers in the US, EU and Japan was furniture with IKEA, Office Depot and others sourcing larger volumes from China. Since 2004, however, clothing exports have increased substantially.

While international sourcing has been a limited feature of retailing for many decades (Shaw *et al.* 1992) it has changed in three ways since the early 1990s. First, there has been a steep increase in the volume of goods sourced internationally such that for some retailers very few products are now sourced from within the country in which they have their main store operations. Second, new sources and

Table 1.2 Exports from China to the US, EU and Japan (US$ million)

	1997	2001	Percentage increase
Clothing			
US	7,770	9,275	19.4
EU	6,715	8,427	25.5
Japan	10,490	14,760	40.7
Toys and games			
US	10,487	13,728	30.9
EU	3,877	5,626	45.1
Japan	1,652	1,949	18.0
Footwear			
US	7,702	10,283	33.5
EU	1,573	1,733	10.1
Japan	1,774	2,017	13.7
Furniture			
US	1,711	5,818	240.0
EU	502	1,196	137.6
Japan	605	1,321	118.3

Source: WTO

structures have been developed, and third there has been more activity on an inter-continental scale. Traditional intercontinental sourcing, for example of meat and fruit products through agents, has given way to direct purchasing by the retailers through their own buying offices. The opening of China and East Asia more gener-ally to the buyers of European and American retailers has been by far the most prominent aspect of this intercontinental sourcing.

Increase in volume of internationally sourced products

The reasons for the increase in international sourcing derive from three directions: the requirements of retailers, the evolving structure of major suppliers and socio-political change.

The major reason for retailers seeking foreign sources is cost reduction. The competitive pressure in terms of price has forced retailers to seek low-cost sources. This has been particularly evident in retailer branded products with the retailer specifying the composition and quality of the product and negotiating lower prices from suppliers, particularly in the emergent economies of Central Europe and East Asia. Major European, American and Japanese retailers, for example Carrefour, Tesco, Wal-Mart and Aeon in the general merchandise sector, provide examples of this approach. It is also very evident in the clothing and house-hold sectors where retailers have a strong brand, for example Fast Retailing, C&A, IKEA and JC Penney. The radical shift in sourcing undertaken by Marks & Spencer, in the late 1990s, when it moved away from UK suppliers in order to reduce costs is further evidence of this generic strategic decision, in retailing, to seek lower-cost sources for products. Retailers have sought foreign sources for products also in order to provide variety in their product ranges. Body Shop and Pier provide examples of this search for variety. As the retailers have become more international in their store operations so a wider net has been cast for suppliers, some of which are local to the foreign store operations but they become suppliers for the firm as a whole. The increase in scale of the major retailers also means that they often have to seek multiple suppliers, potentially from different countries to reduce risks, for some products.

The major suppliers of manufacturer branded items have also encouraged the increase in international sourcing by retailers. Brand rationalization means that retailers in different countries carry the same 'global' brands and when this is coupled with the rationalization of production facilities to obtain scale economies, then increased international sourcing is the inevitable result. Unilever's strategic focus on fewer brands each meeting stringent criteria on brand appeal and brand scale illustrates this phenomenon. Unilever's Pathways to Growth programme resulted in a reduction by 1,200 in the number of brands it supported. Major manufacturers also endeavour to reduce costs by moving or focusing production of their brands into low-cost countries, again resulting in increased international

5

sourcing by retailers, for example Unilever's reduction of manufacturing sites from 400 to less than 300.

Changes in socio-political and socio-technical environments have facilitated the choice of strategic options chosen by retailers and suppliers that result in increased volumes of international sourcing. The trend towards the lowering of international trade barriers within Europe as part of European integration and the creation of a common currency, the collapse of the barriers for trade with Central Europe, and also more widely as part of multilateral and WTO trade agreements have all become significant facilitators of international sourcing by retailers. The willingness of retailers to explore international sources has increased as a result of the greater ease of organizing relationships with foreign suppliers resulting from the reduction in trade barriers. This reduction in transaction costs has also been facilitated by developments in information and communication technologies. Thus, not only has it become possible to link CAD in the retail head office with CAM in a producing country, but also the iterations in the design and development process, for example in fashion clothing, can be undertaken internationally (Azuma 2005). The same advances in ICT have allowed business-to-business exchange over the internet to be undertaken. Costs of the spatial separation of buyer and producer have been reduced. The advances in technology have also affected logistics systems such that the organization of the physical flow of product has become more efficient and able to accommodate different requirements for the different items ranging from highly perishable fashion to live fish. Consumer expectations have changed in ways that have facilitated and encouraged retailers to source products internationally. Consumers seek variety and low prices alongside access to the latest fashions in clothes, food and technology. Meeting these demands inevitably results in wider international sourcing on the part of the retailer.

The organization of international sourcing

The increase in volume and type of international sourcing activity has resulted in the generation of more formal managerial structures to facilitate the activity. Three approaches are evident: internal buying teams including the creation of foreign buying centres, inter-firm buying alliances, and web exchanges. Retailers are using one or more of these approaches to undertake their international sourcing.

Internal buying teams including the creation of foreign buying centres

The increased scale of retailers has allowed them to undertake cost-effective direct sourcing through in-house buying teams. With increasing scale, transaction costs fall and it becomes cost effective to take in-house previously outsourced activities that used agents, importers and wholesalers. There are a range of different models used by retailers depending on the extent to which sourcing is centralized or localized in respect of the international operations.

Carrefour, for example, although undertaking substantial local sourcing, has a group buying organization, Direction Marchandises Groupe (DMG), that consolidates and coordinates international sourcing activity involving about 2,500 suppliers. Since the early 1990s Carrefour has had arrangements in place to coordinate international sourcing activity. Through DMG international negotiations are conducted for manufacturer and retailer branded items, sourcing of Carrefour brand collections is planned, the infrastructure of sourcing hubs and offices is managed and information and knowledge are communicated around sourcing teams. Part of DMG is a dedicated group, Carrefour World Trade (CWT), which negotiates with international suppliers of branded items that have a presence in at least three major markets. The increase in international sourcing since 2000 has resulted in DMG increasing the number of hubs and their associated sourcing offices such that by early 2003, 23 sourcing offices were in place, as shown in Table 1.3. The sourcing hubs coordinate office activities, facilitate information exchange and consolidate the logistics from the region. Sourcing offices vary in size from three to seventy people and tend to focus on a limited number of items; for example, India focuses on clothing and household goods, with the main functions being market search, information transfer back to buyers, negotiation and supplier auditing of quality and performance.

Reflecting the increasing importance of international sourcing, Metro undertook a major reorganization of its sourcing structure effective from January 2004 in order to handle the increasing volumes of international activity and to provide more effective links between the retailer and its suppliers. A single group, Metro Group Buying (MGB), has responsibility for all sourcing activity including the previously used import company Gemex Trading AG and the subsidiary companies

Table 1.3 *Sourcing hubs and offices of Carrefour in 2003*

Region	Sourcing hub	Sourcing offices
Europe	Les Ulis, France	Italy Greece Poland Turkey Morocco
Asia	Hong Kong	China (10 offices) Bangladesh India Pakistan Indonesia Thailand
South America	São Paulo, Brazil	

that were established in Poland, Russia and Turkey for sourcing purposes. MGB also coordinates Asian sourcing through an office in Hong Kong by incorporating the Gemex subsidary that had handled East Asian imports for Metro since 1996, and previously for Kaufhof. The incorporation of Gemex into MGB has consolidated sourcing with over €1.5 billion of products being sourced for the Metro Group through the four foreign buying offices. The main buying office in Dusseldorf sources from domestic suppliers and from suppliers across Europe being responsible for over €44 billion of purchases in 2003.

As international operations become established it is also common for the model to change, often with more local sourcing being introduced. For example, the Swedish-based fashion retailer Hennes and Mauritz, in their stores in the US, initially imported all their products from Europe but by 2003, three years after their launch in America, it was importing directly. By the spring of 2004 approximately 60 per cent of purchases were directly from Asia with the rest still sourced from Europe. An office has been established in Mexico with a view to sourcing from there, at least for the North American stores but also possibly for wider distribution. Adding Mexico to their international sourcing base increased the number of countries from which products are sourced to 22.

The main advantage of in-house buying teams over other forms of organization for international sourcing is the ability of the firm to control all the activities and to tailor these to the needs of the retail outlets. The absence of competitor involvement, compared to buying alliances for example, enables retailer-specific and exclusive sourcing arrangements to be negotiated. Having complete control over the international buying activity can be used as a means of integration within the retailer and ensuring that sourcing is linked to the overall strategic objectives of the firm.

Undertaking the function in-house, however, carries substantial costs with expense incurred in regional buying offices and their management. As such, there are scale economies to be obtained and larger firms can benefit significantly from lower unit costs of sourcing. For the larger retailers, the expansion of their in-house sourcing activities is essential to underpin the international expansion of sales outlets. For several of the large retailers, irrespective of their sector of trading, the experience of substantial amounts of in-house sourcing is still limited and knowledge is being collected rapidly as the firm moves up a learning curve. With this evolution of the knowledge base so the organizational structure of the in-house teams has changed and will continue to change as experience and expectations change. Thus, we are likely to see more variety in the structures being used by retailers and in the mix of functions undertaken by the in-house groups.

Inter-firm buying alliances

Inter-firm buying alliances for international sourcing are of two main types: bi-firm agreements and multi-firm associations. Multi-firm agreements have a long history in no-food sectors where buying groups have been present, for domestic as well as international sourcing, in department stores and sports goods for well over half a century. The international sourcing was largely an extension of the cooperative national sourcing activity of these associations.

In the grocery sector in Europe, international sourcing by multi-firm associations was limited until the late 1980s when a number of groups, which had as their focus international trade, became established in Europe (Bayley *et al.* 1995). Several of the alliances failed with two large ones emerging by the early 2000s. These are European Marketing Distribution (EMD) and Associated Marketing Services.

European Marketing Distribution was established in 1989 and acts as a sourcing alliance for a group of mainly medium-sized firms. By operating in this way these firms are able to access international supply sources at lower costs than would be the case if they sourced individually. Membership of EMD changes periodically (Table 1.4) but generally includes nationally based buying groups of small retailers, thus giving even small retailers an element of internationalization to their sourcing operations. Some members, for example Delhaize, undertake some international sourcing on their own account in addition to that passing through EMD. The international trading volume passing through EMD on behalf of members rose from €700 million in 2002 to €950 million in 2003.

Associated Marketing Services was founded in 1988 and like EMD has had several changes of memberships as firms have withdrawn and others have joined, but in general it limits membership to one per European country. Members are substantial companies operating in mainly national markets (see Table 1.4).

In contrast to the multi-firm alliances several bi-firm agreements have been made to undertake joint international sourcing. Typical is the agreement between Casino and Auchan that created, in 2002, International Retail and Trade Services (IRTS). Each retailer holds a 50 per cent share in IRTS. The two retailers continue to purchase separately but IRTS exists to negotiate and manage international agreements with multinational suppliers as an aid to the retailers' international expansion. It also provides opportunities for smaller suppliers to gain access to the store networks of the two retailers. Intermarché (ITM) also uses bi-firm alliances as

Table 1.4 Membership of the two large sourcing alliances in the grocery trade in Europe in 2004

Group	Membership
EMD	Axfood, Cactus, Euromadi, Markant AG, Musgrave, Nisa Today's, ESE Italia, ZEV Markant, Delhaize, Honiker
AMS	Ahold, Caprabo, Dansk Supermarked, Edeka, Jerónimo Martins, Kesko, Superquinn

a mechanism for international sourcing. Agenor was established in 1998 as a joint agreement between ITM Enterprises and Spar AG, for a while partly owned by ITM. Located in Zurich, Agenor acts as the international purchasing division of ITM. In 2002 ITM created Alidis jointly with Eroski, the major Spanish group with Alidis being responsible for the international sourcing for Eroski. The withdrawal from Germany by Intermarché and sale of assets to Edeka has brought a third party into the alliance as shown in Figure 1.1. The activity is undertaken through Agenor. ITM also has a joint buying agreement with Hagebau, itself a voluntary grouping of German DIY retailers. Links also exist into other similar alliances. These alliances characteristically are very dynamic with changes in members and relationships and this represents one of their weaknesses as an organizational form.

The strength of the buying alliances is their focus on delivering short-term tangible benefits in the sourcing activity. They are very practical in their approach and source what their members say they require. They also are relatively low cost in terms of capital investment, although the opportunity cost of participation by members may be quite large.

Buying alliances of all types have histories of instability. Membership only continues as long as the benefits to a member are greater than the transaction costs involved in membership. Operational costs can be quite high, particularly in multi-firm alliances, with meetings to seek agreement on the common composition of products. Difficulties can also arise between the agreements of the alliance with suppliers and the orders being placed by individual alliance members. Suppliers,

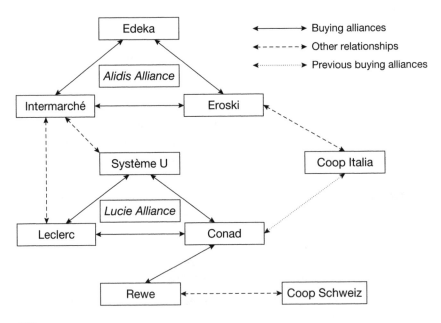

Figure 1.1 Lucie and Alidis alliances

therefore, may complain that negotiations with the central alliance were conducted on the expectation of larger volumes of purchasing by individual members than materialized. Thus, there is not only instability in the membership with firms entering and leaving but also instability in the willingness of suppliers to participate in the joint activity advocated by the central agents of the alliance. Online web exchanges present the greatest threat to alliances because the transaction cost is potentially reduced with electronic interchanges.

Web exchanges

The third main form of organization apparent in international sourcing is the web exchange. These exchanges can have a number of functions but an important one is the potential for international sourcing. This can be accomplished either by linking sellers with buyers in a bilateral way or using the online facilities to create auctions of suppliers wishing to sell to retailers. Exchanges can offer a relatively low-cost way of sourcing for the retailer with the service provider either charging a membership fee to the seller or taking a percentage of the value of each transaction. For retailers who lack the scale to establish their own sourcing group and their own electronic interchange, the exchanges operated by third parties provide a way of accessing international suppliers. The large exchanges also provide a mechanism by which the large retailers can hold auctions for the supply of essentially commodity items.

The increased intercontinental character of sourcing

The increase in volume and the change in the organization of international sourcing have been accompanied by a third major trend, namely a shift towards more intercontinental sourcing by European retailers. This is most evident in the increase in sourcing from East Asia for non-food items but is also apparent with fresh product sourcing. East African countries have become significant sources for vegetables that are flown to the central distribution centres of European retailers (Dolan and Humphrey 2000). Chile and Norway have become major sources of farmed salmon for retailers in Japan. These new and increasingly important sources exist alongside the established ones that have linked, for several decades, Southern Hemisphere meat and fruit commodity producers to retailers in the Northern Hemisphere particularly in Europe and Japan. As consumer demands have become more fragmented and they have required the seasonal characteristic of fresh products to be removed as a limitation on choice, and also as retailers have sought ways to become differentiated competitively through product range diversification, so there has been an increase in the type of products in this intercontinental trade with more specialization in the products being sourced. The trend has been a shift away from commodity items to products for more specialized markets. While cost considerations are present in encouraging intercontinental sourcing, the issue of product availability is more important as retailers have sought ways to differentiate themselves from each other.

The increase in the intercontinental nature of non-food sourcing results from different economic and managerial factors influencing retailers than is the case with fresh food products. The search for low-cost sources becomes the paramount issue in products with a potentially long inventory life. The retailer is able to exploit scale economies of purchasing and use the firm's knowledge base to transfer know-how to a producer who makes the items under contract and to the retailer's specifications. Cost considerations of production and, to a lesser extent, of logistics, and the leveraging of the retailer's knowledge then become the important factors that have encouraged intercontinental sourcing. The lower production costs in East and South Asia in terms of labour, local taxation and compliance with infrastructural directives from government have encouraged retailers to seek producers in these regions. Uniqueness and specialization of product as an element in competition is less important than having low sourcing costs for many of these items.

For products that have a shorter inventory life, for example fresh foods and street fashion, the increase in intercontinental sourcing is only partly on cost grounds but of equal importance is the speed and flexibility of suppliers in responding to the demands of retailers.

There are some important consequences of this increase in international, particularly intercontinental, sourcing. Table 1.5 indicates some of the consequences of the changes taking place in international sourcing.

THE INTERNATIONALIZATION OF THE OPERATION OF RETAIL OUTLETS

It is in the operation of shops internationally where the creation of truly international retailers is most evident. As with international sourcing there is a long history of spasmodic international activity in shop operation but over the last decades of the twentieth century the amount of activity has increased steadily. Hollander (1970) in his classic study provided many examples while Fletcher and Godley (2000) have shown the penetration of UK retailing by international retailers particularly through the first half of the twentieth century. Although in this historical record the activity was important for some individual firms, it represents a very small element in the total volume of retailing and it generally was of very limited spatial extent with firms often only expanding into one or two other countries. Since the 1970s, however, there has been a change with a substantial build up of activity by large and mid-sized firms alike and a generally wider spatial spread of activity with multi-continental activity being pursued by a growing number of firms.

Table 1.5 Some developments in the retailer–supplier relationship in an international context

Change occurring	Reasons for the change	Consequences
1 More volume and variety of products being sourced internationally	Increases in sizes of consumer markets Fragmentation and specialization of demand from consumers	More new product development and range extension Searches for new ways to reduce inventory levels of retailers Increase in demand for specialist logistics markets
2 More complex relationships between retailer and supplier	Increase in diversity of space, time and quantity gaps in the channel Increase in the range of variables used to define the retailer–supplier relationship Changes in organizational buying structures of retailers	More specialist skills need by participants More opportunities for negotiation on more factors Wider and deeper range of information required More promotion by retailer and less by supplier
3 Retailer gaining power in the international channel	Increase in buying scale of retailers Access to/use of information on consumer purchasing activities More knowledge about purchasing processes of consumer Retailer branding of products Tighter control of shelf and store space	Negotiating power firmly held by retailers Relationship more reflective of strategic objectives of retailer Large retailers may dominate small suppliers Brand suppliers search for low-cost production
4 More longer-term relationships	Retailers seek to reduce transaction costs, particularly international search costs Increase in retailer branded products with composition and quality specified by retailer Desire to coordinate the supply chain to remove costs More inertial buying by retailers	Use of ECR-type approaches with supplier required to take part in developments Retailer ROCE stabilized at expense of supplier ROCE Higher levels of trust in relationships; more repeat purchasing
5 More intercontinental sourcing	Lower cost supply base in East Asia Consumer demand for variety	More complex financing of international buying International buying offices become more important Wider search activity by retailers Long-distance logistics increase in importance
6 More new product development	Variety-seeking consumers Attempts by retailers to differentiate by product ranges Shorter product seasons and cycles and even elimination of seasonality	More pressure on store and shelf space Use of rapid NPD processes by retailers Rapid prototyping by suppliers
7 Strong downward pressure on prices in the relationship	Use of lower-cost supply sources by retailers Strong competition among retailers	Medium-sized firms (retailers and suppliers) under considerable competitive and financial pressure from large and small firms

There is an extensive literature that explores the development and expansion of international retailing operations and this is widely available (for example: Alexander 1997; Burt 1993, 1995; Dawson 2001b; Larke 2005; Quinn 1999; Wrigley *et al.* 2005). The substantial range of studies across sector, countries and firms shows that there is great variety in the activity, as might be expected in a sector as diverse as retailing. There are, however, some common factors also but these are less evident. The overriding impression is one of a sector in the early phase of full-scale internationalization with firms trying different approaches as they evaluate local markets and situations. The internationalization of retail operations is at an early stage in its development. While it is not the aim of this chapter to consider the literature in depth, Table 1.6 summarizes the main areas of diversity and consistencies evident from academic studies and the moves of retailers in the last few decades. This is structured in terms of who is involved in the internationalization activity, where does it take place, why and how is it undertaken, when does entry and subsequent growth occur, and what are the consequences of the activity. These are the main dimensions for description of the activity. Although not entirely the case, academic studies have tended to concentrate on describing the nature of internationalization rather than exploring the mechanisms of the process involved. Given the relative infancy of the activity this is a natural consequence and has enabled a sound foundation to be established onto which can be built deeper studies of the processes involved.

THE INTERNATIONAL RETAILER

While the internationalization of operations and of sourcing illustrate major functions of retailing that have become more international in scope since the early 1990s, other activities of retailers also exhibit increased levels of international activity.

Retailers are major employers and there has been an internationalization of employment. Much of the employment in retailing is of relatively low-skilled sales workers. Increasingly, the labour force of retailers has become internationalized with recent immigrant workers being employed in retailers' distribution depots and in stores. The free flow of labour within the European Union since 1992, the extension of the EU to Central European countries in 2004 and the increasing flow of workers from Central America to the US have encouraged relatively low-skilled migrant workers to find employment in retailing occupations in the richer countries. This occurs within the labour market and also within firms. For example, Tesco in 2004 brought workers trained in Tesco Poland to work in stores and distribution centres in the UK in areas of labour shortage including commuter towns in the south-east of England.

Table 1.6 *Diversity and consistency in the analyses of internationalization*

	Diversity and variability in internationalization	Consistency and commonalities in internationalization
Who	Small, medium and large firms involved All types of ownership structure evident All types of store format involved in international operation	More widespread in Europe-based firms than firms based in North America and Asia Successful firms have a very strong domestic market base More prevalent in non-food sector than food sector More prevalent with firms with strong market orientation
Where	Target markets include economies at all levels of development Shotgun and cluster approach to location in target country are apparent All types of location attract international retailers	Border hopping widespread Successful firms have clear view of type of country and type of location in which to operate
Why	Many types of motive for becoming international	No single motive dominates decisions other than the requirement to grow Successful firms have a high level of senior executive commitment to internationalization
How	Approaches can be formal, strategic, tactical or opportunistic Wide variety of growth methods apparent in a country and in a firm Choice of entry method and growth method often different	Four main entry methods: acquisition, franchise, direct creation of outlet, joint-venture Entry method and formula of operation are interrelated Entry method related to perceived transaction costs of entry First mover advantages not consistently apparent
When	Occurs at any stage of a firm's life Speed of development after entry varies widely	Strong balance sheet necessary to sustain successful international entry and growth
Effects	Many types of vertical and horizontal channel and environmental impacts evident	Strategic flexibility is necessary to accommodate inevitable situational surprises Increased risk to firm profitability and continuing existence

The internationalization of management, although less in volume, is of more significance in creating truly international retailers. With international sourcing and international store operation so there is an increasing need for international managers. At the senior levels of management there is also a growing number of international executives. The recruitment of American retailers to run British firms was an early stage of this internationalization but now there is a reverse flow to the US and also a more widespread multilateral flow of senior executives across Europe. In terms of middle management there is substantial use of expatriate managers within firms with international operations. Carrefour and Aeon both typically use expatriate managers for some years after entry into a country to ensure that Carrefour practices are incorporated into sales floor systems.

At senior management levels the international flow of managers remains relatively weak. Most of the members of executive boards of the major firms are nationals of the country of origin of the firm. While boards of operating subsidiaries often contain executives from several countries the pattern is less international with main board membership.

The international movement of senior executives is only one mechanism for the international movement of ideas and know-how. The diffusion of innovations is also undertaken by business consultants who work for different firms across various countries. Ideas and techniques become implemented in the different countries through these consultant networks. Organizations such as ECR Europe aim for the international diffusion of managerial practice such that system developments and operational innovations become widely known internationally quite quickly. The copying of new formats, merchandising methods, promotions and designs has become more common as retailers and consultants visit stores in other countries more frequently, and draw comparisons with domestic operations.

Finance has also become internationally mobile such that the shareholder populations have become more international in composition. Major shareholders resident in one country can have a significant impact on the activities of a retailer based and operating in another country. For example, the role of a California-based investment fund with a major holding in Marks & Spencer was influential in Marks & Spencer's fight against a takeover bid in 2003. The membership of share registers of major firms has become more international over the last 20 years. Joint-venture ownership of foreign operations often also increases the extent of the internationalization of the financing of the international retailer. Both debt and equity ownership patterns show the increasingly international nature of retailing.

All the functions of retailing are now likely to have an international dimension. While most obvious in store operations and sourcing, this international dimension pervades the activities of the large retailers in ways not seen before. The requirements of retail managers in these firms are changing such that an international perspective has become a requirement in all the functional areas. This change in retailing requires that academic analyses of the retail sector take account of the new international influences. Consequently, it becomes an important question whether or not retail management and the academic study of international retailing can draw on concepts, theory and reported practice developed for the international manufacturing sector.

CONTRASTS BETWEEN INTERNATIONALIZATION IN RETAILING AND PRODUCTION

Retailing is not production. This is self-evident, yet it is worthwhile to consider how retailing and production are different. Much of the academic study of internationalization has dealt with productive, particularly manufacturing activities, both explicitly and implicitly (for example, Blomstermo and Sharma 2003; Calori *et al.* 2000; Dunning 1993, 1995). Generally, there is an assumption that these studies are relevant to retailing. The extent to which it is possible to use established models drawn from studies of production depends on the degree to which retailing and production are similar or fundamentally different activities.

In academic terms the study of the internationalization of retailing has a much shorter history than the internationalization of production. It is natural, therefore, in considering the processes of retailer internationalization, initially to look to the larger corpus of research on the internationalization of production for potentially relevant models, concepts and theories. The assumption in such cases is that there is some generic process of internationalization that exists and operates irrespective of economic function. This would seem to be, on deeper reflection, an unlikely situation. There are considerable differences between retailing-based activity and production-based activity. Although the boundaries between firms undertaking different functions are becoming less clear with the emergence of what elsewhere has been termed 'new commerce' (Dawson 2001a) it is clear that the academic models and theories relating to international business are firmly grounded in a more traditional view of economic functions and lag rather in their consideration of the strategies and functions of firms in new commerce. This, surprisingly, is even seen in the attempts to develop concepts of global networks, which, while arguing for the interconnectedness between production and distribution, nonetheless still implicitly take a production-orientated view of the network structures (Dicken *et al.* 2001). For example, Henderson *et al.* (2002), who advocate this approach convincingly, perceive manufacturing firms, rather than integrated firms in commerce, as the main dynamic force in the emerging global networks. Currah and Wrigley (2004) provide one of the few attempts to explore the nature of international retail networks and move the discourse beyond that implicitly developed for manufacturing.

This perception that economic concepts applicable in manufacturing can be transferred comfortably to retailing is widely apparent. The limitations on the extent to which economic and managerial analyses developed for manufacturing can be applied to retailing are seldom explored. Holdren (1960) suggested that:

> the theory of the firm and the theory of consumer choice rarely take explicit cognizance of the fact that manufacturing firms . . . are separated from the final consumer . . . by a distribution mechanism over which the manufacturer has a degree of influence varying from almost none to complete control.

Although this comment is almost 50 years old it remains valid today for many studies. Douglas (1975), slightly more recently, made much the same point and considered the economics of marketing activities with a focus towards retailing, but even here she draws from a base of manufacturing related material. Hall's (1949) classic analysis drew on theory developed outwith distribution. McClelland (1966), Nooteboom (1980) and, more recently, Betancourt (2004), Filser et al. (2001), Sciarelli and Vona (2000) and Spranzi (1991) all move along similar lines, drawing essentially on economic concepts, originally formulated from studies of production to analyse the economics of retailing in domestic markets. Nooteboom (1980) admits that: 'In spite of the problems concerning the plausibility of neo-classical theory, especially in the context of retailing, we started out with a neo-classical approach' (p. 22).

With the increase in size and power of retail firms, particularly since the early 1980s, and their simultaneous internationalization, so it becomes increasingly evident that many of these earlier approaches are unsuited to the analysis of retailing and distribution processes. Pellegrini (1990, 1996) has begun to develop these arguments and to explore an alternative basis for the study of retailing but this has been taken up by few other scholars.

The lack of applicability to retailing of many concepts is particularly the case with internationalization where the established literature in international business (Björkman and Forsgren 1997; Buckley and Ghauri 1993; Chryssochoidis et al. 1997; Contractor and Lorange 1988; Dunning 1993; Harzing 1999; Young et al. 1989) explores issues of joint-venture production in foreign countries, foreign direct investment in production facilities, the export/import of products and other aspects of international business, but ignores issues on retail internationalization. Welch and Luostarinen (1988) in exploring how the concept of internationalization evolved in the academic literature show, implicitly, that retailing has not been considered as an activity that is susceptible to the internationalization process. Even the few attempts to consider service industries in a generic way from an international business perspective are approached within the production-orientated OLI paradigm (Arvidsson 1997; Buckley et al. 1992; Dahringer and Mühlbacher 1991; Erramilli 1990; Valikängas and Lehtinen 1991). The increased expansion of retailers into foreign markets makes this view unsustainable for the analysis of retailers. Nonetheless, the theoretical literature remains firmly in the production arena (Nielsen *et al.* 1999; Oviatt and Mc Dougall 1994).

Features of retailing as a social and economic activity result in its management and its economics being different in nature from management and economics in production. These differences are important to understanding international retailing and it is useful to explore the main differences in order to better understand the nature of the internationalization of retailing.

Multi-establishment form of retailing

While micro-firms in retailing have few operating establishments, the common form for medium and large firms is to operate through many outlets. It is not unusual for retail firms to have 500 or more outlets from which they trade. In many cases these shop units and other outlets are relatively small. Examples from Europe are Euromarché (over 8,000 stores), Boots (over 1,500 stores), Aldi (over 6,000 stores), Schlecker (over 13,000 stores), Douglas (1,600 stores), Benetton (over 4,000 stores) and Euronics (over 9,000 stores). Within Europe in 2003 among the largest 100 retailers there were 46 organizations with over 1,000 stores and only four of the largest 20 retailers had fewer than 500 outlets in Europe (Mintel 2004). The contrast with manufacturing is illustrated in the work in France by Hecquet and Roualdes (1999). For the period 1985–93, they showed that 55 per cent of companies with more than 50 employees in manufacturing have only one establishment while less than 40 per cent of firms of this size in commerce have only one outlet. Furthermore, of the commerce and service companies with more than one outlet, 40 per cent have ten or more but for manufacturing companies with more than one establishment only 10 per cent have ten or more local units. This pattern of retail sector structure is generic to Europe and North America.

Retailing has the characteristics of being spatially disaggregated and networked. These features result in different economic relationships from those of fewer but larger operations in manufacturing firms. The efficiency of operation of the network and the flows among the shops are critical aspects of retailer operation. The links and relationships of local unit to head/regional office and to other local units are a major factor affecting the efficiency of the local unit and overall cost functions. In the manufacturing sector operational efficiencies at the local unit are generally more in the control of management at the local unit than is the case with retailing. Without the efficiencies in the network elements of the retail firm, service levels fall and shops do not have goods to sell. Thus, the flows of goods, information and knowledge across the network take on very important roles in the retail context. While the Network School of research in international business (Hakansson 1982; Johanson and Mattsson 1988; Welch and Welch 1996) has shown the importance of networks in internationalization processes, much of the work concentrates on the limited networks of manufacturers. Surprisingly, few studies of international retailers with extensive networks of operating outlets and company interactions have been undertaken. A recent exception is the study by Jonsson and Elg (2005) of the knowledge network in the internationalization of IKEA. The importance of extensive networks linking local units to centres of managerial control is important to an understanding of the process of internationalization of retailing.

Local nature of the market

In retailing the market is local, even for large international retailers. Only for internet-based retailers is this not the case. By contrast, large manufacturers can consider their market as international or even global. The local nature of the market requires retailers to be aware of local aspects of consumption and of local attributes of culture. Situational aspects of consumption and buyer behaviour are more important in retailing than in manufacturing. The consequence for the retail internationalization process is the requirement placed on retailers to understand consumer cultures that can be very different from those in the home market. While manufacturers may vary the product for local markets they are unlikely to vary the systems and processes in a way that is a requirement for retailers.

Large number of suppliers

Retailers often have a relatively large number of suppliers. The demise of merchant wholesalers has increased the size of the supply base for many retailers. A firm operating large department stores, for example, may have many thousands of suppliers from which it sources items. Even a large firm operating limited range discount stores with 800 or so items may have a hundred or more suppliers. A small firm with sales of no more than €2 million in the gift shop sector, for example, needs around 350 suppliers in order to create appropriate ranges throughout the year. The relationships of the retailer with this large number of suppliers are central to the nature of the retail firm and the functions the retailer performs. Filser (1989) is one of the few to explore this view of retailing and builds his analysis around channel relationships.

Relationships with suppliers span a wide range of types from short-term transactions to long-term strategic alliances. A retailer manages a portfolio of relationships of these many different types. Rather than generating value through transforming physical items, as in the case of manufacturers, the retailer generates value through the management of relationships with suppliers and the creation of ranges of items for sale. Relationships with suppliers may be an intangible asset that is larger for retailers than for manufacturers. The relationship depends heavily on the knowledge of those involved and the concentration of this knowledge can be considered as 'ba' in the nomenclature of Nonaka and Konno (1998; Nonaka *et al.* 2001). As such, this 'ba' location and the relationships in it attract a greater level of investment by retailers than by manufacturers. The investment by retailers in relationships with suppliers is generally believed to have increased and retailers have taken more control over functions such as quality specification and branding of items produced by suppliers. In the context of international retailing there may well be a different portfolio of suppliers, and supplier relationships, for stores in different countries but within the same firm.

The large number of suppliers is related to the complexity of the mix of items in the range and dynamic nature of these ranges. While in manufacturing the parts and components are assembled in the same way to create each product this is not the case in retailing where items for resale can be assembled in many different ways, and in ways that can be changed. This idea of an assembled assortment is an aspect of retailing without equivalence in manufacturing and is important in internationalization as Mukoyama (2000) indicates, because of the need for different assortments in different local markets.

The outlet is the retailer's product

The retailer sells services not items.

> The customer of a retail store . . . buys from the retailer . . . not goods but services, such as the retailer's anticipation, transactions services, product mix, financing, delivery, and information.
> (Douglas 1975: 220)

> In retailing the 'product' is in fact a 'bundle of services' . . . in a marketing mix which is not homogeneous across competitors.
> (Nooteboom 1980: 18)

These services, including physical items, are brought together by the retailer in a sales outlet. The sales outlet is designed to be 'consumed' by the customer. The outlet may have many alternative physical forms and contain many different attributes. Thus it may be, for example, a shop, vending machine, mail order catalogue, website or otherwise. Because the sales outlet is created by the retailer it is, in effect, the product of the retailer and has to be considered as such in any economic analysis of the retail firm. While this product is the most evident aspect of a retailer's international activity, it is, effectively, only the external manifestation of the retail internationalization process. The product is the result of a process of creating economic value. The contrast with manufacturing is obvious with the factory not seen as the manufacturer's product. In an international context, the condition that the product of the retailer is anchored in a specific social, economic and political environment means that cultural inputs into the product design and operation are considerable.

Different cost structure

Cost structures in retailing result in different sources of operating efficiencies compared to production activities. The cost of goods for resale is very important and, although there is variation by type of retailer, may constitute 80 per cent of the overall costs. This puts a premium on gaining scale economies in these costs. The search for and evaluation of suppliers, and managing these supplier relationships, have particular importance. For retailers with a higher gross margin, for example in the specialist clothing sector where cost of goods may be less than 30 per cent, the economies of scope associated with creating the right range become very important. Minimizing markdowns in such a business is the basis of profitability.

The terms of trade with suppliers of goods for resale often mean that retailers operate with a negative working capital, in effect selling the goods to consumers before payment is made to suppliers. For example, working capital as a percentage of sales in 2001 for Carrefour was −9.5 per cent, for Tesco −8.8 per cent, and for Sainsbury −6.1 per cent. For large retailers current liabilities may be higher than current assets. Table 1.7, from the Eurostat BACH Database, shows the situation for large retailers in France during the 1990s. Over the decade the cost structure changed with current liabilities as a percentage of sales becoming greater than current assets. Although for manufacturers such a position may alarm management, this is not the case in retailing and is actively sought by retailers. This becomes an important support to the internationalization activity where the availability of short-term capital at zero cost is a benefit when store construction and opening projects are delayed, a situation more likely to occur in an international rather than a domestic context.

Space costs for many retailers are also a critical element in the cost structure with small differences in costs being important in the success or failure of a shop at a particular location. There is, within retailing, a great variety of cost structures with very different costs associated with different formats. For example, retailing through mail order has a very different cost structure from retailing through kiosks, or through hypermarkets, or specialist shops, or convenience stores and so on. The extent of this variety in cost structure is considerable and while it may not be greater than in manufacturing, the role of the different elements in the structure is distinctive.

Within international retailing the cost structure of foreign operations may be very different from those in the home market with cost perhaps being higher in the foreign market. For the retailer, therefore, these higher costs of foreign operations have to be supported by strong performance in the domestic market. This contrasts with manufacturing where usually a reason for a move to a foreign

Table 1.7 Current assets and current liabilities as percentage of sales for large firms in France

	Retailing		Manufacturing	
	Current assets	Current liabilities	Current assets	Current liabilities
2001	47.40	53.62	56.11	40.63
2000	48.93	52.61	57.10	40.83
1999	51.68	61.12	55.15	39.14
1998	50.80	55.10	54.91	37.51
1997	46.56	51.44	58.88	38.30
1996	39.40	44.13	56.69	38.01
1995	50.39	54.22	58.25	40.19
1994	52.11	55.20	56.31	38.73
1993	54.43	52.78	55.95	37.82
1992	51.48	51.22	57.28	37.88
1991	58.49	50.74	57.83	38.76
1990	56.44	52.72	58.72	39.70
1989	63.89	57.84	61.38	41.76
1988	64.07	55.11	65.00	45.02
1987	57.54	51.60	66.54	47.01
1986	61.40	57.55	67.82	48.57
1985	61.85	59.25	66.75	48.69
1984	63.11	59.44	67.56	50.98

Source: Extracted from BACH database

manufacturing base is a search for lower costs. Retail internationalization may not necessarily be a search for lower costs but a search for larger markets.

High level of customer contact

In retailing there are large numbers of customers and hence large numbers of transactions. This also makes retailing different from manufacturing. Royal Ahold claimed in 2004 to have 40 million customers per week across its 9,000 stores. The close contact with the consumer results in the need for cultural responsiveness in the interface with consumers. While manufacturers may seek to standardize the products they make, the retailer attempts to particularize both the items and the product (retail outlet) they sell in order to respond to the needs of their potential customers. This high level of customer contact is carried through to the need for alignment of managerial style with consumer culture. The debate on standardization versus localization, which is common in the research on internationalization, has a different context in the retail internationalization process where *all* retail internationalization has to be localized to some extent.

Numerous market imperfections

Although there is a high degree of transparency in store operations and often an immediacy to competitive response there are many market imperfections. These are associated with:

1   The way items are bundled for resale in a format, the way formats are bundled in a firm and the associated economies of scope; this bundling can change rapidly and transparency as to what exactly is happening in a competitive sense is often lost.
2   The many forms of public policy intervention in the markets for retail resources with policies on land use and retail location, licensing of establishments and items for sale, trading hours, and relationships with suppliers, and many other areas of intervention; these interventions by public agencies attempt to manage the competitive position but often, mainly inadvertently, result in reduced levels of competition.
3   The potential for spatial quasi-monopoly; by the nature of retailing (other than internet retailing) being fixed in space so the opportunity for local monopolies arises.
4   The large number of opportunities for non-price and very complex price competition; the nature of the retailer's product enables a wide variety of forms of non-price competition while the bundling nature of assortments enables complex pricing across ranges.

While there may be market imperfections in production they are often of a different nature in retailing.

Despite these market imperfections some aspects of retailing engender a more competitive situation than is found in manufacturing. The openness of retail operations enables direct price comparison of many items but the comparison of value remains very complex and difficult. Copying of the 'product' is relatively easy in retailing with no protection of store design so 'look alike' stores are commonplace. It is also possible, although to a lesser extent, to copy the systems of a retailer. This copying of knowledge or intellectual capital is much easier in retailing than in manufacturing and is a notable feature of the retail internationalization process.

The differences between production and retailing mean that most of the existing models of internationalization have limited applicability in the retail context. The retail internationalization process has attributes that are particular to it because of the nature of retail activity. It is with great care, therefore, that analyses of retail internationalization can draw on theories developed in the production sector and when this is done the substantial differences in process and structure of the two sectors needs to be constantly borne in mind.

RETAILING BECOMES COMMERCE[1]

Through the second half of the twentieth century there was an apparent change in many of the structures that define retailing. The condition of retailing at the end of the century was the result of the cumulative impact of the three fundamental innovations that enabled managerial changes in the sector over the previous half-century (Dawson 1999). These were:

1 the acceptance of 'self-service' as the principal form of relationship between retailer and consumer in almost all types of retailing;
2 the acceptance of formalized marketing activities as a major element of managerial activity at strategic and operational levels in retailing;
3 the convergence of information and communication technologies.

These innovations enabled the emergence of larger and more complex firms and have facilitated the increase in international activities of retailers. Many of the structures that define retailing have changed, for example the role of economies of scale, scope and replication, the nature of relationships between retailers and suppliers, the development of retail formats and formulae, and the role played by retailing in generating the social values of consumers, not least through branding. The three fundamental innovations have also changed the speed of development of retailing with changes taking place at a faster rate now than formerly. These changes in retailing in the late twentieth century constitute more than superficial changes in institutional and managerial behaviour. They are generating, as Ishihara and Ishii (1996; Ishihara 2000) also suppose, a deep restructuring of the economic constructs of retailing that result in boundaries of activities being extended both spatially and organizationally. It thus becomes more appropriate to consider 'commerce' as the descriptor of this integrated activity rather than the term 'retailing'. In most cases it is retailers who have taken on the role of integrators and have extended their activities to encompass commerce.

While this change in concept has been discussed more fully elsewhere (Dawson 2001a; Hayashi 1999) it is useful in the current context to provide illustrations of the nature of this change from 'retailing' to 'commerce' as it has impacts on the nature of the internationalization of 'retail' firms. Examples of the change are:

- The emergence of multi-channel operation with firms using several different channels simultaneously, including different types of electronic, physical and mixed channels. Firms in commerce can then develop different channels in different countries.

- The blurring of functional boundaries between production, wholesaling and retailing as viewed traditionally such that a single firm may manage (although not necessarily own) all the functions in taking a good or service to market. Firms selling to final consumers can then develop relationships with production facilities in one country with a view to managing the export of the items to stores in other countries.

- The growth of inter-channel competition with profit considered as an output of the channel rather than an output of a function, but at the same time costs and values of each function are individually identified. This generates different operational modes in different countries, for example, with the firm operating franchises in one country and wholly owned subsidiaries in another.

- The extension of 'retail' management methods into other consumer service sectors, notably finance, health, leisure and education. The diversification into other service sectors provides additional opportunities for international expansion.

- The intensification of volume and range of international activity in both buying and selling activities. This generates the need for new organizational structures, for example, regional buying offices and global sourcing strategies and a wider knowledge base for the firm.

- The increase in activities aimed at adding value at point of sale such that item (service) transformation may be undertaken at the time of purchase by the final consumer. These activities enable more sophisticated adaptation to local buying needs and local cultures in the international operations.

- The shift in consumer channels from transactional relationships to administered and integrated relationships between firms in commerce and suppliers and also between commerce and customers. The impact on the internationalization process is a requirement for the firm to have a deeper understanding of the commercial and consumer cultures of the countries in which it operates.

In the context created by the changes in activity, the identification of retailing activity as previously defined becomes very difficult and new definitions have to be sought. Whether viewed from the viewpoint of a consumer or a firm it is now necessary to consider the interaction between consumer and firm as part of an integrated commercial process, not simply 'retailing'. When this interaction is considered as commerce, the concept of internationalization of commerce can be viewed in a more holistic way than the views usually taken of the internationalization of retailing. This more holistic view has to be accommodated in any new model of the internationalization of commerce/retailing.

A model of the internationalization process in new commerce-retailing has to accommodate not only issues within the retail organization but also the issues associated with interactions with consumers and with the wider socio-political environment in which the firm is operating. Situational factors have substantial influence on the processes such that the same inputs can have different outputs in different situations of space, time and culture. In considering the dynamics and measurement of the process, non-linear as well as linear processes have to be accommodated as do sub-processes that operate at different rates. The development of a model, therefore, is a complex activity that requires an integrated framework in which to consider the activities of internationalization.

NOTE

1   The term 'commerce' has different interpretations within different languages. In the current context it signifies an integrated group of activities that connect production to consumption and involves the process of 'going to market'. Retailing, whole-saling, distribution, etc. refer to specific functions. While 'commerce' is often used to describe activities prior to the industrial revolution it subsequently has declined in use as the various separate functions have become more clearly differentiated.

REFERENCES

Alexander, N. (1997) *International retailing*. (Oxford: Blackwell)

Arvidsson, N. (1997) Internationalisation of service firms; strategic considerations. In: G. Chryssochoidis, C. Millar and J. Cledd (eds) *Internationalisation strategies*. (Basingstoke: Macmillan Business) pp. 71–89

Azuma, N. (2005) The paradox of competition in the world of volatility: an analysis of the drivers in the middle market of international fashion retailing. *Journal of Global Marketing*, 18(1/2): 45–72

Bayley, J., Clarke-Hill, C. M. and Robinson, T. M. (1995) Towards a taxonomy of international retail alliances. *Service Industries Journal*, 15(4): 25–41

Betancourt, R. R. (2004) *The economics of retailing and distribution*. (Cheltenham: Edward Elgar)

Björkman, I. and Forsgren, M. (1997) (eds) *The nature of the international firm*. (Copenhagen: Copenhagen Business School Press)

Blomstermo, A. and Sharma, D. (2003) Three decades of research on the internationalization process of firms. In: A. Blomstermo and D. Sharma (eds) *Learning in the internationalization process of firms*. (Cheltenham: Edward Elgar)

Brown, S. and Burt, S. (1992) Retail internationalisation: past imperfect, future imperative. *European Journal of Marketing*, 26(8/9): 80–84

Buckley, P. J. and Ghauri, P. (1993) (eds) *The internationalization of the firm.* (London: Academic Press)

Buckley, P. J., Pass, C. L. and Prescott, K. (1992) The internationalization of service firms: a comparison with the manufacturing sector. *Scandinavian International Business Review*, 1(1): 39–56

Burch, D. and Goss, J. (1999) Global sourcing and retail chains: shifting relationships of production in Australian agri-foods. *Rural Sociology*, 64(2): 334–350

Burt, S. (1993) Temporal trends in the internationalisation of British retailing. *International Review of Retail, Distribution and Consumer Research*, 3(4): 391–410

Burt, S. (1995) Retail internationalisation: evolution of theory and practice. In: P. J. McGoldrick and G. Davies (eds) *International retailing: trends and strategies*, (London: Pitman) pp. 51–73

Calori, R., Atamer, T. and Nunes, P. (2000) *The dynamics of international competition.* (London: Sage)

Chryssochoidis, G., Millar, C. and Cledd, J. (1997) (eds) *Internationalisation strategies.* (Basingstoke: Macmillan Business)

Contractor, F. J. and Lorange, P. (1988) *Cooperative strategies in international business.* (New York: Lexington Books)

Currah, A. and Wrigley, N. (2004) Networks of organizational learning and adaptation in retail TNCs. *Global Networks*, 4(1): 1–23

Dahringer, L. and Mühlbacher, H. (1991) Marketing services internationally: barriers and management strategies. *Journal of Services Marketing*, 5(3): 5–17

Dawson, J. A. (1999) The evolution and future structure of retailing in Europe. In: K. Jones (ed.) *The internationalisation of retailing in Europe.* (Toronto: Centre for Study of Commercial Activity) pp. 1–13

Dawson, J. A. (2001a) Is there a new commerce in Europe? *International Review of Retail, Distribution and Consumer Research*, 11(3): 287–299

Dawson, J. A. (2001b) Strategy and opportunism in European retail internationalization. *British Journal of Management*, 12(4): 253–266

Dicken, P., Kelly, P. E., Olds, K. and Yeung, H. W. (2001) Chain and networks, territories and scales: towards a relational framework for analyzing the global economy. *Global Networks*, 1(2): 89–112

Dolan, C. and Humphrey, J. (2000) Governance and trade in fresh vegetables: the impact of UK supermarkets on the African horticulture industry. *Journal of Development Studies*, 37: 147–176

Dolan, C. and Humphrey, J. (2004) Changing governance patterns in the trade in fresh vegetables between Africa and the United Kingdom. *Environment and Planning*, A36: 491–509

Douglas, E. (1975) *The economics of marketing.* (New York: Harper & Row)

Dunning, J. H. (1993) *Multinational enterprises and the global economy.* (Wokingham: Addison-Wesley)

Dunning, J. H. (1995) Reappraising the eclectic paradigm in an age of alliance capitalism. *International Journal of Business Studies*, 26(3): 461–491

Erramilli, M. K. (1990) Entry mode choices in service industries. *International Marketing Review*, 7(5): 50–61

Filser, M. (1989) *Canaux de distribution.* (Paris: Vuibert Gestion)

Filser, M., des Garets, V. and Paché, G. (2001) La distribution: organisation et stratégie. (Colombelles: EMS)

Fletcher, S. R. and Godley, A. C. (2000) Foreign direct investment in British retailing 1850–1962. *Business History*, 42(2): 43–62

Gereffi, G. (1999) International trade and industrial upgrading in the apparel commodity chain. *Journal of Industrial Economics*, 48: 3–70

Gereffi, G. and Korzeniewicz, M. (1994) (eds) *Commodity chains and global capitalism.* (Westport, CT: Greenwood Press)

Hakansson, H. (1982) (ed.) *International marketing and the purchasing of industrial goods.* (Chichester: Wiley)

Hall, M. (1949) *Distributive trading.* (London: Hutchinson University Library)

Harzing, A. W. K. (1999) *Managing the multinationals: an international study of control mechanisms.* (Cheltenham: Edward Elgar)

Hayashi, S. (1999) *Modern commercial science.* (Tokyo: Yuhikaku) (Japanese)

Hecquet, V. and Roualdes, D. (1999) Companies and local units: the employment trends in France. In: S. Biffignandi (ed.) *Micro and macro data of firms.* (Heidelberg: Physica-Verlag) pp. 587–597

Henderson, J., Dicken, P., Hess, M., Coe, N. M. and Yeung, H. W. (2002) Global production networks and the analysis of economic development. *Review of International Political Economy*, 9: 436–464

Holdren, B. R. (1960) *The structure of a retail market and the market behavior of retail units.* (Englewood Cliffs, NJ: Prentice Hall)

Hollander, S. (1970) *Multinational retailing.* (East Lansing, MI: Michigan State University)

Hughes, A. and Reimer, S. (2003) (eds) *Geographies of commodity chains.* (London: Pearson)

Ishihara, T. (2000) *Internal reorganization of commercial structure.* (Tokyo: Chikurashobo) (in Japanese)

Ishihara, T. and Ishii, J. (1996) (eds) *Integration of manufacturing and commerce,* (Tokyo: Nikkei-Shinbunsha) (in Japanese)

Johanson, J. and Mattsson, L.-G. (1988) Internationalisation in industrial systems – a network approach. In: N. Hood and J.-E. Vahlne (eds) *Strategies in global competition.* (Beckenham: Croom Helm)

Jonsson, A. and Elg, U. (2005) Knowledge and knowledge sharing in retail internationalization: Ikea's entry into Russia. Paper given to EAERCD conference, Lund, June 2005

Larke, R. (2005) The expansion of Japanese retailers overseas. *Journal of Global Marketing*, 18(1/2): 99–120

Leslie, D. and Reimer, S. (1999) Spatializing commodity chains. *Progress in Human Geography*, 44: 401–420

Leslie, D. and Reimer, S. (2003) Fashioning furniture: structuring the furniture commodity chain. *Area*, 35: 427–437

McClelland, W. G. M. (1966) *Costs and competition in retailing*. (London: Macmillan)

Mintel (2004) *European retail rankings* (London: Mintel)

Mukoyama, M. (2000) The standardization-adaptation problem of product assortment in the internationalization of retailers. In: M. R. Czinkota and M. Kotabe (eds) *Japanese distribution strategy*. (London: Business Press)

Nielsen, K., Pedersen, K. and Vestergaard, J. (1999) *Internationalization of SMEs*. (London: Macmillan)

Nonaka, I. and Konno, N. (1998) The concept of 'Ba': building a foundation for knowledge creation. *California Management Review*, 40(3): 1–15

Nonaka, I., Konno, N. and Toyama, R. (2001) The emergence of 'Ba'. In: I. Nonaka and T. Nishiguchi (eds) *Knowledge emergence*. (New York: Oxford University Press) pp. 13–29

Nooteboom, B. (1980) *Retailing: applied analysis in the theory of the firm*. (Amsterdam: J. C. Gieben)

Oviatt, B. M. and McDougall, P. P. (1994) Toward a theory of international new ventures. *Journal of International Business Studies*, Spring: 45–64

Pellegrini, L. (1990) *Economia della distribuzione commerciale*. (Milan: Egea)

Pellegrini, L. (1996) (ed.) *La distribuzione commerciale in Italia*. (Bologna: Il Mulino)

Quinn, B. (1999) The temporal context of UK retailers' motives for international expansion. *Service Industries Journal*, 19(2): 102–117

Sciarelli, S. and Vona, R. (2000) *L'impresa commerciale*. (Milan: McGraw-Hill)

Shaw, S., Dawson, J. and Blair, L. (1992) Imported foods in a British supermarket chain: buyer decisions in Safeway. *International Review of Retail Distribution and Consumer Research*, 2(1): 35–58

Spranzi, A. (1991) *La distribuzione commerciale*. (Milan: F. Angeli)

Valikängas, L. and Lehtinen, U. (1991) Strategic types of services and international marketing. *International Journal of Service Industry*, 5(2): 72–84

Welch, D. E. and Welch, L. S. (1996) The internationalization process and networks: a strategic management perspective. *Journal of International Marketing*, 4(3): 11–28

Welch, L. S. and Luostarinen, R. (1988) Internationalization: evolution of a concept. *Journal of General Management*, 14(2): 34–55

Wrigley, N., Coe, N. M. and Currah, A. (2005) Globalizing retail: conceptualizing the distribution-based transnational corporation (TNC). *Progress in Human Geography*, 29(4): 1–21

Young, S., Hamill, J., Wheeler, C. and Davies, J. R. (1989) *International market entry and development: strategies and management*. (Hemel Hempstead: Harvester Wheatsheaf)

Chapter 2

Retail internationalization as a process

John Dawson and Masao Mukoyama

INTRODUCTION

The internationalization of retailing is a process, not a series of events. It is a complex process that has changed in recent years. It has become more widespread. This internationalization process has an increasing influence on corporate strategies and has extended its effects on the development of the retail sector. The magnitude, the form and the function of the process have all changed. A body of research on internationalization in retailing has grown (for example, Akehurst and Alexander 1995; Alexander 1997; Alexander and Myers 2000; Burt 1991, 1995; Dawson 1994; and Rugman and Girod 2003), yet much of this research has focused on events. The links and relationships between the events often have not been explored, although there has been a move towards this approach in more recent work, notably the study of Royal Ahold by Wrigley and Currah (2003). A limited amount of research, often in case studies, has explored the sequences of events. Often the work is descriptive and considers the unique situation of the case study company, for example the detailed work of Laulajainen (1987, 1991, 1992). Such descriptions are useful and insightful but provide a partial perspective on the overall process. There is little research that considers the processes associated with the sequence of events before placing these processes in a model. Such a model is essential to a theoretical and conceptual understanding of retail internationalization if it is to be of use to academics concerned with how firms function and to managers who are charged with directing the firm. The model of retail internationalization must encapsulate a process that permeates through the whole of the retail firm, influences competitor actions and changes the environment in which the firm and its competitors operate. Internationalization, when viewed as a process, enables a retail firm to exploit innovation and so to grow and evolve.

DIMENSIONS OF THE FRAMEWORK DEFINING THE PROCESS

The framework to the process can be hypothesized to comprise a number of dimensions. These dimensions can be related to the content of the process, the results of the process and the framing of the process.

We can consider three dimensions that relate to the content of the process:

1 the form of the internationalization process;
2 the temporal stages or sequence through which the process moves;
3 the transformations of resources and technology transfers within the process.

There is a dimension that draws together the results of the process:

4 the outputs of the process.

There are three dimensions that can be considered as relating to the framing of the process:

5 the value system on which managerial decisions are based;
6 the scale of the process;
7 prevailing environmental and situational conditions.

These seven suggested dimensions to the process interact but it is useful to consider each in turn as a way of trying to characterize the process.

DIMENSIONS OF CONTENT OF THE PROCESS

Form of the process

It is possible to distinguish four broad forms to the process of internationalization of retailing in its guise as new commerce.

Functional This form of the process relates to the functions that are affected by the internationalization activity. Chapter 1 has explored these functions. The dominant functional form of the process discussed in this book is the operation of sales outlets in a country other than the country of origin of the firm. Other functional forms of the internationalization process involve the use of other resources obtained from another country. Often these resources are products for resale, but they may include items, services and labour used in the retail firm. As discussed in Chapter 1 the international sourcing of items for resale is long established and involves increasing volumes of goods as international trade increases. International sourcing of items used in the firm includes, for example, computer equipment, logistics equipment, packaging materials, vehicles, consultancy and so on. There are few studies of this feature of retail purchasing but the international element is likely to be increasing. The use of internationally mobile labour and of international capital are examples of other input resources that represent different functional forms of the internationalization process. The international operation of sales outlets is, however, the focus of this chapter.

Spatial This form of the process involves the way information passes through geographic space, the nature of decisions over space, the spatial diffusion of know-ledge and how investment is allocated spatially. Examples are: the way that a spatial network of stores is created so increasing the market power of a retailer, the way that information is diffused through the consumer body in the 'foreign' market and the way that a spatial supply network using regional distribution centres is created for the store network. At a global level, for example, we see this form of the process in the way IKEA has established stores across 32 countries by opening each store through direct investment in a community and in how Ahold had established stores across 28 countries by 2003 generally by a process of acquisition and joint-venture investment with retailers already in the countries. In both companies there is spatial form to the internationalization process but the mechanisms are different. There is a growing literature using the concept of 'embeddedness' to explore this spatial aspect of the form of the process (Dicken 2003, 2004; Wrigley *et al.* 2005).

Temporal This form to the process relates to the period of its activity, the speed at which it operates and the extent to which it is cyclical, staged or repeated over time. Some retailers have been involved in international activity for a long period, for example Aldi, and C&A in Europe. For others it is a recent activity although the retailer may have been in existence for a long time, for example Tesco, and El Corte Ingles. Marks & Spencer have passed through a process of market search, market entry, store development and then exit, from a considerable part of its international activity in a little over 20 years (Burt *et al.* 2002; Mellahi *et al.* 2002). The corporate learning activities associated with foreign retailer ventures clearly have a temporal dimension with some firms able to learn more quickly than others (Currah and Wrigley 2004). Carrefour, for example, has entered several markets and learnt quickly whether the market holds potential for future development; if not withdrawal has been relatively rapid as in the US, UK, Germany and Japan. Within a firm, therefore, we can see different time lines to developments in different countries and so a complex temporal form exists for the process.

Structural This form of the process relates to the structure of the firm and its markets and the changes associated with the internationalization process. Structure in this context is the nexus of relationships that exist between variables that define the firm and its market. Thus, the cost structure, governance structure, relationships with suppliers, competition in the sector, and so on, together constitute the overall structure. Internationalization causes changes in this structure. Wrigley and Currah (2003) have explored transfers of intellectual capital and knowledge that occur as part of the structural transformation of the firm on internationalization. A further example of this form of process was the change in relationships with suppliers that occurred when Promodès entered the Greek food sector. Promodès required longer payment periods and lower prices from its Greek suppliers than had previously been the case and when these were achieved Greek retailers sought similar conditions from the suppliers. A similar process was evident in Japan after the entry of Carrefour.

All four aspects of the content of the process exist simultaneously, interact, and so help to define the specific nature of the generic process associated with particular internationalization events.

Stages of the process

The retail internationalization process can be hypothesized as comprising a sequence of stages. Passage from one stage to the next is characterized by a distinctive set of activities. Some type of trigger or catalyst is likely to mark the move from one stage to the next. The key stages are:

- pre-entry
- entry
- post-entry development
- assimilation
- exit.

The amount of time in each stage is highly variable across firms and markets. Managerial activity is also very different at each stage.

These stages differ from the stage models in the international business literature that emphasize the change in organization as a manufacturing firm moves from exporting to establishing branch plants (Calori *et al.* 2000; Johanson and Vahlne 1977, 1990). Although Bell and Young (1998) and Turnbull (1993) have criticized this approach, the alternatives of Dunning's eclectic paradigm and the network/ interaction approach also are not easily applicable to retailing as has been argued in Chapter 1. These approaches focus on accessing markets from a distance rather than being present in the market as is essential in a retail context.

There exists a substantial amount of research on aspects of pre-entry and of entry, particularly the different entry mechanisms and the advantages and disadvantages of each (for example, see Alexander 1997; Alexander and Myers 2000;

Dawson 2001; Doherty 1999; and Evans *et al.* 2000). Such studies are useful but represent only a part of the overall process of internationalization. The stages of 'assimilation' and 'exit' effectively mark different end states of the international-ization process. Assimilation occurs when the firm changes from being a foreign firm to being a domestic one. Exit can be of many types from complete withdrawal to reduced levels of activity (Burt *et al.* 2003, 2004).

Examples of the relationships between forms of process and the stages of the process are illustrated in Table 2.1. It may also be possible to explore phases within each of these major stages. Table 2.2 presents, for example, a possible sequence of phases during the post-entry phase.

The transformation of resources and knowledge transfer

The internationalization process causes the transformation of resources within the firm as it operates in a foreign market. This transformation process often involves some form of knowledge transfer within the firm and from the internationalizing firm into the host market (Currah and Wrigley 2003; Wrigley and Currah 2003).

Table 2.1 *Activities illustrating the relationships between stages and form of processes*

Stages of process	Form of process			
	Functional – operation of international stores	Spatial	Temporal	Structural
Pre-entry	Knowledge review Market research	Local market research	Extent of earlier experiences	Strategy evaluation
Entry	Formula design	Market choice	Timing of entry	Entry method Relations with suppliers
Post-entry	Retail brand development Knowledge transfer to Head Office	Network development	Rate of expansion	Management of cost structure Competitive activities
Assimilation	Social integration of firm	–	Trigger to establish independent firm	Creation of subsidiary company
Exit	–	Sales unit closures	–	Sales of operations to other retailer

Table 2.2 Phases of internationalization of a retailer on post-entry stage

	Stabilization phase	Consolidation phase	Control phase	Domination phase
Dynamics	■ Uncertainty in formats, formula and markets ■ High rate of formula innovation and high degree of operational flexibility ■ Fluctuations in demand ■ Low volume of sales ■ Formula functionality more important than brand name ■ Erratic competitive actions ■ Test relationships with suppliers	■ Appearance of dominant format ■ Clearer understanding of customer needs ■ Increased process innovation ■ Introduction of retailer branding ■ Competition based on quality and availability ■ Network expansion	■ Strong pressure on margins ■ Formula differences emphasized ■ Retail brand product development specific to market ■ Convergence of product, formula and process innovations	■ Multi-format and multi-formula development ■ Obsolescence of earlier assets ■ New competition from many directions ■ Increase of channel power ■ Options to break subservient position in respect of group
Priorities	■ Development of formula ■ Understanding customer ■ Acquiring knowledge (tacit and explicit) from competition ■ Establishing the formula as benchmark format	■ Fine-tuning of formula ■ Market exploration and learning about market ■ Pursuit of growth strategy to increase sales space ■ Improve logistics	■ Cost-control focus ■ Branding of formula ■ Customer service levels defined and delivered ■ Extend power over suppliers	■ Brand development of formulae and items ■ Increase social role ■ Explore new formula for growth sub-markets ■ Outsource non-core activity
Strategic alliances	■ Formation of alliances with business services providers ■ Evaluation of franchising	■ Joint-ventures and alliances to increase network density ■ Alliances with marketing service agencies	■ Retailer-controlled alliances with suppliers	■ Alliances with innovative channels
Mergers and acquisitions	■ Acquisitions to gain tacit knowledge ■ Acquisitions to gain operational scale	■ Opportunistic acquisition of competitors	■ Acquisitions to become dominant retailer in the market ■ Acquisitions to enter new markets	■ Acquisitions of niche players ■ Divestment of non-performing formulae

Source: Dawson (2003a)

The transformation occurs through various economic and social mechanisms that operate in different ways in a foreign context than in the domestic one. Examples of these mechanisms are:

- Economies of scale, scope and replication operate at different speeds and with different intensity in different countries. Scale economies in buying relate to the size of the market and the structure of the supply sector, both of which vary considerably across countries.
- Social mechanisms of communication and decision making inside the firm vary from country to country. The extent of local control varies with firm and by country within a firm. For example, Lidl, the food discount retailer, has a highly centralized system of managerial control while DM, the drugstore discount retailer, has a very decentralized decision-making structure. Within Reitan-Narvesen, the food discount retailer, the level of control over the Rema discount store formula varies considerably by country.
- Differences in the transaction costs associated with decisions on alternative organizational structures, for example, with franchise operation, wholly owned subsidiaries and joint-ventures. Marks & Spencer used a different organizational structure in different countries in recognition of the different transaction costs.
- Inter-country variations in the social mechanisms of power relationships that govern interaction with the external environment of consumers, firms and public policy agencies. Western retailers entering China have found difficulty accommodating the different nature of social and power relationships even to the extent that some, notably Ahold and Obi, have withdrawn from the market.
- Differences in the managerial capabilities relevant to an ability to operate in a different country and to transfer organizational capabilities across markets (Florida and Kenny 2002). The extent of the international perspective and international culture of a firm will affect the nature of perceptions of different countries and will affect the mechanisms that are put in place to develop managerial knowledge and to transfer it. In this respect we can contrast IKEA and Boots. In IKEA the commitment to internationalization is strong and capabilities are transferred internationally despite the commonality of item ranges in stores. In Boots there has been, over many years, a history of failed international expansion with an apparent inability to operate in other countries and an apparent low level of commitment to the foreign operations.

This dimension of resource transformation is of particular importance because it deals with the nature of the retailer's 'product' in the foreign market (Goldman 2001). The retailer will be experienced and have knowledge in the operation of a format that is adjusted to their home country, and is their brand of a format, which we can call their store formula. This is then transferred to the new market. Each firm will have its own formula and will adjust in a slightly different way to the new market. The formula also will be adjusted as experience of the foreign market is gained.

For example, the hypermarket format operated by Tesco in the UK is the branded Tesco Extra formula. The generic hypermarket format has a number of characteristics associated with size, product range, merchandising systems, and so on, and the Tesco Extra formula builds on and adjusts these core characteristics and possibly adds particular innovations. The nature of the formula is an important output from the strategy of the firm, in this case Tesco. Similarly, Carrefour has its own branded hypermarket in France which is different from Tesco but is still a hypermarket format. In the decision to become international the strategy for internationalization will include consideration of the market to enter, the entry mode, the managerial control mechanisms and organizational structure to be used. This international strategy will also reflect the culture of the firms and its core competencies that may be able to be transferred to the new market. The implementation of this strategy may require the creation of a new formula, probably as an adjustment to the one already in operation in the home market. Thus, for example, the Tesco hypermarket in South Korea is a different formula to that in the UK. Those in Taiwan or Poland or Hungary are different again although all have core features of the Tesco branded hypermarket developed in the UK. The Tesco formula in South Korea initially involved a joint-venture organization, different sourcing systems for items, a different balance of categories of items, different customer service provision, and so on. The variables that define the Tesco hypermarket are interpreted in a different way in each market. There is a transformation of resources and a transfer of knowledge. In the same manner, Carrefour and other retailers undertake comparable transfers of knowledge to create country-specific formulae.

This knowledge transfer will be somewhat different when the retailer establishes individual stores from when the retailer buys an existing firm. This again can be illustrated with Tesco's international operation of hypermarkets. In Poland, Tesco has established their hypermarket formula, transferring knowledge into the Polish market from its experiences in the UK and also from the other Central European markets where it has operations. In addition Tesco, in 2002, purchased a chain of HIT hypermarkets. This chain was the Polish version of the hypermarket formula of Dohle, a firm based in Germany. In acquiring these HIT stores and changing them to the Tesco formula there is, again, a knowledge transfer but one that is influenced by the formula designed by the previous owner.

In this transformation of resources and transfer of knowledge there are three distinct aspects:

1   the transfers in the firm needed to establish a new formula in the new market – both in individually developed and in acquired outlets;

2   the transfers within the firm of knowledge gained from experience in the new market;
3   the transfers to other firms and from other firms operating in the same market.

These three aspects of resource transformation and technology transfer operate at two levels in respect of the operational aspects of the firm:

1   The level of the core format and the relationships that define it and its evolution, for example the hypermarket, convenience stores, etc.
2   The changes to the format made by a firm to make it a formula of that firm in a particular market, for example, Tesco hypermarket in UK, Seven-Eleven convenience store in Japan. Within each market these changes are adjusted to make the formula specific to the local market, for example, Tesco Taiwan, Seven-Eleven Taiwan.

THE DIMENSION OF OUTPUTS OF THE PROCESS

The three issues considered so far are internal to the firm and part of decision-making activity inside the firm. There is a set of issues to be considered in a model of the internationalization process in commerce (retailing) that relates to the output of the process at its various stages. The output or impacts of the processes, on the firm, consumers, channel relationships, public policy and society, have been considered elsewhere in a conceptual framework. There have been few rigorous studies of the impacts and of the ways these impacts are felt. More are needed.

In considering the impacts of internationalization, it is suggested (Dawson 2003b) that it is necessary to distinguish between:

■   types of impacts
■   the processes of impact, and
■   the level of intensity of impacts.

Figure 2.1 illustrates the range of types of impact anticipated as outputs of the internationalization process. Each of these types of impact have associated processes so that, for example, processes of marketing management and retail operations management are important in determining the competitive impacts while processes of channel management and logistics, management of the technology of flows and buying and supplier management are critical in changes in the effectiveness of the demand chain (Takahashi 1994). Clearly there are interactions between these outputs and internal aspects of the internationalization process, notably the resource transformations and knowledge transfer in the firm. These issues are explored in more detail in Dawson (2003b).

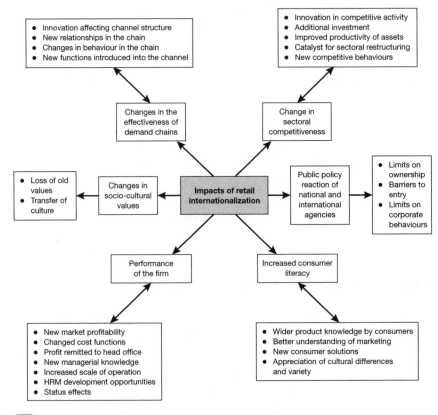

Figure 2.1 *Types of impact of retail internationalization*

THE DIMENSIONS FRAMING THE PROCESS

The third group of dimensions frame the internationalization process. These are factors that can be hypothesized as mediating influences that shape the process but are not exclusive to it. These framing dimensions exist outside the process of internationalization but influence the content and the outputs.

Managerial value systems

The operation of the internationalization process in retailing is influenced by the managerial cultures of both the firm and the country. Managerial styles differ in response to historical and cultural factors that underpin social value systems. This is particularly the case in retailing, as pointed out above, where the link between managerial culture and consumer culture is important. In the context of international retailing at least four main distinct managerial styles can be hypothesized:

North American, European, Asian and Islamic. Child *et al.* (2001) suggest a wider range of styles within Europe in their analysis of international acquisitions, but for our purposes broader cultural values are of more importance (Nisbett 2003).

These styles of managerial culture are broad over-generalizations of the subtle effects of culture on management methods and each broad style contains some substantially different cultural approaches. Thus, within the European managerial culture realm it is possible to distinguish differences in managerial and consumer culture. For example, it may be appropriate to distinguish different styles in firms based in macro regions, for example, Mediterranean, Scandinavian, French and Anglo-Saxon. It is argued by practitioners, for example, that there is a French style of hypermarket, typified by Carrefour and Casino, and an Anglo-Saxon style typified by Real and Tesco (Ducroq 2003). This approach applies to retailing some of the conclusions of Child *et al.* (2001). The interplay between consumer-market cultures and the culture of the firm is complex and not well understood.

In respect of retail internationalization, relatively few European retailers have been successful in North America, with the most successful adopting American-style management within relatively devolved subsidiary companies. European retailers have been more successful in their international moves within Europe. Few American retailers have been successful in Europe when they have sought to use American managerial style. American retailers have shown a preference to move into Canada. Asian retailers, with a few exceptions, have remained within the Asian countries and the exceptions have tended to operate highly devolved subsidiary companies. Rugman and Girod (2003) consider this macro-regional nature of internationalization but do not hypothesize any explanations. Recent moves by North American and European retailers into Asia have met with mixed fortunes; some of the lack of success may be due to the managerial culture of the foreign firm.

The managerial style is manifest in many features of commerce including formula design, customer relationships and customer interactions, knowledge management and transfer, technology responsiveness and possibly even the nature of innovation. We can, therefore, expect the process of retail internationalization to be heavily influenced by the cultural style of the internationalizing firm and the cultural values of managerial structures in the market.

Scale

Scale is a further factor that has a direct influence on the process. Any model of the process of retail internationalization must accommodate this factor. Size of firm, size of shop and size of market all appear to influence the way the process operates. Some examples can be used to illustrate these three aspects of scale.

International moves by firms inevitably dilute earning for the firms and larger firms are more able to accommodate this dilution. The transfer of scarce managerial resources from domestic operations to foreign operations is more likely to be possible in the larger firms. In respect of size of shop, then the site acquisition process for smaller units in the foreign market is likely to be easier and certainly lower cost than the acquisition of sites for large shops. The size of the market influences, among other factors, the degree of commitment a firm may have in a new market and the level of resources the firm is willing to allocate to that market.

Prevailing environmental conditions

A final influential factor of relevance is the prevailing environmental conditions in host and home countries. This influences the speed at which the stages of the process operate, the outputs of the process, the responsiveness to managerial style, the form of the process and the mechanisms of resource transformation and knowledge transfer.

The level of consumer wealth can be a significant factor in this respect. Wealth is not evenly distributed so the spatial pattern of development of an international retailer will be influenced by spatial differences in wealth and spending power. In the moves of Western European retailers into Central Europe in the 1990s most firms moved first to the major cities with their concentration of consumer spending power. There are several other aspects of the consumer environment that influence the internationalization process, for example, household structure and familial relationships, durable and home ownership, availability of personal living space, and so on. Many other aspects of the prevailing environment are also relevant. Studies of international retailers moving into China, for example, emphasize the importance of Chinese socio-political networks as a cultural feature of importance. Such a basic feature of culture is likely to have a deep and lasting effect on the internationalization process. Other environmental factors may be more short-term, for example the problems of logistics for foreign retailers in China. In all cases, however, it is the managerial perception of these aspects as much as the aspects themselves that is significant. This managerial perception will be influenced by the managerial style of the firm.

MEASUREMENT

The second part of this chapter considers some of the issues of measurement of the internationalization process. The dimensions, discussed above, that characterize the internationalization process in retailing are complex and not easily measured. Nonetheless, in order to develop a model of the process some form of evaluation or measurement is necessary. Qualitative assessment as well as quantitative measurement is possible in this respect. Measurement of the process is required for accurate description, comparison, understanding of the interactions, and also for explanation.

Measurement to describe the process

The process can be described with four main measurements:

The retailer involved   This addresses the question 'who?'. This goes beyond a simple name but includes consideration of the people who are making the decisions, the organizational structure of the firm, the size of the firm, the items sold by the firm, its ownership, and so on. In effect, a full description of the retailer is relevant because many of these aspects of the firm affect the way the process operates. The location of the head office is part of the overall description of the firm. A retailer, particularly a smaller firm, with a head office close to a national border may find border hopping easier or a more obvious strategy than a firm headquartered at a great distance from a border. The people may also be important.

The activity involved   This addresses the question 'what?'. The retail format and formula are major aspects for measuring the activity involved. Some formats appear easier to internationalize than others. Department stores, in general, appear to be difficult to internationalize but discount food stores appear to be more suited to the internationalization process. The number of SKUs in a format may be a factor but other factors are also involved, for example, managerial structure and cultural preferences of consumers. The management of the format and its trans-formation into the retailer's formula are also to be considered, for example, the type of organization involved (joint-venture, franchise and so on), the extent to which expatriate managers are used, the use of retailer branding, the specific item ranges on sale, the retail logistics system, and so on. The activity need not involve shop formats but can be in remote shopping formats, automated non-store formats or personal selling formats.

The location of the activity   This addresses the question 'where?'. The location can be considered in respect of country and type of location in the country – size of market, type of site, etc. Type of site may mean, for example, location at trans-port nodes, out-of-town green field sites, city centre, etc. Location may also be relative to another retailer with advantages in being associated with proximity to the other firm, with an approach through concessions in other stores being the extreme position. Measurement of 'where' has to be undertaken in order to describe the process fully. This measures the access to the market.

The time of the activity   This addresses the question 'when?'. The time can be considered in an absolute sense of a date and also in a relative sense in respect of conditions in the firm and in its environment. For example, achieving a certain market share in the home market may become the trigger for starting the pre-entry aspects of the overall internationalization process, or sustained losses for a particular period may mean that exit occurs. Time may also be judged in respect

43

of the likely acceptance of the retailer by the consumer in the host market. Time may also be influenced by the financial position of the firm with a strong financial base being needed to sustain the profit dilution that occurs on market entry.

From the information on these aspects of description, so comparisons and relationships among them can be determined. Thus, we can identify changes in the patterns of movements, the preferred activity of particular companies, the temporal form of the intensity of the overall process, and so on. Burt (1991, 1993) and others have undertaken significant work in this measurement for descriptive purposes.

In making the comparisons we can:

- Compare the activities of one retailer across countries, and possibly across culture realms; for example, comparing the experience of Carrefour in its activities in American, European and Asian culture realms.
- Compare the activities of several retailers in one country or culture realm; for example, comparing American, European and non-Chinese Asian retailer activity in China.
- Compare the activities of several retailers in several countries; for example, within the clothing market, by comparing the international activities of Gap, H&M, Zara, Fast Retailing and others.
- Compare the totality of international activities across several countries; for example, comparing a range of firms at a specific stage, for example initial entry mechanisms.

The database required for such exercises increases in complexity as we add more activities and more countries. The difficulty of development of a comprehensive database should not be underestimated. None exists. One is needed.[1]

Measurement to explain the process

To move towards explanation we have to address the question 'why?' not only in respect of undertaking international activity of any kind but also in respect of the specific nature of the activity undertaken by a firm at a particular time. Measurement to explain the process inevitably is closely related to the framework, considered above, that has been used to establish the process.

Why internationalize?

The motives for internationalization have been studied through several surveys by Alexander (1997) and others. It is necessary to measure the situation of the firm both internally and within the environment of its home market. It is appropriate to identify:

- what constitutes sufficient conditions;
- what the triggers to action are; and
- what constitute the discriminating success factors that underpin the decision to internationalize.

The triggers for action will be within the firm and in the target country and there needs to be an alignment such that actions are stimulated. It is unlikely that there are clear quantitative measures of these conditions but there are likely to be qualitative measures that relate to the resources of the firm.

Why internationalize in a particular way?

A second set of qualitative measures are associated with managerial competencies. The learning ability of the firm may be used to explain why internationalization is undertaken in the way it has been. It would be expected that different resources and competencies will be used depending on the ways that internationalization is undertaken (Hunt 2000). Thus, for example, different resources, even within a single firm, are used in international franchising from those used when internationalization is by acquisition. Different resources are needed to internationalize hypermarkets from those needed to develop convenience stores (Chang 2002). Different resources are needed to expand rapidly from those associated with slower development of a network. The measures to describe internationalization require to be related to the resource base of the firm.

The way that internationalization is carried out will also be related to the managerial perceptions of the market and of the competition. The ability of the management of the firm to see and analyse the catalysts and constraints in the foreign market is an important factor in explaining the patterns of international activity. The socio-economic conditions in the host market, and the evolution of these conditions as perceived by the retailer, will affect the way the internationalization process is pursued by different retailers. The same market conditions may be perceived differently by different retailers; for example, the perceptions of Russia as a target market vary greatly among retailers depending on the retail firm's evaluation of risk.

In all cases public policy intervenes in the internationalization process and affects the ways that retailers make decisions. The policies may stimulate and encourage, either directly or indirectly, particular directions of internationalization (Davies 1993). Commonly, public policy introduces constraints on particular aspects of the internationalization process and thus shapes the way it operates. For example, the opening of the Carrefour store in Cracow, Poland in July 2002 was halted by city authorities who refused the opening permit because the associated public infrastructure, a bus station, to be provided by Carrefour, was not complete.

The competitive reactions of retailers already present in the market are also important in shaping the way the process operates. The internationalization process acts alongside the processes of retailing undertaken by domestic retailers and interacts with them. This interaction helps to shape the internationalization process within a market.

In measuring the various factors of why internationalization is undertaken in a particular way it is necessary, throughout, to distinguish *sufficient conditions* from *discriminating conditions*. Conditions may have to be present for the process to operate but their presence does not necessarily mean the process will operate. These sufficient conditions are also not those that explain the different mechanisms through which the process operates.

Evaluation of internationalization

Measurement in this context addresses the question 'Has internationalization been a success?'. Measurement is needed for the outputs of the internationalization outlined above. The level of success or otherwise is an important feedback factor in the overall process and affects explanation of temporal forms of the process. There are several aspects to measurement of success depending on the stakeholders involved:

- ■ Financial measures. The amount and type of investment and the return on this investment are typical areas of measurement, in a similar way to the evaluation of any domestic activity of the firm. What may be different is the expectation of the size of investment needed and the rate of return that is considered to be acceptable, both initially and after a number of years.
- ■ Knowledge transfer to other parts of the firm. The extent to which the resources of the firm generally are enhanced by activities in the foreign market.
- ■ Stimulus to competition. The extent to which there is a higher level of competition and more competitive behaviour in the sector as a result of the international activity.
- ■ Improved quality of retail provision. The extent to which there are improvements in the consumer perception of satisfaction with retail provision.

The obverse of these issues of success are the issues of 'failure'. Measures of failure can range from complete withdrawal to limited network reorganization.

These various issues of measurement are related to the framework of the processes considered. The different aspects of the framework can be measured but different approaches are required in respect of the different aspects of the framework.

CONCLUSIONS

Figure 2.2 summarizes the thesis of this chapter. Retail internationalization is a process. The process in commerce is not a simple linear and sequential process but there are complex interactions among variables that provide the framework in which internationalization occurs. The core of the process is a mechanism to sustain innovation with the transfer of knowledge within the firm and between the firm and its environment (Gallouj 2002). The transfer of knowledge enables the transformation in the resources of the firm. The process involves not just the retailer who moves internationally but also many other groups including competing firms, suppliers, consumers and public policy agencies.

In moving towards a model of the internationalization process we need to identify the framework of the process and establish the architecture of the process. It is hypothesized that there are seven dimensions to this framework. These dimensions, comprising the content of the process, are related to the way in which the process is described with the questions of who, what, where and when being applied to each dimension. From this description it is then possible to build

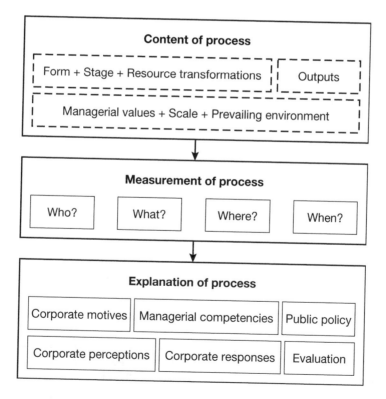

Figure 2.2 *Hypothesized dimensions of the internationalization process*

hypotheses of explanation that relate the activities of the firm to the environment in which it operates.

NOTE

1 With the greatly increasing importance of international retailers within the world economy, the opportunity exists for a supra-national agency, for example the WTO or UNCTAD, to develop such a resource that would help in understanding the process and inform policy makers.

REFERENCES

Akehurst, G. and Alexander, N. (1995) The internationalisation process in retailing, *Service Industries Journal*, 15(4): 1–15

Alexander, N. (1997) *International retailing*. (Oxford: Blackwell)

Alexander, N. and Myers, H. (2000) The retail internationalisation process, *International Marketing Review*, 17(4/5): 334–353

Bell, J. and Young, S. (1998) Towards an integrative framework of the internationalization of the firm. In: G. Hooley, R. Loveridge and D. Wilson (eds) *Internationalization: process, context and markets*. (Basingstoke: Macmillan) pp. 5–28

Burt, S. (1991) Trends in the internationalisation of grocery retailing: the European experience, *International Review of Retail, Distribution and Consumer Research*, 1(4): 487–515

Burt, S. (1993) Temporal trends in the internationalisation of British retailing. *International Review of Retail, Distribution and Consumer Research*, 3 (4): 391–410.

Burt, S. (1995) 'Retail internationalisation: evolution of theory and practice'. In: P. J. McGoldrick and G. Davies (eds) *International retailing: trends and strategies*. (London: Pitman) pp. 51–73

Burt, S., Dawson, J. and Sparks, L. (2003) Failure in international retailing: research propositions. *International Review of Retail, Distribution and Consumer Research*, 13(4): 355–373

Burt, S., Dawson, J. and Sparks, L. (2004) The international divestment activities of European grocery retailers. *European Management Journal*, 22(5): 483–492

Burt, S., Mellahi, K., Jackson, P. and Sparks, L. (2002) Retail internationalization and retail failure: issues for the case of Marks & Spencer. *International Review of Retail, Distribution and Consumer Research*, 12: 191–219

Calori, R., Atamer, T. and Nunes, P. (2000) *The dynamics of international competition*. (London: Sage)

Chang, F. (2002) *Analysis of competition in the convenience store industry in Taiwan*. Ph.D. thesis, University of Edinburgh

Child, J., Faulkner, D. and Pitkethly, R. (2001) *The management of international acquisitions*. (Oxford: Oxford University Press)

Currah, A. and Wrigley, N. (2004) Networks of organizational learning and adaptation in retail TNCs. *Global Networks*, 4(1): 1–23

Davies, B. K. (1993) Trade barriers in East and South East Asia: the implications for retailers. *International Review of Retail, Distribution and Consumer Research*, 3(4): 345–366

Dawson, J. (1994) The internationalization of retailing operations, *Journal of Marketing Management*, 10: 267–282

Dawson, J. (2001) Strategy and opportunism in European retail internationalization. *British Journal of Management*, 12(4): 253–266

Dawson, J. (2003a) Introduction. In: J. Dawson, M. Mukoyama, Sang Chul Choi and R. Larke (eds) *Retail internationalisation in Asia*. (London: RoutledgeCurzon) pp. 1–5

Dawson, J. (2003b) Towards a model of the impacts of retail internationalisation. In: J. Dawson, M. Mukoyama, Sang Chul Choi and R. Larke (eds) *Retail internationalisation in Asia*. (London: RoutledgeCurzon) pp. 189–209

Dicken, P. (2003) 'Placing firms': grounding the debate on the global corporation. In: J. A. Peck and H. W. Yeung (eds) *Remaking the global economy: economic-geographical perspectives*. (London: Sage) pp. 27–44

Dicken, P. (2004) Geographers and 'globalization': (yet) another boat missed. *Transactions of Institute of British Geographers*, NS29: 5–26

Doherty, A. M. (1999) Explaining international retailers' market entry mode strategy: internalization theory, agency theory and the importance of information asymmetry. *International Review of Retail, Distribution and Consumer Research*, 9(4): 379–402

Ducroq, C. (2003) *La nouvelle distribution*. (Paris: Dunod)

Evans, J., Treadgold, A. and Mavondo, F. T. (2000) Psychic distance and the performance of international retailers: a suggested theoretical framework. *International Marketing Review*, 17(4/5): 373–391

Florida, R. and Kenny, M. (2002) Transfer and replication of organizational capabilities. In: G. Dosi, R. R. Nelson and S. G. Winter (eds) *The nature and dynamics of organizational capabilities*. (Oxford: Oxford University Press) pp. 281–307

Gallouj, F. (2002) *Innovation in the service economy*. (Cheltenham: Edward Elgar)

Goldman, A. (2001) The transfer of retail formats into developing economies: the example of China. *Journal of Retailing*, 77(2): 221–242

Hunt, S. (2000) *A general theory of competition*. (London: Sage)

Johanson, J. and Mattsson, L.-G. (1988) Internationalisation in industrial systems – a network approach. In: N. Hood and J.-E. Vahlne (eds) *Strategies in global competition*. (Beckenham: Croom Helm)

Johanson, J. and Vahlne, J.-E. (1977) The internationalization process of the firm – a model of knowledge development and increasing foreign market commitment. *Journal of International Business Studies*, 8 (Spring/Summer): 23–32

Johanson, J. and Vahlne, J.-E. (1990) The mechanism of internationalisation. *International Marketing Review*, 7(4): 11–24

Laulajainen, R. (1987) *Spatial strategies in retailing*. (Dordrecht: D Reidel)

Laulajainen, R. (1991) International expansion of an apparel retailer: Hennes and Mauritz of Sweden. *Zeitschrift fur Wirtschaftsgeographie*, 35(1): 1–15

Laulajainen, R. (1992) Louis Vuitton Malletier: a truly global retailer. *Annals of the Japan Association of Economic Geography*, 38(2): 55–77

Mellahi, K., Jackson, P. and Sparks, L. (2002) An exploratory study into failure in successful organizations: the case of Marks & Spencer. *British Journal of Management*, 13(1): 15–29

Nisbett, R. E. (2003) The geography of thought. (New York: Free Press)

Rugman, A. and Girod, S. (2003) Retail multinationals and globalization: the evidence is regional. *European Management Journal*, 21(1): 24–37

Takahashi, Y. (1994) Toys R Us fuels changes in Japan's toy distribution system. *Journal of Marketing Channels*, 3(3): 91–112

Turnbull, P. W. (1993) A challenge to the stages theory of the internationalization process. In: P. J. Buckley and P. Ghauri (eds) *The internationalization of the firm*. (London: Academic Press) pp. 172–185 (reprint of a paper published in 1987)

Wrigley, N. and Currah, A. (2003) The stresses of retail internationalization: lessons for Royal Ahold's experience in Latin America. *International Review of Retail, Distribution and Consumer Research*, 13(3): 221–243

Wrigley, N., Coe, N. M. and Currah, A. (2005) Globalizing retail: conceptualizing the distribution-based transnational corporation (TNC). *Progress in Human Geography*, 29(4): 1–21

Chapter 3

Building an international retail strategy

Marc Dupuis and Jean Fournioux

INTRODUCTION

Already well under way by the 1970s, retail internationalization accelerated in the mid-1990s. The internationalization process for companies and for store formats is, however, a long, risky, complex, expensive and non-linear one. Failure rates have been high and, since the turn of the century, some of Europe's major firms, such as Marks & Spencer, Royal Ahold, and more recently Carrefour, have instigated a series of new international launches and withdrawals. Could these groups have avoided failure? Did some of them neglect their home market? Analysing the cause of a failure is often as important as analysing a success; mounting the learning curve provides rich experience. Moreover, and despite the current trend of standardization towards a single consumer, each country continues to require a specific approach (Colla and Dupuis 1997). In a number of emerging economies, distribution maturity has accelerated, whether Chile, South Korea or China, with the emergence of strong local retailers who understand how to copy overseas retailers' know-how, correct mistakes, and develop hybrid formulae that are better adapted to the local setting.

The first part of this chapter focuses on the strategic conditions for successful internationalization. The second part explores the management cycle of retail internationalization.

FROM OPPORTUNISM TO A CONTROLLED STRATEGY

The decision to enter overseas markets is often the decision of one person or a small group of founding shareholders or local affiliates who take the initiative. The initial decision maker can be a key shareholder or manager. Interviews with retail managers in France showed that the basic decision to internationalize was often founded on the intuitive conviction that certain store formats and aspects of the retail business formula could be carried over to other cultures because they work well in the home country. A number of failures, however, can be attributed to individual decisions, which although they seize opportunities, are not based on a coherent strategy. We have noted that in the literature, opportunism and opportunities are sometimes confused.

Opportunism occurs when the decision to internationalize, and its concrete modalities, is taken in the absence of rational criteria, acquired experience, and a detailed evaluation of risks. Opportunistic behaviour can result from many causes that are internal or external to the company. Decisions may be taken hastily by managers regarding the choice of the country or the timing of internationalization. There may be pressure from the stock market or financial analysts. Other causes are cases of competitors attempting to keep up or the sudden availability of real estate.

Opportunism often leads to under-performance in the market entry phase, which eventually leads to the company's withdrawal from the country or to a lag in moving to the growth phase. Movement up the learning curve, however, may signify going from opportunism to a prepared decision. After a first phase marked by opportunistic decisions, there is a second phase that involves the definition of objectives, country groups and pre-defined missions.

Opportunity occurs when the time and the methods selected to internationalize mean that the firm can currently or potentially fulfil key criteria that it has set for itself, in applying the formats on an international level.

The distinction between opportunism and opportunity is important and it reinforces the need to develop corporate strategy within a strategic ensemble.

THE BASIS OF AN INTERNATIONAL RETAIL STRATEGY

A move from opportunism to opportunity implies the formulation and implementation of an international strategy that builds on the firm's core competencies. This is illustrated in Figure 3.1.

The retailer's core skills lie in its capacity to adapt its business formula, which consists of store concepts, logistics, and organizational capacity, and, finally, its capacity to organize its relationships with suppliers and customers. These competitive advantages must be understood and applied successfully within the domestic market before successful transfer is possible to new countries.

Four types of key strategic decision must be taken:

1   What store formats and formulae should be internationalized in priority (assuming a multi-format group)?

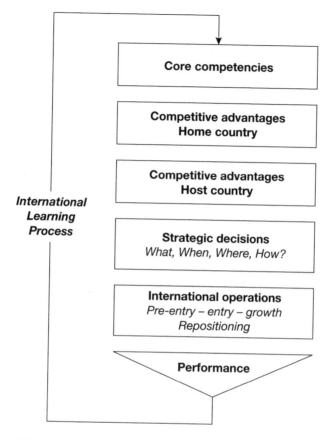

Figure 3.1 *Building an international strategy*

2   In what country or group of countries should investment occur?
3   When should international moves be made?
4   How should internationalization be achieved?

Once these decisions have been taken, the operational phase of the internationalization process follows. This leads to measurable performance and the enrichment of skills via experience.

The effective order of these operations is far from being totally rational, and firms who internationalize often forget to ask simple questions: Why internationalize? Are we strong enough in our home market? Do our formulae provide international added value? If so, what markets are appropriate? Do we have the financial and human resources to go international without jeopardizing our home market? What is the economic maturity of the economies and distribution systems in the target markets?

The prerequisites for international success

Strong retail business formula in the home market

Academics and professionals (Pederzolli 2001) agree that creating a strong proven formula is a prerequisite to launching retail operations on international markets. The vocabulary relative to the retail formula, however, needs some background information. The business formula is a combination of material and non-material elements owned by the retail firm and providing solutions that are both global and specific to the consumer in terms of sale of goods and services. This is somewhat different from, but relates to, the store formulae referred to in Chapter 2, whereby individual store formats undergo a shift in formula as required by local markets and cultures.

Carrefour Annual Reports indicate that its formula revolves around three points:

1 controlling the sales model (assortment, discount strategy, innovation);
2 establishing the economic model (revenues and investment on a square metre basis);
3 determining the financial model (site ownership or rental).

A retail business formula's strength can be evaluated on various criteria both qualitative and quantitative. These include true perceived differentiation, market share, and profitability by providing the revenue stream needed to finance an international launch.

Size of domestic market

A second prerequisite is the importance of the domestic market as the base that can guarantee future development. For Wal-Mart, for example, the large size of its domestic market has helped subsidize considerable losses on international ventures, for example, the acquisition in Germany (Knorr and Arndt 2003). A strong home market position allows for losses over a sustained time period in new markets and in later phases of international development. On the other hand, Ahold, which sought to refocus international activity in the early years of the twenty-first century, was hindered by the smallness of its home market in the Netherlands.

Exportability of the retail formula

The ability to 'export' a store formula lies in the formula's capacity to create real added value, which can be perceived by the consumer in other countries and other cultures. The failure of 'French-style' hypermarkets in the US in the 1980s and

1990s (Tordjman 1988) points to the fact that the perceived value of a formula in a country is not the same when transposed to another country. If the formula already benefits from an international reputation and strong differentiation, acceptability could be the target of consumers who are familiar with the store brand abroad or who are highly sensitive to innovation, for example, tourists, diaspora, students and executives. The launch of Starbucks in France was made easier by the brand's reputation being already established, not just as a place at which to drink coffee, but as a place to spend a moment of life.

This is also seen in the experience of Grand Optical in the UK. The group Grand Vision has two store formulae based on the same offer: 'making glasses in one hour'. In France, Grand Optical built the initial business formula and later acquired Vision Express in the UK. The key factors of the Grand Optical formulae are unique locations, usually requiring a high investment, high-quality service, with the laboratory integrated on site, consumer confidence and limited advertising. The second business formula originates from the Vision Express acquisition in the UK which is driven by a strong sales promotion policy accompanied by a high advertising budget. The quality of service comes second.

When Grand Vision wanted to change the Vision Express brand to Grand Optical, the company ran into a number of problems. For the company's managing director, Jean Luc Sélignan, an exportable formula must above all be accepted in the host market. The acceptance level is based not only on the sales aspects of the formula, but also extends to its front and back office operations.

Customers of Vision Express in the UK are accustomed to frequent promotions. The issue was to increase the focus on service and, more importantly, have the Grand Optical total formula accepted by customers. A mainstay of the Grand Optical strategy is site location. Grand Vision came to the conclusion that merging business formulae and cultures was not so simple and the company backtracked on its rebranding decision, but introduced a key Grand Optical element: an integrated laboratory.

Control of the supply chain

The ability to export a formula is greater when its international differentiation level is high for all of its key skills. The formulae that fully or partially dominate a value chain acquire a competitive advantage when they are moved internationally. These formulae can, therefore, be better differentiated by offering only their own labels and consequently build on a symbiosis between store atmosphere and the products presented and services provided. Mastering the supply chain means the retailer having access to more of the overall margin in the channel including the design margin, as is the case for IKEA. In the case of Zara and Yves Rocher, the retailer even has access to the production margin. Figure 3.2 indicates this relationship.

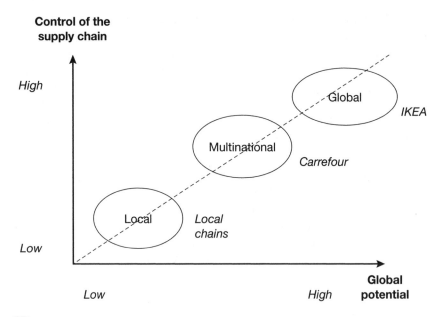

Control of the supply chain

High

Global

IKEA

Multinational

Carrefour

Local

Local chains

Low

Low

High

Global potential

Figure 3.2 Supply chain control and extent of internationalization capacity

Exportability of a formula and competitive advantage

The success of a firm's internationalization lies in the existence of competitive advantages in other markets. The competitive advantages theory explained by Hunt and Morgan (1995) contrasts with the neo-classical theory of perfect competition. Indeed, Hunt and Morgan's theory considers that, depending on the firms involved, competition is imperfect and unequal. A firm's advantage lies in the dual aspects of comparative advantage in terms of internal resources (financial, information, human resources and organization) and competitive advantage on the market, allowing for a quicker adaptation to market needs and expectations. Firms combining these advantages yield better financial performances, combined with a greater propensity to innovate.

By adapting the theoretical framework to an international retailer's issues we can distinguish:

- comparative advantages linked to a firm's resources, the retail formula, management of various chains (physical, financial and information), capacity to organize on an international level, create lasting relations with players who are both internal and external to the sales network;
- the competitive advantages linked to the store's position in its competitive environment, relevance of choice in terms of the retail formula to take international, and timing of market entry.

Given these persistent differences between country and culture, the international competitive advantages lie in the company's ability to appreciate a country's or group of countries' promise based on its specific competitive environment.

Defining the 'glocalization' level

The word 'glocalization' is the contraction of the terms globalization and localization. A firm may discuss replicating its retail formula worldwide, but this overlooks the problems of adapting to local and national cultures (Dupuis 2000). Glocalization pushes the company to adopt the local retail mix (sales offer, location, pricing, talent management and communication), sometimes referred to as the store formula (see Chapter 2). The advantage of global strategies is that they may provide economies of scale. IKEA, for example, prints some 145 million copies of its catalogue in 25 languages using the same photo base, regardless of the country. Localization is necessary to respond to local cultures of consumption.

Glocalization can be defined as:

■ The determination of key characteristics and intangibles that define the core retail formula. These constitute the global aspects of the formula. For example, the French Leclerc retail business is characterized by a combination of low prices and decentralized management based on a group of associates.

■ The local elements are the adaption of assortment and specific services, local talent, adapted communication, as well as competitive advantages that vary with each local level. Hygiene and mastering the cold chain, for example, in certain emerging countries, innovation in products and services compared to the local market.

These global and local features are shown in Figure 3.3 (based on Courbon 1994). This illustrates Carrefour's hypermarket applied to Taiwan in the 1990s, which served as a bridgehead for its subsequent development in mainland China.

Figure 3.3 The 'glocal' differentiation: Carrefour in Taiwan

MANAGING THE RETAIL INTERNATIONALIZATION PROCESS

Phases in the internationalization process

Figure 3.4 illustrates the phases for the internationalization of a retail formula.

- The pre-entry or preparation phase entails a number of choices and decisions to make, establishing a process to choose the host country, undertaking market studies and environmental studies, selecting and adapting the store formats, deciding on the mode and time of entry.
- Entry relies on the search for a partner, choosing the first market launch store format and planning corrections after market reaction. At the end of this phase, and if at this point the launch is a failure, a decision might be taken to withdraw from the market. If, on the other hand, the first phase is a success, the network and/or deployment might be extended. Firms tend to anticipate the growth phase very early, without being certain of the profitability level of the first wave of store openings, which further heightens the level of investment risk.
- The growth phase builds on the first launch to create a network. This phase usually entails a better geographic coverage and the deployment of logistics throughout the country (or sometimes a group of countries).
- Repositioning when the network has reached maturity with little or no growth or the entry of local or international challengers. The company should foresee this phase by a total repositioning, and/or the set-up of a multi-format or multi-channel strategy.

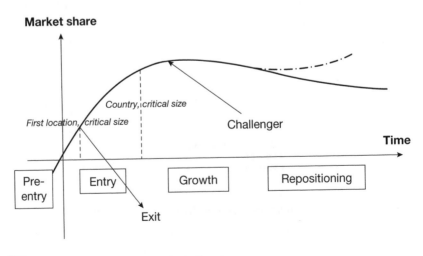

Figure 3.4 The international retail cycle

During the pre-entry phase the retailer has to take three types of decision: choosing the retail formula to export; choosing a target country; and choosing an entry mode.

Choosing the retail formula to export

A firm may have more than one retail formula to export and will probably combine its key skills and its experience by target country. The group will logically choose the formula that it normally employs, so reducing risk. Yves Rocher uses a number of multi-channel formulae via its own-name sales network and catalogue. A mail order catalogue keeps investment to a minimum, requires no geographic location, and introduces consumers of the host country to the products.

Choosing a target country

When choosing a country the following criteria must be considered:

- Geographic distance. Taking a formula to a country that is geographically close helps limit investments, especially logistics costs in the entry phase.
- Cultural proximity. This broad concept can be a key factor in choosing a country. Wal-Mart, for example, has not successfully transferred to all its foreign markets, but the company has affirmed its presence most in countries that share a cultural proximity, notably Canada, and the UK via the Asda acquisition.
- Maturity of the distribution system. This can be measured by the market share of modern retailing contributing to a country's retail revenues. This has grown over the past decade, especially in the large cities of emerging countries. Generally speaking, the more mature a country the harder it is to enter. Maturity is based on economic factors as well as the distribution system.
- Economic and political stability. The legal and regulatory environment and acceptance of foreign investment is an important variable to be considered. This aspect may be seen in the changed perceptions of Moscow as a potential market of interest for international retail ventures (*Le Monde* 2005). Moscow has some 10 million inhabitants whose purchasing power is growing rapidly but unequally, with salaries increasing by an average 10 per cent a year. This growth is marked compared to Russia's other 13 cities with over 1 million inhabitants. As a result, malls are being opened in Moscow. After the launch of Méga 1 in the capital's South East, Méga 2 opened in December 2004 in the northern suburbs. These centres target middle-class consumers and not just the newly rich. Stores such as Auchan, Metro, IKEA, Leroy Merlin, Obi and other major international firms are present.

Three types of markets can be identified:

1 Mature markets. The countries are characterized by high competition and sophisticated consumer demand. These markets are difficult to enter without a strong local network and/or a highly differentiated retail formula.
2 Poor countries with no short-term development prospects. This group includes countries or groups of countries that have not developed economically and whose inhabitants' standard of living and/or incomes are not high enough to foresee economic development. For a number of retailers, however, the presence of expatriates, tourists and wealthy local families constitutes sufficient rationale for a local deployment.
3 Emerging economies. This group offers strong growth and progressive opening to foreign investment. These countries are attractive markets for retailers and include countries in Central and Eastern Europe, Asia and Latin America.

As defined, emerging economies represent a diverse group of countries, but share a common factor: strong economic growth, starting from an initial low point and leading to a political liberalization process spanning regulatory and economic issues. As a result, retailing has developed and modernized, meaning that it has introduced new techniques (Amine *et al.* 2005).

Measures of attraction, that are country specific and that apply to retailing, have been developed. The *Global Retail Development Index* (GRDI), is an annual multi-criteria index composed of four weighted variables that rank 30 emerging economies based on their attraction level for retailing groups wishing to internationalize. Country risk is measured on a scale of 0 (high risk) to 100 (low risk). In Table 3.1 we see that the investment risk is higher in Russia than in Slovakia, for example. To rank a market's attraction level a grade of 0 corresponds to a very low attraction level for international retailers. Vietnam, for example, has a very low attraction level. A second group of variables assesses business saturation. This shows a 0 for countries in Western Europe where markets are saturated, but Vietnam provides more opportunity because of its low saturation. The time factor, in terms of the urgency required in taking a stance in a country, has a 0 when it is neither urgent nor opportune in the short term to enter into a market, as the retail market is evolving slowly. Russia is considered first in terms of the investment window.

The final ranking shows that, between 2003 and 2004, Eastern Europe and Asia gained in attraction. Russia maintained its first place, while India was second, gaining three places despite a political and regulatory framework that remains restrictive for foreign firms. China is still third followed by Slovenia, which is now part of the top ten. The countries that have fallen in the GRDI ranking of ten attractive emerging countries for distribution in 2004 are for the most part based in the

Table 3.1 *The ten most attractive emerging countries for mass retailing (2004)*

Country	Score	Country risk	Market attraction	Market saturation	Time
Russia	100	56	56	77	100
India	88	62	34	92	72
China	86	71	42	62	90
Slovenia	84	83	60	43	76
Croatia	83	61	53	55	93
Latvia	82	64	55	54	89
Vietnam	76	52	29	90	66
Turkey	75	50	58	67	65
Slovakia	74	69	48	35	100
Thailand	73	68	38	60	76

Source: *2004 GRDI, Emerging Market Priorities for Global Retailers*, A. T. Kearney

Mediterranean (Morocco, Egypt, Tunisia). The limits of this ranking system stem from the rapid evolution of national situations, as well as the possibility that major retail firms will choose to enter a country with a low attraction level. The case of the Bourbon Group entering Vietnam is one such case of the latter problem.

Choosing the entry mode

Choosing an entry mode into a country designates the selected organizational structures for initial development. The main entry modes include creating a subsidiary, joint venture, franchise, corporate buyout or network acquisition (see Table 3.2).

- Subsidiary: this comprises a direct investment with total control on the introduction and development of the retail formula. Choosing to employ a subsidiary as the entry mode is recommended in cases where the retail formula in question is very different from that operating locally and where firms already enjoy a highly developed acquired skill set.
- Joint-venture: a joint-venture or joint subsidiary creates a company to manage one or more retail formulae and/or the back office. A majority controlling stake is needed to drive decision making in the initial launch and subsequent network development. The advantage of the joint-venture is to benefit from an initial set-up via a local partner. The problem is finding a sufficiently capable local partner.

Table 3.2 The key entry modes

Entry mode	Advantages	Disadvantages	Examples
Subsidiary	Total control of the formula	Major self-financing	H&M, Fast Retailing
Joint venture	Presence of an established partner	Partner reliability Little control unless majority stake	Carrefour, Tesco
Franchise	Low investment level Quicker development	Risk of deforming a formula Requires rigour and high level of control and major formula differentiation	Yves Rocher, Body Shop
Buyout or acquisition	Immediate network	Risks in terms of partner Possible cultural and formulae conflicts	Wal-Mart

- Franchise: a contract is established between a franchiser who provides the know-how and brand and the franchisee who invests providing initial capital. The franchise provides excellent leverage for a company to launch into a new market. The franchise requires extreme rigour in terms of determining the transfer and control of deployment. If the contract is signed with a firm that will develop the retail formula itself, this is referred to as a master franchise.

- Buyout or acquisition: a key way to enter a mature market is by buying a chain, if possible a market leader, to reap immediate critical mass. Acquisitions, however, require that the buyer integrate the corporate culture or even different formulae. This may delay network profitability. A buyout also implies massive investment to standardize and update systems and these costs must be integrated in the business plan's return on investment.

A reference model for the international mode of entry has been developed by Dunning (1988). According to this model the firm chooses the entry mode that provides the best return on investment after accounting for the entailed risk. Dunning looks into three types of comparative advantages (OLI): the advantages linked to ownership, especially the advantage linked to control, costs; advantages linked to location, access to supplies, human resources, and so on; and, finally, the advantages of internalization which help lower transaction and coordination costs. Transaction costs include all the costs linked to the market launch of a retail formula in a country. Coordination costs relate to costs linked to relationship management between the exporting company and its co-contractors.

The Dunning model is predictive in terms of impact on the entry mode for a direct industrial investment made by multinational companies in a host country. One of the best ways to enter a mature market is to buy a leader ensuring immediate mass effect. An acquisition supposes that the buyer integrates the corporate culture or even different formulae, which can push back the break-even point. An acquisition also entails a number of investments for 'standardization', which must be integrated in the calculation of the return on investment. In an interview, Jean Luc Sélignan of Grand Vision stated that:

> Changing an existing formula with an existing clientele base takes longer than creating [a retail company] from scratch. A company is like a human being and trying to turn around a newly acquired company, by administering a dose of horse medicine can be fatal.

Taking a company international also means paying a certain price to cover all of the investments before entering the market: market studies, searching for the first site, local partners, and the cost of contracts with local partners. This is usually from the home country operation with requirements for return on investment as the network develops. This is part of the pre-entry costs.

The entry phase

Setting up operations in a host country entails making good use of the firm's knowledge. This set-up is best achieved when the retailer already benefits from an international reputation, if the company already has ties with suppliers in the target market, or if the company has a 'scout' operation in the country. The performance effects of some key strategic decisions during the entry phase have been measured with a sample of 75 European food retailers by Gielens and Dekimpe (2001). They showed that better performance in terms of sales growth and turnover per square metre could be achieved by the first movers entering on a large scale, without partners, using a business model that was both familiar to them and new to the target market.

Choosing the timing of entry

Choosing the timing to launch onto a market translates into finding the strategic window that is the most opportune for a company. According to Jean Fournioux, former Business Development Director of Fnac: 'The timing to enter a market is key: the company has to be ready as does the market. For Fnac, the Berlin population in 1991 did not have the required revenues to launch our formula store.'

Being the first mover in a market is an advantage. This is seen in respect of Carrefour in Brazil and in Taiwan. When the firm is the first, it limits other firms from launching, particularly in less developed markets. For the consumer, the first mover becomes a reference to that particular retail formula. The firm can acquire the best locations and create barriers to entry via its established strength, and its share of voice (media) in terms of competitors. On the other hand, if the company has made a mistake choosing the target country, for example, in terms of the retail formula's acceptance, a first-mover position can become a handicap. For example, Ahold wanted to pave the way in Central Europe and encountered difficulties. Both Fnac and Galeries Lafayette, which tried to set up operations in Berlin just two years after the fall of the wall, were based on debatable locations and market positioning, forcing them to withdraw. A further example is provided by Auchan in Argentina. Auchan entered Argentina in 1997 and withdrew in 2005. In 2001, Argentina underwent one of the most serious financial and economic crises a country has ever undergone. The country's foreign debt quadrupled between 1993 and 2000, and the purchasing power of the average salary was halved between 1974 and 2002. At the time of the crisis Auchan had not even broken even on its operation and, given these conditions, and having already withdrawn from the US and Mexico, it decided in 2005 to withdraw from Argentina to focus on Southern and Central Europe.

Seeking the location for the first outlet

The first store location in a host country implies a key value, since the company's success or failure largely depends on the future developments of the network. Indeed, competitors and sector analysts will study the first store location. Arnaud Périssé of Yves Rocher states: 'The first opening involves good knowledge of the country's real estate position and from there, to determine the best site locations.' Retailers, therefore, have to choose their first location by making sure that they do not overpay for the site.

The first critical financial threshold for international firms is the profitability of the first sales point. It is important that the retailer choose this first location very carefully. The first site has to become profitable rapidly in order to amortize the structural costs of the network's bridgehead. A gap frequently appears at this level between the return on investment for shareholders and the required time-frame for the first sites to break even and become profitable. The speed at which profitability is obtained is affected by the network strategy adopted. Two strategies can be seen in operation:

1 A one-off strategy: this was adopted by a number of French retailers (Promodès, Carrefour, Auchan, Leclerc) when they tried to enter the US market in the 1980s and 1990s. These were not successful, but a few years later Wal-Mart used a similar approach with its super-centres in the US market.

2   Setting up new sites in groups: this implies a ramp up to meet growth pre-requisites during the network growth by programming a large number of openings to break even financially.

Launch and early adaptation

Launching a new retail formula is not only a communication action, it also encompasses symbolic and political dimensions. The first opening of a Toys 'R' Us in Japan was preceded by a visit from the US President. The launch of the Virgin store in Beirut, based in the former Opera House, was accompanied by the arrival of the Virgin founder and the Lebanese Prime Minister in a tractor. Both are examples of retailers well aware of the public relations effect of new launches overseas.

In the entry phase, changes to the retail formula for overseas markets are made quickly. The firm must have a relevant, efficient and quick control system, which should be:

■   relevant, because the indicators prior to the launch must span all marketing, economic and financial data to make the right decisions;
■   efficient, because measurement tools must be set up for the both front and back offices; and
■   quick, because the information has to be transmitted in real time or very shortly afterwards to operational teams.

A number of firms give free rein to their overseas managers in the international decision-making process, making it a key part of their strategy. The autonomy of the decision-making process can be a part of the company's business culture, with Grand Optical's Jean Luc Sélignan stating: 'When a salesperson interacts with a client s/he is the company's boss.'

Other firms follow a different route with limited autonomy given to IKEA managers and the firm favouring strong centralization. In the initial store in a country, IKEA sends a team, which takes all decisions in coordination with the head office. This system also seeks to shorten the decision-making process.

Analysing failure leading to a withdrawal from a country

Academic literature on internationalization frequently refers to the success of retailers, often ignoring their failures (Dupuis and Prime 1996). The reasons are simple; companies communicate little about their failures. But they know that analysing the failure provides a key part of the company's black box. Failures, although not well documented include:

■   The retail formula–country combination does not work. Successive attempts to set up French hypermarkets in the US led to failures in the 1980s.

- Competition is too intense. Access to highly developed markets such as the US and Germany may be limited by the intensity of competition.
- Strategic reorganization. The capacity to reposition over the long term for companies that are considered international models, such as Marks & Spencer, may lead to some withdrawals (Burt *et al.* 2002).

Burt *et al.* (2003) list ten research propositions linked to international retail failures. Propositions are grouped in four major failure categories:

1 mistakes as to the choice of target markets due to poor evaluation of the economic risk and the target country's cultural distance;
2 poor assessment of the intra-type (identical, or almost, formats) or inter-type (different formats) competition, as well as the force of competitors in terms of size, access to supplies and the capacity to change quickly;
3 organizational failure due to insufficient experience in the target country;
4 management failure due to insufficient management experience, as well as defaults in the transfer of corporate culture and formulae.

Entry strategy

A successful acquisition strategy is, in part, linked to the firm's position in the host country. The Wal-Mart case in Germany and Japan bears testimony to this point. In Germany, Wal-Mart encountered a number of difficulties. After purchasing Wertkauf from Spar and Intermarché, another French failure, in 1997, Wal-Mart became number four in Germany's hypermarket sector, although it had a limited presence on the German retail market. While Wal-Mart planned to extend its network by 50 stores in early 2001, it was forced to close two stores and reno-vate three others to present a store format similar to the supercentres used in the US. The reasons for this degree of adaptation point to a number of factors:

1 difficulty in transferring the basic competitive advantages to a country where discount retailers Aldi, Lidl and Norma are strongly placed in the market;
2 difficulty in providing a purchase alternative to local market leaders, given the insufficient presence of the acquisition, as well as the poor quality of the Wertkauf chain locations.

In Japan, Wal-Mart has adopted a more refined strategy by progressively taking over Seiyu, although it has still not made the company a wholly owned subsidiary. This strategy sought to move progressively upstream in the value-chain and inject its know-how, without changing the retail banner, and more specifically by intro-ducing its IT system to yield better stock management. The approach has met with strong local criticism, however.

The growth phase

Whereas in the 1970s, retail companies launched international operations relying heavily on opportunism, more recently the definition of the format's international strategy is apparent. This has posed some new problems for retailers with strategies generating obstacles on competitive grounds, the evolution of the environment and the impatience of shareholders in terms of profitability. The growth phase can be defined by the development of the network in a country or a group of countries as well as dedicated logistics. In the entry phase, management and coordination costs are covered by one or two sales points, and in the growth phase these costs will be spread over the entire network.

Strategies for international expansion by major retailers are often ambitious. In many cases they seek to achieve a high market share in a short time achieving a threshold for sustained growth (Filser 1998). The growth threshold is attained by realizing a minimal standard of performance at the first series of stores. A retailer should not embark on a growth phase without first having reached a profitability level that covers the operating costs of the first units. As of early 2005 a number of international firms were focusing on countries where they could reasonably attain this profitability although they were in a loss-making phase in other countries from which they eventually withdrew.

The repositioning phase

Few international retailers have successfully completed the repositioning phase, corresponding to a certain maturity level in the life cycle of store formula. A number of factors highlight this phase, for example:

- The retail formula has aged, as was the case for Marks & Spencer at the end of the 1990s, parallel to the growth of more innovative and better performing companies, for example, H&M, Zara and Mango.
- Local challengers grew by watching, learning and moving beyond their competitors with the local competitors being better able to meet local needs. This is seen by Carrefour in South Korea where E-Mart, the local leader, has cut personnel costs to 12 per cent of sales versus 19 per cent at Carrefour Korea, with an annual stock rotation of 30 compared to 12 at Carrefour Korea.

Repositioning must take place as soon as necessary. Carrefour believes that its international repositioning strategies should take place every three years.

Toys 'R' Us Japan illustrates the importance of repositioning. Whereas its French counterpart took time to modernize its initial entry position, Toys 'R' Us Japan managers realized within four years that the American retail formula had to be temporarily readjusted to reach the growth phase. This largely meant switching from a direct procurement system to one that included traditional wholesalers. However, having made this adjustment, Toys 'R' Us Japan achieved significant growth and chain development. With more than 100 stores in operation, it then reversed the original adjustment, reverting to the original formula of direct procurement.

The rate of maturity of retail markets can be seen in the rise of the number of local challengers to the international firms in Chile, Korea and Russia. Leaders are often local retailers who not only knew how to copy, but also how to create new retail formulae, building on their own skill set and going beyond the copied formulae. The South Korean E-Mart illustrates this trend. E-Mart is a retailer larger than Samsung-Tesco, Lotte-Mart and Carrefour and illustrates the growing retail maturity in South Korea. In 1993, E-Mart developed a large supermarket based on the Western discount format, with low prices, a simplified environment and minimal service. The firm then combined low prices with an enhanced environment and added a number of services. E-Mart's evolution mirrored the country's growing economic maturity following rising consumer demand in terms of quality and service and the concomitant rise of the middle class.

Internationalization carried out in a number of countries in the same geographic region allows a retail brand to share costs and benefits across several markets. Functions such as logistics, purchasing, management and real estate purchasing can be shared among several countries. Toys 'R' Us, for example, set up a centralized purchasing office in Europe. This consolidation is not always possible. For example, Séphora also wanted to set up central logistics but could not change local habits and pressure from suppliers who wanted to deliver to each site independently, making it impossible to operate a central purchasing warehouse.

A further way of sharing costs is through a multi-format strategy. This has three advantages:

1 the selected formats can be adapted more precisely to the host country or at market launch;
2 they can eventually lead to developing local retail brands or finding the best-suited positions;
3 the retailer has the means to cover a larger product offering in the country.

As of the beginning of 2000, Carrefour was able to use a format portfolio, built up after its merger with Promodès, and launched Dia and Champion in Asia after using the Carrefour hypermarket as an initial format.

But the multi-format strategy can have the negative effect of dispersing scarce resources. Each format must establish its own credibility on the market and reach critical size independently of the other formats present on the same market. Profitability of the host country can be delayed by the format with the longest returns on investment.

CONCLUSION

Retail internationalization is an extended and risky process. The decision to internationalize too often remains an opportunistic decision with no real strategy. To define a strategy, decision makers must ask themselves a set of questions and in developing the strategy it is useful to consider several phases to the process. The major phases are pre-entry, entry, growth and repositioning. Each of these phases is associated with a critical threshold that facilitates moves into the next phase. Table 3.3 provides a summary of these thresholds.

Table 3.3 *Prerequisite and critical thresholds of the internationalization process*

Phase	Prerequisite	Critical thresholds
Pre-entry	Strong business formula in the domestic market International perceived added value	Size of the host market Network critical size and profitability in the national market
Entry	Added value for the host country	Acceptability and profitability and adaptation of the first site launch in the host country
Growth	Capacity to be a leader in the host country	Network's critical size Network's profitability
Repositioning	Capacity to reshape the business formula and/or to develop a mutli-format, multi-channel, multi-structure strategy	Quick test phase and generalization of the renewed format over the entire host country

REFERENCES

Amine, A., Dupuis, M., Obadia, C. and Prime, N. (2005) Characteristics of an emerging distribution industry: the case of Lebanon. Paper to Indian Institute of Management, Ahmedabad International Conference, 'Marketing for Emerging Economies', 12–13 January, 2005

Burt, S., Dawson, J. and Sparks, L. (2003) Failure in international retailing: research propositions. *The International Review of Retail, Distribution and Consumer Research*, 13: 355–373

Burt, S., Mellahi, K., Jackson, T. P. and Sparks, L. (2002) Internationalization and retail failures: issues from the case Marks and Spencer. *The International Review of Retail, Distribution and Consumer Research*, 12: 191–219

Carrefour (2000, 2001, 2002, 2003) Annual report and accounts

Colla, E. and Dupuis, M. (1997) *The global challenge of low prices*. (Paris: Publi-union)

Courbon, P. (1994) *Carrefour in Asia: case study*. (Fontainebleau: INSEAD)

Dunning, J. H. (1988) The eclectic paradigm of international production, a restatement and some possible expansions. *Journal of International Business Studies*, 19: 1–31

Dupuis, M. (2000) Réussir sa 'glocalisation'. *Market-Management*, 1: 1–3, 35–40

Dupuis, M. and Prime, N. (1996) Business distance and global retailing: a model for analysis of key success/failure factors. *International Journal of Retail and Distribution Management*, 24(11): 30–38

Filser, M. (1998) Critical size and retail strategies. *Décisions Marketing*, 15: 7–16

Hunt, S. D. and Morgan, R. M. (1995) The comparative advantage theory of competition, *Journal of Marketing*, 59: 1–15

Gielens, K. and Dekimpe, M. G. (2001) Do international entry decisions of retail chains matter in the long run? *International Journal of Research in Marketing*, 18: 235–259

Knorr, A. and Arndt, A. (2003) Why did Wal-Mart fail in Germany (so far)? Working paper, University of Bremen, Department of Business Studies & Economics

Le Monde (2005) The mega development of Moscow's retail distribution. 2 February

Pederzolli, D. (2001) Elaboration et test d'un modèle d'interprétation des stratégies d'internationalisation des grandes entreprises de distribution des pays occidentaux. Thèse pour le Doctorat en Sciences de Gestion, Université de Rennes (IGR-IAE)

Tordjman, A. (1988) The French hypermarket: could it be developed in the United States? *Retail and Distribution Management*, 16(4): 14–19

Chapter 4

Inditex-Zara

Re-writing the rules in apparel retailing

Steve Burt, John Dawson and Roy Larke

INTRODUCTION

Inditex is regarded as in international phenomenon in the apparel industry. When a Zara store opened in the International Finance Centre in Hong Kong on 21 May 2004, it represented the group's 2,000th store in its 50th country. By providing good value, design-led fashion clothing in a much reduced lead time, Zara has challenged many of the traditional ways of operating within the retail clothing sector. Inditex-Zara is an example of a firm that has harnessed communication technologies within a traditional supply chain to redefine how a retail sector works and to invert many of the accepted drivers in the channel. At virtually every stage in the channel the tasks, roles and responsibilities of actors and intermediaries have been altered as established business processes have been reconfigured to harness a demand-driven view of the channel. The Zara approach has epitomized what has become known as 'fast fashion', and reflects a view of retailing as an integrated commercial process rather than a channel activity. This approach has, to date, provided a source of competitive advantage that has allowed rapid retail internationalization and generated a financial performance (Table 4.1) that has been the envy of many of its established competitors. The figures for financial year 2003 show the first dip in what has otherwise been an unblemished record of growth.

BACKGROUND AND HISTORY

Until its flotation in May 2001, Zara was a secretive, family-owned firm located in Galicia, a peripheral region in north-west Spain. This geographical location helped to keep Zara from the public eye, as did the reclusive, publicity-shy stance

Table 4.1 Inditex – financial performance, 1996–2003

	1996	1997	1998	1999	2000	2001	2002	2003
Net sales (€ million, exc. VAT)	1,008.5	1,217.4	1,614.7	2,035.1	2,614.7	3,249.8	3,974.0	4,598.9
% annual change	–	+20.7	+32.6	+26.0	+28.5	+24.3	+22.3	+15.7
Operating income (€ million)	150.3	192.6	241.5	296.2	379.9	517.5	659.5	627.0
% annual change	–	+28.1	+25.4	+22.7	+28.3	+36.2	+28.4	–4.9
as % of sales	14.9	15.8	15.0	14.6	14.5	15.9	16.6	13.6
Net income (€ million)	72.7	117.4	153.1	204.7	259.2	340.4	438.1	446.5
% annual change	–	+61.5	+30.4	+33.7	+26.6	+31.3	+28.7	+1.9
as % of sales	7.2	9.6	9.5	10.1	9.9	10.5	11.0	9.7
Return on equity (%)	20	25	25	26	25	26	27	23
ROCE (%)	29	35	36	33	34	39	41	32

Source: derived from Annual Reports

of the company founder Amancio Ortega Gaona. The press consistently claim that only two photographs of Ortega are in the public domain.

Ortega, the son of a cleaner and a railway engineer, began his working life in the textile industry as a runner for a shirtmaker (Roux 2002). In 1963 he formed Confecciones Goa and started out on his own as a lingerie and nightwear manufacturer. The cancellation of an export order led to an unplanned diversification into retailing in May 1975 with the opening of the first Zara store in La Coruna. Originally a lingerie store, the product range expanded to incorporate women's fashion, menswear and children's clothes. A decade later Inditex (Industria de Diseno Textil) was created as a holding company to manage the growing business.

The international adventure began in 1988, with the short move from Galicia into Oporto, Portugal, and the formation of a subsidiary company, Zara BV, in the Netherlands to oversee retail internationalization. The Portuguese store was followed a year later by outlets in New York and Paris. However, international expansion was steady rather than spectacular until the late 1990s when Inditex, through Zara and its other retail chains, exploded onto the world stage. In 1996 Inditex operated 142 international stores in ten countries, accounting for 36 per cent of group sales. By January 2004 the number of countries had more than quadrupled, and the 792 international stores generated 54 per cent of group sales.

The Inditex portfolio expanded through a combination of internal brand development and acquisition during the 1990s. Acquisition has added the Massimo Dutti (1996) and Stradivarius (2000) brands, while Pull & Bear (1991), Bershka (1998) and Oysho (2001) have been developed by Inditex. Over the last decade other subbrands such as Kiddy's Class, Bretto's, N&B and Lefties have been trialled but most of these are now found as concessionary brands within Zara outlets, with the exception of Kiddy's Class which is now being rolled out as a store brand. The most recent addition to the portfolio is the Zara Home concept that appeared in 2003.

The rapid expansion of the group was financed internally, partly through negative working capital, and during the 1990s Inditex undoubtedly became one of Spain's retail success stories, particularly as its international profile rose. When the group was floated on the Madrid stock exchange in 2001, through the placement of 26 per cent of the share capital, the offer was heavily oversubscribed. Shortly after flotation Inditex announced an employee share participation scheme which dispersed a further 4.3 million shares (0.7 per cent of the stock) to staff in Spain, Portugal, France, Belgium and Greece. Despite these moves, industry observers stress that Amancio Ortega remains firmly at the helm (retaining 61.2 per cent of the share capital).

THE ZARA CONCEPT: 'THE DEMOCRATIZATION OF FASHION'

The 1998 Annual Report defined the principles of Inditex as: 'creativity, painstaking design, innovation, fast response to the market, special attention paid to the interior design of the shops and flexible management.'

Although the group now comprises seven established retail clothing chains, the flagship brand, Zara, accounts for 70 per cent of sales and 76 per cent of operating profit, and epitomizes the group approach to retailing.

Zara's success has been built around business process re-engineering, with the company seemingly breaking all the established rules within apparel retailing. The core competence is the implementation of rapid reaction, just-in-time principles in the fashion industry:

> For Inditex, time is the main factor to be considered, above and beyond production costs. Vertical integration allows us to shorten turnaround times and achieve greater flexibility, by reducing stock to a minimum and diminishing fashion risk to the greatest possible extent.
>
> (Zara Press Dossier 2004)

Inditex has developed and implemented systems and processes that allow customer demand for up-to-date, design-based fashions to be brought to the market with lead times dramatically shorter than the industry norm. This underlying business process is summed up by Revilla Bonnin (2002) as: 'the establishment of a complete, integrated system of communication between points of sale and central offices with the purpose of defining demand at each establishment and translating it into the production schedule of the factories.'

Despite the ownership of significant manufacturing capacity (22 manufacturing companies are shown in the 2004 Annual Report) in a sector which has seen most leading clothing retailers divest of manufacturing, Inditex's operation is undeniably market led.

> The client is the base that supports the strength of the Group. Knowing their desires, responding promptly, maintaining a constant dialogue with them in those meeting points which are the shops; here we have the pivots upon which fashion rests.
>
> (Annual Report 1998)

This market-pull, demand chain approach drives the whole 'Zara system'.

The hub of the operation is a large manufacturing and logistics centre at Artexio near La Coruna. Inditex creates most of its product range with a team of in-house designers, typically turning out 10,000 new items per year from a base of 40,000 design ideas. According to Ferdows *et al.* (2002, 2004), a commercial team comprising designers, market specialists and buyers operate on a multi-tasking basis to ensure that design, sales and production considerations are integrated at an early stage. The physical proximity of these teams shortens communication channels and speeds up the product development process. Design ideas observed on the catwalk and in 'youth' arenas, such as university campuses and nightclubs, are brought back to La Coruna and interpreted by the commercial team (Vitzthum 2001). The designers sketch out and prepare a portfolio of base models (incorporating designs, fabric selections, prints and colours) for each season, use CAD tools to produce variations, and make final adaptations when customer reactions to the latest fashion trends have been assessed. New products are tested in certain stores before production runs are finalized, reducing failure rates to around 1 per cent compared to the industry average of 10 per cent (D'Andrea and Arnold 2003). Production runs are typically limited to between 100,000 and 350,000 items, produced in five to seven sizes and five to six colours for each design.

The design, production, to market cycle has been reduced to 22–30 days, in an industry where nine months was the traditional lead time. Harle *et al.* (2002) report that typically this cycle is made up of 1 day for final design, 3–8 days for manufacture, 1 day for transport, and 17–20 days for selling. Significant investment in information technology drives the demand chain, particularly at the production and logistics end of the chain. The five-storey, 500,000 square metre, distribution centre contains over 200 kilometres of moving rails, and automated routing systems deliver electronically tagged garments to the appropriate loading bays for dispersal via third-party sub-contracted distributors. Products are ready for dispatch eight hours after arrival, and road haulage is managed to a set timetable for country deliveries (Ferdows *et al.* 2002; Points de Vente 2000). Overseas dispatches are usually routed through the local Santiago di Compostela airport, to cut delivery time. Zara claims that distribution is 98.9 per cent accurate. Shrinkage is less than 0.5 per cent. Growth has been such that a new logistics centre 'Plataforma Europa' for Zara was opened at Zaragoza in northern Spain during May 2003.

Whereas perceived wisdom in the apparel industry is that production should be outsourced to low-cost countries, Zara claims to produce the bulk of its product in-house within Europe. Annual Reports regularly note that over 80 per cent of Zara's production takes place on the Continent. What is meant exactly by 'in-house' is open to interpretation as Zara utilizes a network of over 500 sub-contractors in Spain and Portugal to assemble pre-cut material. Hellier (2001) argues that this system allows Zara to retain control over the capital-intensive elements of production while outsourcing the most labour-intensive aspects. The use of this sub-contracting network for assembly provides access to labour costs that may be as low as those found in the developing economies used by competitors. This implied criticism may partly explain the introduction of an ethical code of conduct during 2001.

Raw material is sourced from a wide supplier base on a global level to reduce dependency and is delivered to La Coruna (Christopher 1998). Ferdows *et al.* (2002) report that 40 per cent of fabric is sourced through a company-owned subsidiary, Comditel, and a network of over 250 other suppliers. Fashion 'basics' are sourced from Asia via 50–60 key suppliers to obtain lower costs on simple, standardized, products, whereas the more complicated garments are manufactured in Europe. As with Benetton, 'postponement' principles are applied with around 50 per cent of fabric sourced as undyed until colour trends are confirmed. On arrival the fabric is dyed and cut in the Inditex factories and sent out to sub-contractors for sewing. The assembled garments are then returned to the Inditex-owned factories for final finishing, quality control, price tagging and packing, before being sent to the distribution centre.

This network of sub-contractors, allied to daily feedback from store managers on how ranges are performing, allows industry beating flexibility. The production pipeline can be turned on or off as the market dictates, as José Maria Castellano (the former CEO) comments: 'We have the ability to scrap an entire production line overnight if it is not selling' (Crawford 2000a).

Christopher (1998) also suggests that production is deliberately planned for a level slightly below projected sales – opting for a strategy of under supply rather than over supply and obsolete stock. Zara's pre-season inventory level (the production committed before the season begins) is 15–20 per cent, compared to the industry norm of 40–60 per cent, with the in-season commitment, made possible by the fast response, flexible production process, in the 40–50 per cent region. This approach allows a closer alignment of production to sales forecasts, reducing the need to clear unwanted stock. It is claimed that Zara retails 85 per cent of its stock at full price, compared to the industry norm of 60–70 per cent (Ferdows *et al.* 2002). Such ratios are historically unheard of in the retail clothing sector.

At the retail end of the concept, continuous replenishment and the regular introduction of new lines encourages customers to return to the stores and increases footfall. Store replenishment operates on a staggered three-day cycle depending on location. Store sales are recorded daily on hand-held computers (PDAs), and store orders are made at predetermined times: Wednesday by 15.00 hrs and Saturdays by 18.00 hrs in the case of Spain and Southern Europe; Tuesdays before 15.00 hrs and Fridays before 18.00 hrs for the rest of the world. Store managers select from an 'offer' displayed on the PDA allowing replenishment of existing lines and requests for new garments (McAfee *et al.* 2004). This deadline-based ordering discipline, allied to predetermined dispatch times at the warehouse, provides control and reduces costs. Deliveries reach stores twice a week and observers claim that over a two-week period around 70 per cent of merchandise in the stores will have changed. Furthermore, the continual churn of stock encourages customers to purchase when they visit, rather than delay purchase. Director Luis Blanc says: 'We want our customers to understand that if they like something, they must buy it now, because it won't be in the shops the following week. It is all about creating a climate of scarcity and opportunity' (Crawford 2000b).

Consequently, items are only available within the store for a four-week period. Flexibility in supply and the 'fast fashion' approach also provides some protection against other suppliers copying Zara products. By the time competitors respond the item may already be out of the Zara range.

The stores, as the source of customer information, are recognized as the key component of the business: 'The point of sale does not close the process but rather renews it, acting as a market information collection system that provides feedback to the design teams and reports the trends demanded by consumers' (Zara Press Dossier 2004).

Store managers determine their product ranges based upon local sales data and informal customer contact. Sales, customer reactions and comments on the range are reported on a daily basis. Accordingly the cashier is recognized as a key occupation and these positions are not rotated. In the store, remuneration is based on a salary plus a bonus based on overall store sales to provide an incentive to maximize outlet level performance.

Although information flows are crucial to the Inditex system, McAfee (2004) stresses that: 'Zara runs an information intensive business with remarkably little information technology.'

This is perhaps best illustrated by the limited use of IT within the store. The PDAs are seen as a key tool, being introduced in 1995 to replace a daily end-of-business fax. POS terminals are not networked, and inventory cannot be tracked from the store. The emphasis is firmly placed on information as an aid (not a substitute) to decision making. The Inditex process is the focus of the whole operation, and information technology is therefore targeted at and developed in-house for very specific business needs, rather than purchasing off-the-shelf solutions (McAfee et al. 2004).

A further difference from traditional behaviour within fashion retailing is a very low spend on marketing. Inditex does not have a formal marketing department and Zara neither advertises, nor supplies samples to magazine photo shoots. Zara's advertising expenditure is claimed to be 0.3 per cent of sales, and dedicated to supporting the annual sales and new store openings. Publicity and communication is 'mouth to ear'. Product is showcased through stores located on prime sites. High-profile sites are chosen for large flagship stores, often in architecturally interesting buildings to reinforce the style and design message. Stores are typically spacious and limited stock availability reinforces the impression of fashionability and exclusiveness. A great deal of attention is given to product presentation and window display, and the group has a separate Window Dressing Department alongside the Store Design Department. In Italy, the absence of large display windows was seen as an initial barrier to expansion. Beneath Inditex's headquarters an area housing 25 full-size store windows is used to establish window designs and test different light conditions. The approved look is then rolled out to all Zara stores worldwide (Hellier 2001). Products are not displayed by line (e.g. skirts, trousers) but by outfit to try to maximize customer spend. Store décor and furniture is changed every two years to ensure a fresh look is maintained.

THE RETAIL CHAINS

All the retail chains within the Inditex portfolio operate autonomously as semi-independent businesses. Each chain has its own management team with no cross-integration between formats, although a range of support functions is provided by the corporate HQ (e.g. IT, legal, accounting and real estate). The oldest brands, Zara and Pull & Bear are based in Galicia, while Massimo Dutti, Stradivarius and Bershka have their headquarters in Catalonia (Barcelona).

Currently Inditex operates eight brands (Table 4.2), whose positioning and target market can be gleaned from the website and company documentation:

■ Zara – '*dressing ideas, trends and tastes*'
The flagship brand, launched in 1975 and moved international to Oporto (Portugal) in December 1988, followed by Paris (France) and New York (US) in 1989. Originally aimed at the mass-market, fashionable womenswear segment, a menswear range has since been added. The values of the brand are defined by the Inditex website as:

> ZARA is in step with society, dressing the ideas, trends and tastes that society itself has created. This is the key to its success among people, cultures and generations that, despite their differences, all share a special feeling for fashion.

In August 2003 the Zara brand was extended into home furnishings with the opening of the first Zara Home store in Spain. Providing 'articles to dress and decorate the home', the textile, tablewear and décor lines are presented in four decorative atmospheres – contemporary, classic, colonial and white.

■ Pull & Bear – '*a way of life*'
Launched by Inditex in 1991 and introduced into Portugal in 1994. Originally positioned below Massimo Dutti to provide 'basic apparel for the young urban man' in the 14 to 28 age group. A womenswear range was added in 1998 and over time the brand has evolved to focus on casual and urban fashion. The chain now retails men's and womenswear, accessories, perfume and home décor. The brand concept is expressed through the store:

Table 4.2 *Inditex – contribution of retail brands, 2003*

	Total Inditex	Individual retail brands							
		Zara	Kiddy's Class	Pull & Bear	Massimo Dutti	Bershka	Stradivarius	Oysho	Zara Home
Net sales (€ million)	4,598.9	3,219.6	89.7	287.9	388.9	395.0	162.0	45.1	10.6
Operating income (€ million)	627.0*	476.1	18.0	18.9	60.1	57.3	4.4	2.1	-0.5
as % of sales	13.6	14.8	20.0	6.6	15.5	14.5	2.7	4.6	-4.5
Number of stores (n)	1,922	626	103	350	297	253	191	76	26
– domestic	1,130	221	90	241	181	167	159	49	22
– international	792	405	13	109	116	86	32	27	4
Sales area ('000 sq m)	988.3	686.1	20.6	67.2	62.1	85.8	49.8	10.9	5.8
Number of countries (n)	48	46	2	18	23	13	4	8	4

* Total includes –€9.4 million goodwill

Source: derived from Annual Reports

For them, Pull and Bear is not just a store anymore. The wide range of clothes, accessories and cosmetics available is complemented by a number of added services: from good music to video images, from a cup of coffee to videogames areas, from the XDYE Magazine to the web site. All this in order to make a shop, clothing, a brand into a whole way of life.

(www.inditex.com)

■ Massimo Dutti – *'fashion and quality'*
This is the first of Inditex's acquired brands. Founded in Barcelona in 1985 as a menswear chain, Inditex acquired a 51 per cent stake in COFIR (which, in turn, owned 72 per cent of Massimo Dutti) in 1991. Full control was achieved in March 1996. With a target market of urban, independent and cosmopolitan men and women in the 25–45 age range, Massimo Dutti offers traditional styles updated by new fabrics. The offer is defined as high-quality clothing at affordable prices for the modern urban customer, sold in shops that are characterized by a 'subdued and studied atmosphere' offering comfort. As with Pull & Bear a womenswear range was added in 1995, and a Dutti Boys childrenswear range was trialled in 2003.

■ Bershka – 'not just a product, more an attitude'
Launched in April 1998 as 'trendy fashion for the urban young girl', Bershka opened in Portugal and Cyprus in the same year. The Bershka concept is aimed at the younger female market (13–23 age group) and in keeping with the lifestyle theme running through the Inditex brands, the store format is where 'the shopping experience turns into a socio-cultural immersion into youth aesthetics of the new century'. This is achieved through large, spacious stores designed to create a modern, urban and fun environment – 'a meeting place for fashion, music and street art'. In the winter 2002 season, Bershka added a menswear collection.

■ Stradivarius – 'always the latest trends'
Inditex's second acquisition. Originally founded in 1983 as a competitor to Zara, Inditex acquired 90.5 per cent of the Barcelona-based chain from Pigaro 2100 in November 1999. The founding Triquill family retained the remaining equity. At acquisition Stradivarius had 75 stores and was already present internationally in France, Portugal and Taiwan. The chain targets young women in the 15–25 age bracket. Spacious stores provide a young, dynamic atmosphere, with a strong emphasis on providing latest fashion trends in design, fabrics and accessories. The product range is positioned at a slightly higher quality and price point than Bershka.

■ Oysho
The most recent clothing chain, launched in September 2001. Oysho brings the Inditex principles to the lingerie category, and is targeted at the Zara customer

base. The offer comprises high-quality, fashionable lingerie, informal home wear and swimwear at attractive prices. Designed to be an international concept at its birth, by the end of 2001 the chain had 34 outlets in 7 countries and 76 in 8 countries at the end of 2004. Stores are larger than average for the sector and are either stand-alone or distinct spaces in other group outlets.

At various points in Inditex's history other brands have appeared. The 1998 Annual Report records eight Bretto stores – targeted at the 'trendy young suburban woman', and two Lefties stores, but these had disappeared two years later. In 2004 Pull & Bear was piloting a new menswear concept, called Often, providing the 20–45-year-old urban male with 'comfortable and new basics through a wide variety of styles that get a "total" look from sports to urban wear'. More enigmatic is Kiddy's Class, a childrenswear concept originally launched in 1991. In the late 1990s, 45 stores under this name were in operation. The stores then seemed to disappear from company documentation but reappeared in 2002, with a statement that the concept, previously accounted for within Zara, would now be expanded. The strategy is to open in smaller towns or commercial centres unable to support a full Zara store or in sites complementary to existing stores. Since 2003 the financial accounts have presented the Kiddy's Class concept as a separate brand, with adjustments to store number data revealing that previously these units had been accounted for within the Zara brand. The concept is now presented as a separate brand on the Inditex website and a stand-alone website is under development.

RETAIL INTERNATIONALIZATION

Internationalization has a clear place in the Inditex vision and the overarching philosophy of the group:

> International expansion, carried out both independently and through agreements with other companies, is the objective that cannot be delayed and will allow us, through diversity, to enrich our culture and vision of the market.
>
> (Annual Report 1998)

This is reinforced as a core business objective for each of the retail chains, whose stated aim is 'to be leaders in their market segment by means of a flexible business model, in which a vocation for international expansion is a reality' (Annual Report 2000). The extent to which individual chains have internationalized varies (Figure 4.1), but all have a significant non-domestic contribution to sales and profit.

Origin of sales

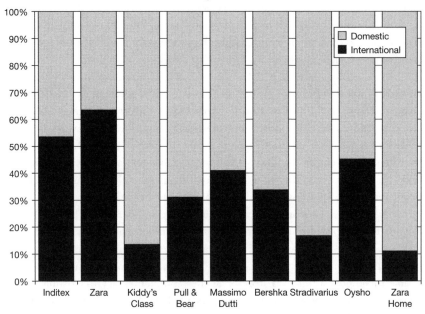

Location of stores

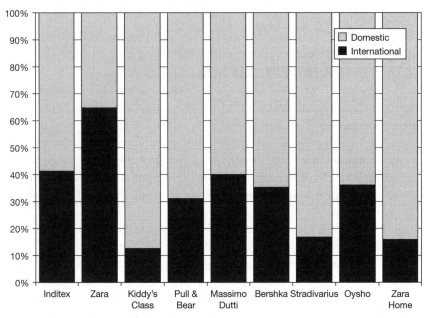

Figure 4.1 *International contribution of retail brands, 2003*

As shown in Table 4.3, international sales have grown steadily from 25 per cent of total sales in 1994, to 54 per cent in 2003, as the portfolio of stores outside Spain has increased from 81 (19.1 per cent of the total) to 792 (41 per cent) over the same period. Although all the retail chains have an international presence, Zara inevitably dominates with 405 or 51 per cent of these stores. In the case of the Zara chain, over 63 per cent of sales are now achieved from its international stores, and, with the exception of Stradivarius, each of the other established clothing chains achieves between 30 and 40 per cent of sales internationally. It is clear from these ratios that Oysho has been seen as an international brand from its inception, benefiting from the established expertise and existing sites of Zara.

As recounted earlier, the internationalization process began in 1988 with a short border-hop into Oporto in Portugal, followed by store openings in the important fashion cities of New York and Paris. In the early 1990s, Zara entered Mexico (1992), Greece (1993) and Belgium (1994). A widening of operations occurred during the late 1990s as Zara spread its wings and the other retail chains began to open abroad. A step-change in the pace of international activity occurred in 1998–99, when further expansion in Europe (including the UK and Germany) was matched by growth in Latin America (Venezuela, Argentina, Chile, Brazil and Uruguay), entry into the Middle East (Israel, Kuwait, Lebanon, Saudi Arabia and Bahrain) and tentative steps into Asia with Japan. To date, expansion in the Asean region has been limited. The Japanese market was entered in 1998, through a joint venture with Bigi Group. A move into China in the late 1990s with Pull & Bear ended in 1999, although Zara opened in Singapore in 2002, Malaysia in 2003 and the Philippines in 2005. While most of the internationalization effort centred on Zara, inevitably Pull & Bear and Massimo Dutti took advantage of this experience and opened in some of these markets during the same period.

The step-up in internationalization since 1998 is perhaps most marked in the case of Zara and Bershka. In the case of Bershka, given the age of the chain, this is inevitably from a low base, and like Oysho internationalization occurred in the same year as the launch on the Spanish market. Zara now operates in 46 different countries, compared to 16 in 1998, with Massimo Dutti present in 23 countries and Pull & Bear in 18. The stated strategy, which is reflected in the activity recounted above, is to consolidate position in the largest markets and spread into new growth markets: 'We plan to continue consolidating our presence in many of the international markets that we have recently entered, paying special attention to Europe, but without overlooking our expansion in other parts of the world' (Annual Report 2000).

While the rapid expansion of the late 1990s has given Inditex a diverse range of stores in a number of markets, the strategy in all has been to enter with high-profile capital city stores (the 'London–Paris–New York' syndrome). Typically a single store is opened in a high-profile location, the performance is closely monitored, and expansion decisions are then made. A small number of countries have become key markets (Table 4.4). Given the proximity to the Galician base, it is

Table 4.3 Inditex – number of stores, 1994–2003

	1994	1995	1996	1997	1998	1999	2000	2001	2002	2003
Total Inditex (n)	424	508	541	622	748	922	1,080	1,284	1,558	1,922
– Spain	343	391	399	433	489	603	692	769	918	1,130
– % of total	80.9	77.0	73.8	69.6	65.4	65.4	64.1	59.9	58.9	58.8
– International	81	117	142	189	259	319	388	515	640	792
– % of total	19.1	23.0	26.2	30.4	34.6	34.6	35.9	40.1	41.1	41.2
Net sales (€ million)	N/A	N/A	1,008.5	1,217.4	1,614.7	2,035.1	2,614.7	3,249.8	3,974.0	4,598.9
% of sales international*	25	30	36	42	46	48	52	54	54	54

* Declared in Annual Reports

Source: Annual Reports

Table 4.4 Inditex – international presence of retail brands, 31 January 2004

Country	Zara	Kiddy's Class	Pull & Bear	Massimo Dutti	Bershka	Stradi-varius	Oysho	Zara Home	Total Inditex
Spain	221	90	241	181	167	159	49	22	1,130
Portugal	40	13	47	40	26	20	10	2	198
France	76			2	3	1			82
Belgium	16		1	16	4				37
Netherlands	4			1	2				7
UK	25			6				1	32
Germany	26			4					30
Sweden	1			2					3
Norway				1					1
Andorra	1		1	1					3
Austria	4								4
Denmark	3								3
Luxembourg	2			1					3
Iceland	1								1
Ireland	1		6						7
Finland	3								3
Italy	12				1		2		15
Switzerland	3			3	2				8
Poland	6								6
Czech Rep	1								1
Greece	25		8	5	9		1	1	49
Slovenia	1								1
Slovakia			1						1
Malta	1		3						4
Cyprus	3		2	1	2	2			10
Israel	12		13						25
Lebanon	2		1	2	1				6
Turkey	10								10
Kuwait	3		2	1		1	1		8
UAE	4		3	4	3	2			16
Saudi Arabia	12			4		3	1		20
Bahrain	1		1	1					3
Qatar	1		1	1		1			4
Jordan	1		1	1		2			5
Canada	10								10
USA	12								12
Dominican Rep	1								1
Mexico	33		12	17	25		11		98
Venezuela	8		6	2	8		1		25
El Salvador	1								1
Brazil	13								13
Argentina	5								5
Chile	5								5
Uruguay	2								2
Japan	9								9
Singapore	2								2
Russia	1								1
Malaysia	2								2
Total	626	103	350	297	253	191	76	26	1,922

Source: Annual Report

not surprising to discover that Portugal has the largest number of Inditex stores outside Spain (198), with all the retail chains well established. In France, Zara has grown to a 76-store chain, but it was only in 2001 that the second chain, Stradivarius, opened, followed by Massimo Dutti in 2002 and Bershka in 2003. Within Europe, Greece is also a major market with six of the brands present through 49 stores and the Inditex presence is growing in Belgium, the UK and Germany. In terms of store numbers, as well as these European markets we find significant numbers of stores in Mexico (98) and Venezuela (25), and the more recent expansion into other Latin American markets implies a strong commitment to the region despite the economic instability. This is further reflected in the decision to commission another integrated factory in Mexico in 1998 to support the North and Central American market, after the NAFTA Treaty imposed heavy import duties (Harle *et al.* 2002). Operating in the Southern Hemisphere, however, creates the 'problem' of managing reverse seasons and has led to a cautious approach to some Southern Hemisphere markets. Other countries exhibiting significant growth in numbers include the Middle East markets of Israel, Saudi Arabia and the UAE with 25, 20 and 16 stores respectively – which may reflect the use of franchise contracts in these markets. In contrast, despite relatively early entry into the US (1989), store development has been slow with only 12 Zara stores open in January 2004.

Internal growth has been the preferred entry mechanism. Although 12 per cent of the stores, and 10 per cent of sales were through franchises in 2003, franchising tends to be concentrated in the Massimo Dutti (33 per cent of stores) and Stradivarius (19 per cent of stores) chains, both of which are acquired chains, or in more 'sensitive' markets, such as the Middle East. In a response to an FAQ on franchising the website comments that:

> Due to the complex commercial dimension of our chains, the Inditex Group only chooses this business formula (franchising) in order to enter certain markets where, whether owing to requirements of the country or to specific characteristics of the same, collaboration with a local company is needed or considered advisable.

Franchise or joint venture partners are either established retail textile groups, such as Otto Versand in Germany, Reitmans in Canada, Stockmann in Finland and Russia, and Royal Clicks (part of Royal Sporting House) in Singapore, or companies with access to specific assets required for rapid expansion. A typical illustration of the latter being the joint venture with Percassi, a real estate company (and Benetton franchisee), to enter Italy. In recent years there have been signs of consolidation of control in some of the more important markets. The Italian subsidiary is now 80 per cent owned, the Japanese venture 85 per cent owned and early in 2005 the Massimo Dutti franchise in Mexico was bought out.

The managerial approach to retail internationalization is based on a global vision and strategy, with core concepts and policies determined and controlled at head office. This is reflected in the 1998 Annual Report:

> The conviction that frontiers will not prevent the sharing of the same clothing culture is the main principle of the expansion process in progress which, although adapting itself to the peculiarities of each country, has common guidelines such as privileged locations in the main cities, and exquisite care of the facades, shop windows and interior designs.

Although, as an integral part of the Inditex approach, local market adaptation determines the product range, Inditex retains a highly centralized approach to core strategic issues such as product design and development, price, selection of local management and processes (logistics and inventory control and market information systems).

The design team in each chain determines the core brand concept, product range and pricing strategy which is then implemented in each country. An important element in the selection of markets is the ability to price an item at the right level for that market. Consequently, the group argues that entry decisions are market price driven not cost driven. Initial attempts to operate a uniform pricing policy have given way to market variable pricing as international expansion gathered pace. One casualty of this switch has been the distinctive Zara price tag, which listed the different prices in each country identified by a flag. The complexities for both the company and customers of producing and interpreting a price label covering 46 markets in the case of Zara, has seen this system replaced by store level tagging in each country. Inevitably, owing to variations in market conditions and positioning, pricing varies. D'Andrea and Arnold (2003) show that prices typically vary from the Spanish benchmark by +10 per cent in Southern Europe; +70 per cent in Northern Europe and the US; and +100 per cent in Japan, while material on the Inditex website suggests pricing variations within Europe from the Iberian base of +10 per cent in Greece; +25 per cent in 'Euroland'; and +35 per cent in the UK, Scandinavia and Switzerland.

According to Bonache and Cervino (1997), in the early years of expansion Zara took a very ethnocentric approach to retail internationalization, with stores built and managed to replicate the Spanish model. Spanish executives were sent out into the field to manage the business and establish identical management. The company, however, experienced some cultural differences, particularly in relation to work practices and behaviours, and has now, depending on cultural distance and experience curve considerations, decentralized various operational elements (e.g. local recruitment, internal communication, sales promotion, merchandising, and so on) to take on board market sensitivities. The approach now is to find local managers to develop and grow the business, although the initial set-up is still managed by

Head Office staff sent on placement for up to three months. Once recruited, country managers are brought to La Coruna to experience a complete immersion in the Inditex-Zara way of doing business.

The company also aims to develop a Zara culture across international markets, through a shared set of values and norms that bind the business together. Although this is recognized by both observers and the company itself, it is difficult to articulate what this culture represents. Informality and teamwork are encouraged and form central tenants of the organizational culture, with the Head Office designed as an open plan operating environment with plenty of social and meeting space to encourage discussion and the exchange of opinions across traditional job boundaries. In such an atmosphere of informality, there is little formal explicit knowledge retained in the business, with very little written down. The cross-pollination of ideas is achieved through organizational learning mechanisms such as a subsidiaries management committee, which holds regular quarterly meetings to exchange experiences and know how, and which also performs an auditing function. The auditing function is managed by Head Office staff from the commercial department who act as international area managers, monitoring country level implementation. Bonache and Cervino (1997) argue that this mixture of bureaucratic and cultural control mechanisms reinforces the global approach to international markets.

THE FUTURE OF INDITEX

The distinctive Inditex approach of market-driven flexibility has provided the basis for rapid growth and expansion in both the domestic and international market. The group has developed an innovative business process covering the whole channel, and by reconfiguring how the traditional apparel channel operates has provided itself with the skills and competences to internationalize its activities. To date, the business model has provided a competitive advantage that can be leveraged in a wide range of markets.

The 2003 financial figures represented the first 'blip' in this seemingly inexorable growth. Warm weather in Europe, discounting pressures in key markets, currency fluctuations in the Americas, and underperformance of some brands were given as the reasons for this slowing of growth (George and Levitt 2002; Scaher 2003). Stradivarius and Pull & Bear were identified as the culprits and an Inditex team was placed in Stradivarius to oversee changes in sourcing and store management, including the 'full replication' of the Inditex model. In the case of Pull & Bear a poorly performing collection was blamed. Despite these problems, plans for a further 300 plus new stores during 2004 were achieved. The plan was to concentrate on growing the newer concepts in Spain while consolidating store numbers in key European markets. This 'in-fill' strategy appears logical given the range of formats and countries where the company is present. It is not yet clear where the Asean region fits into this agenda, but there is clearly scope for future development.

In the long term, like all retail organizations, Inditex-Zara must assess the sustainability of its business approach. A stock market listing brings its own pressures. Based on past performance, expectations on sales growth and earnings are high, and the extent to which sales growth can be maintained by like-for-like growth, if new store openings and new formulae options slow, is unclear. As other firms adopt the 'fast fashion' model questions over the extent to which Inditex (like Benetton before it) can hold on to its intellectual capital and unique selling proposition come to the fore. If the basic business model is imitated, then attention switches to unique features of the Inditex approach as a means of sustaining competitive advantage. At the production end of the channel, the ability to organize low-cost production in Europe, close to the key markets, currently provides advantages. With China gaining WTO membership and textile quotas being eliminated in 2005, sourcing structures within the industry are liable to change, presenting new challenges. At the retail end of the channel, the low expenditure on traditional marketing activities such as advertising is replaced by high rental costs for prime sites. This, in turn, raises rental and advertising costs for competitors, allowing Zara to manage industry and (competitor) cost structures. To sustain this position in the future the retail sector as a whole must be capable of paying increasing property costs. Innovation in retailing is notoriously easy to imitate, but tends to be more sustainable if it is grounded in the culture and behaviour of a business. Ultimately the work practices and culture of Inditex-Zara may prove to be the greatest asset of the group.

REFERENCES

Bonache, J. and Cervino, J. (1997) Global integration without expatriates. *Human Resource Management Journal,* 7(3): 89–100

Castellano Rios, J. M. (2002) El processo de internacionalizacion de Indtiex. *Empresas Multinacionales Espanolas,* 799, April–May: 209–217

Christopher, M. (1998) Zara: time-based competition in a fashion market, (Case Study). In: M. Christopher (ed.), *Logistics and supply chain management,* second edition. (London: Financial Times/Prentice Hall) pp. 155–157

Crawford, L. (2000a) Zara set for a stylish debut. *Financial Times,* 2–3 September

Crawford, L. (2000b) Putting on the style with rapid response. *Financial Times,* 26 September, p. 17

D'Andrea, G. and Arnold, D. (2003) *Zara*. Harvard Business School Case Study, 9–503–050

Ferdows, K., Machuca, J. and Lewis, M. (2002) *Zara*. Georgetown University/ Universidad de Sevilla/University of Warwick Case Study, 603–002–01

Ferdows, K., Lewis, M. A. and Machuca, J. A. D. (2004) Rapid-fire fulfillment. *Harvard Business Review*, 8(11): 104–110

George, N. and Levitt, J. (2002) Retail leaders hope to show they're more than just a passing fashion. *Financial Times*, 18 September

Harle, N., Pich, M. and Van der Heyden, L. (2002) *Marks & Spencer and Zara: process competition in the textile apparel industry*. INSEAD case study

Hellier, R. (2001) Inside Zara. *Forbes.com*, 28 May

Inditex Annual Report 1998, 1999, 2000, 2001, 2002, 2003

Inditex Press Dossier 2004

McAfee, A. (2004) Do you have too much IT? *MIT Sloan Management Review*, Spring: 18–22

McAfee, A., Sjoman, A. and Dessain, V. (2004) *Zara: IT for fast fashion*. Harvard Business School Case Study 9–604–081

Points de Vente (2000) Le rouleau compresseur Zara. *Points de Vente*, 3 May, pp. 26–27

Revilla Bonnin, A. (2002) The fashion industry in Galicia: understanding the 'Zara' phenomenon. *European Planning Studies*, 10(4): 519–527

Roux, C. (2002) The reign of Spain. *Guardian*, 28 October, pp. 6–7

Scaher, T. (2003) Hot summer hits Zara fashion group. *Financial Times*, 15 December

Vitzthum, C. (2001) Zara's speed sells fashion. *The Wall Street Journal Europe*, 11–12 May

Websites

www.inditex.com

www.zara.com

www.pullandbear.com

www.massimodutti.com

www.bershka.com

www.e-stradivarius.com

www.oysho.com

www.zarahome.com

www.often.com

www.kiddysclass.com

Chapter 5

Carrefour

Being aware of the domestic market!

Marc Dupuis, Sang Chul Choi and Roy Larke

INTRODUCTION

Carrefour is the second largest retailer in the world by sales. This position was achieved following the merger with French retailer, Promodès, in September 1999. Even as the second largest, Carrefour's turnover is only a third that of Wal-Mart, at €79 billion in 2004, but it is a leading global retailer with a significant international presence. At the end of 2004 Carrefour was established in 29 countries. It operated stores in each of the four major continents and sub-regions of Western Europe, Central Europe, South America and Asia. It was a multi-format group operating hypermarkets, supermarkets, discount stores and convenience stores, but the hypermarket has been the core format for Carrefour in almost every market in which it operates.

HISTORICAL BACKGROUND

The story of Carrefour begins with the alliance of two French families, the Fournier and the Defforey families, both of whom had already operated small shops for generations. In 1960, Marcel Fournier and the Defforey family founded a company named 'Carrefour Supermarkets' and began self-service retailing by opening the first supermarket in Annecy.

Historically, Carrefour has been recognized as the inventor of the hypermarket store format, the very first of which opened in the outskirts of Paris in 1963. The hypermarket format has been, and remains, Carrefour's primary retail format and it has played a key role in the company's internationalization process. The original 1963 store was 2,500 square metres in area and the format has since proved to be one of the retail innovations of the twentieth century. The core of the hypermarket format was, and remains, a method of retailing that relies on the three main pillars of low prices, large parking lots and the aim of providing customers with a one-stop shopping location.

Based on these three pillars, the hypermarket format became the leading type of store in terms of market sales share in France. By the late 1960s and early 1970s (Burt 1986), the expansion of the hypermarkets slowed as competition from hard discount supermarkets and large-scale speciality retailers began to expand, but it remained the most important type of store overall. By 1973, Carrefour was the leading French retailer, but in that year legal restrictions in the form of the Loi Royer were introduced further restricting the expansion of large-scale retail stores. This proved to be the signal for Carrefour to begin exploring opportunities outside its domestic market. The internationalization process had begun.

Although restrictions on expansion in its domestic market led Carrefour to begin its ventures in other countries, it did not abandon the hypermarket format. This particular retail type continues to be one of the fastest growing in the world today, particularly in emerging markets, and not least as Carrefour itself has pioneered the format on a global scale.

CARREFOUR'S INTERNATIONALIZATION PROCESS (1973–2003) FROM LOCAL TO GLOBAL

The 'Latin' step, 1973–1982

The first ten years of Carrefour's international expansion were focused on Latin countries in Europe and South America. The selection of the countries appears to be based on the criteria of geographic and/or cultural proximity as well as ease of entry. Carrefour entered Spain in 1973, followed by Brazil in 1975 and Argentina in 1982. The retail markets in these countries were just on the point of opening up to modern mass retailing when Carrefour began its entry phase, providing significant opportunity to develop a first mover advantage.

The multi-continental step (US and Asia), 1988–1989

In 1988, Carrefour opened two hypermarkets in the US. The entry of Carrefour into the world's largest and most developed consumer market proved to be far more difficult than expected. Carrefour soon faced problems dealing with a market that was culturally different and economically more advanced than those it had attempted to date. Not that such problems were unique to Carrefour. Other French hypermarket companies, such as Euromarché, Auchan and Leclerc, also tried to enter the US market around the same time. Carrefour gained little success in the US market and withdrew its activities in 1993.

A number of possible reasons for the failure of Carrefour in the US can be suggested:

- The maturity of the US consumer in terms of mass retailing presented a much more difficult market to work in.
- It was not a Latin market but, rather, presented a consumer culture in which Carrefour had little experience.
- Tough competition from domestic retail leaders such as Wal-Mart meant that Carrefour had problems making a profit as quickly as elsewhere.
- The small size of the initial investment was not enough to achieve a local critical size quickly enough to achieve sustainability.

Only one year after its initial US entry, however, in 1989 Carrefour began its activities in Asia through entry into Taiwan, this time through a joint venture with the President Group.

In the early 1990s, therefore, despite setbacks in North America, Carrefour had become a multi-continent retailer, with stores in Europe, America and Asia.

Toward a global strategy, 1990–2004

Following the decision to enter the US and Asia, over the next 14 years, Carrefour developed a multi-continental strategy of expansion. It now sees itself as a global retailer with a presence across the world, despite difficulties in highly developed markets. In addition to Western Europe, Carrefour, in late 2004, operated in the areas and countries shown in Table 5.1.

In addition to exiting the US market in 1993, Carrefour also withdrew from the UK after two attempts to enter the market, finally leaving in 1996 following a failed attempt to operate hypermarkets and a discount format called ED. It withdrew from Hong Kong in 2000 after four years in the country. Arguably, the most important factors that initiated such high-profile withdrawals were similar to the case of the US:

- high levels of domestic competition from mature local players in the same market;
- relatively high costs of operations in a developed, modern retail market;
- difficulty in achieving a necessary critical size in terms of store numbers in these countries.

In 2000, Carrefour became the first multinational food and general merchandise retailer to establish stores in Japan, another mature and highly competitive market. Here, Carrefour faced similar problems and, despite expanding to eight stores, announced its withdrawal in early 2005.

Table 5.1 Regions and countries where Carrefour operated retail stores

Region	Countries (December 2004)
Asia	Malaysia Thailand China Taiwan South Korea Singapore Indonesia Japan
Latin America	Brazil Argentina Mexico Colombia
Central Europe	Poland Czech Republic Slovakia Romania
Near and Middle East and North Africa	Egypt Turkey Morocco United Arab Emirates Qatar Tunisia Oman

A LEADERSHIP STRATEGY

A key goal for Carrefour is to be one of the three leading retailers in each country that it enters. In 2002 Carrefour was ranked number one for international retailers in 13 of the 31 countries in which it operated. This strategy is explained by Carrefour's CEO Daniel Bernard as follows:

> Carrefour is faced, like its other competitors, with a battle for new market shares. It doesn't mean anything to be ranked as the worldwide number two retailer if you are weak in each country. You have to be number one in Buenos-Aires, number one in Argentina, and finally to be number one in South America.
>
> (Bernard 2002)

Before merging with Promodès, the Carrefour home market was France, but the Promodès chain was more widely dispersed across Europe. In the new merged company, Carrefour considers Europe as a whole as the 'core market' (Table 5.2).

Table 5.2 *Carrefour's globalization: the European core market remains dominant*

Countries	% of total turnover
Core market (Europe)	87
Home market (France)	36
Rest of Europe	51
South America	7
Asia	6
Total	100

Source: Carrefour Annual Report, 2003

Home market: France

Carrefour was the number one retail group in France in 2001 with a 28 per cent share of the total retail market, followed by the independent discount group, Leclerc, with 26 per cent. Both internationalization and the process of merging with Promodès caused problems that weakened Carrefour's performance in its own home market during the 2000–2002 period (see below), leading to a loss of 1.2 per cent of market share. This loss of share for Carrefour has been the gain of independent retailers and cooperative groups such as Leclerc and Système U. These groups are more decentralized and less internationalized and have been able to concentrate more on competing with Carrefour at home.

There have been a number of explanations as to why Carrefour has had problems maintaining its market share in France. First, Carrefour faced considerable difficulties in merging the differing corporate and retail cultures between itself and Promodès. The most difficult problems arose from combining buying and logistics functions. Historically, Promodès was a wholesaler dealing with a mostly franchised retail network while Carrefour has developed as a retail chain.

Second, Carrefour has also lost ground in terms of image and values, shopping experience, and staff and services compared with its main French competitors Leclerc, Auchan, Casino, Système U and Intermarché (IGD 2002).

Third, through a greater emphasis on qualitative aspects of its business, with more sophisticated communication and merchandising, Carrefour has lost ground in the discount market as its image has moved more upscale as compared to its competitors. Consequently, a rise in gross margin from 20.1 per cent in 1997 to 22.5 per cent in 2003 has also had a negative impact on Carrefour's price image (see Table 5.3). A survey made in 1991 ranked Carrefour as cheaper than Leclerc, Intermarché and Auchan, but in ten years the relationships had changed.

Finally, some of the company's most experienced managers have been dedicated to Carrefour's international development and expansion, causing a slight, but possibly significant reduction in ability within its home market.

Table 5.3 Price index of the main hypermarket fascias in France in 2002

Fascias	Structure	Price index*
Leclerc	Associated independents	97.6
Auchan (Mulliez group)	Family chain	98.5
Intermarché	Associated independents	98.6
Carrefour	Public company	98.6
Géant (Casino)	Public company	99.2

* Index 100: average 12 fascias

Source: *Les Echos,* 21 February 2003

During 2002, Carrefour focused on restoring its discount image with a very important promotion programme. In 2003 it launched price promotions for its fortieth anniversary with a new advertising slogan, 'Everyday Carrefour is cheaper', emulating the 'Every Day Low Price' theme at Wal-Mart. The opening of a new hypermarket at Collegien (France), featuring an adjusted formula, was considered by Carrefour to be a new start for its home market. However, a survey published in November 2003 by the French professional journal *LSA* still ranked Carrefour third in terms of perceived price attribute in its format sector (*LSA* 2003).

Core market: Europe

Carrefour is ranked as the number one retailer in Europe by sales. Since 1999 (and the merger with Promodès) Europe has become the company's core market in terms of strategy. It has a leading position in Southern Europe (France, Spain, Italy, Portugal, Greece) and has acquired important companies in Switzerland and Belgium. Together, Europe accounted for 86 per cent of Carrefour's total turnover in 2003 and was vital in providing cash flow for expansion of operations in other parts of the world. As noted above, Carrefour was still absent from the major markets of the UK and Germany, but it entered Norway in 2003 through an agreement with Norges Gruppen, with a plan of 137 supermarkets for the Champion fascia by 2005.

As with some of its key competitors, the markets of Central and Eastern Europe may be a way for Carrefour to expand further, although it will face strong international competition there. Carrefour currently operates in Poland, the Czech Republic, Slovakia and Romania, but has yet to enter Hungary, for example.

South America: an Eldorado for Carrefour

Carrefour has led the expansion of international retailers in South America and has achieved remarkable success in these markets (Table 5.4). It was the first

Table 5.4 *Carrefour in Latin America*

Countries	Year of entry	Rank (food retailing)
Brazil	1975	2
Argentina	1982	1
Mexico	1994	8
Colombia	1996	5

Note: Carrefour announced a withdrawal from Mexico in 2005

Source: Annual Report 2002

international retailer to open stores in South America, especially in Brazil and Argentina, where it has achieved a leading position through a combination of organic growth and company acquisition. In Latin America Carrefour has enriched its experience in working in unstable political and economic environments and in countries with very high inflation levels. According to a report by financial analysts Standard & Poor, 'Carrefour has successfully weathered the Latin American hyperinflation crises and has a superior know-how in adjusting its concept to local economies' (AGSM 2000). This know-how seems particularly fruitful in the context of the Argentinian financial crisis where Carrefour decided to focus on its low-price policy and gained increased market share as a result. Equally, low land prices in Brazil allowed the chain to expand rapidly, achieving critical mass in terms of store numbers and establishing its own logistics operations at an early stage.

Asia: the European leader

Similarly in Asia, Carrefour has been the European leader in terms of international retail expansion in the region (Table 5.5). It has expanded widely, entering Taiwan in 1989, followed subsequently by China, Thailand and other Asian markets. Of the foreign retailers operating in Asia, in 2004 it ranked number one in Taiwan, number two in Thailand and number four in South Korea. It ranked as the fifth largest retailer overall in China, and, although exact figures are unavailable, the second largest foreign retailer in Japan if luxury brand companies are excluded.

Hong Kong is a relatively advanced and developed economy with numerous non-domestic retailers operating in the territory. This proved to be unsuccessful for Carrefour. In Singapore, Carrefour currently operates two stores but both are very popular despite a number of competitors operating similar retail stores on the island. As for many international retailers, Singapore is too limited in terms of market size to have very much ultimate importance and is unlikely to receive significant development in any case.

Table 5.5 Carrefour in Asia

Countries	Year of entry	Rank (food retailing)
Taiwan	1989	1
South Korea	1996	4
China	1995	3
Thailand	1994	5
Malaysia	1994	3
Indonesia	1998	1*
Japan	2000	–
Singapore	1997	5

* Hypermarkets only

Source: Company Report 2002

South Korea

Following the complete opening of the retail market in 1996, South Korea has attracted numerous overseas chains. Regulations on floor space and shop numbers were abandoned and the retail market was liberalized (Choi 2003), and Carrefour entered the market soon after. It was then followed by Makro in a joint venture, and has since been joined by Costco, Wal-Mart and Tesco. Even so, the first hypermarket in Korea was built in 1993 by a domestic chain, E-Mart, and E-Mart is still the largest company operating the format today. The entry of Carrefour added the concept of low price and reasonable quality to Korean consumers and this has now become standard in the market.

At the end of 2000, Carrefour remained the second largest hypermarket company in South Korea in terms of store numbers. In 2004 Lotte Mart overtook Carrefour in terms of store numbers, pushing it to number three. Sales rankings are believed to be in line with store numbers.

Carrefour was criticized by the Korean press for being a global company and for not taking enough account of differing Korean consumer culture. In response, in early 2003, Marc Oursin, the then CEO of Carrefour Korea said:

> We are going to concentrate on providing our customers with the best service through competitive price, best quality and various service programs, especially 'Back to Customers', which places importance on improving stores in line with Korean customers' delicate expectations, for example lower shelf heights.

In the same context Carrefour attempted to reduce friction with local employees by the expanded use of Korean managers. The company was planning a new expansion of stores for 2005.

Carrefour in China

In July 1992, the Chinese retail market was partially opened to overseas companies on a highly restricted basis. Firms were forced to establish separate joint ventures in different regions, but the size of the market and its future potential proved attractive nonetheless. At the end of 1995, Carrefour opened its first hypermarket with the store name of Jialefu in Beijing. In January 1996, it opened a second store in Shanghai through a partnership with Lianhua, the largest supermarket chain in China at the time. It then added stores in Shenzhen and other cities. It was by far the largest and quickest rollout of stores of any overseas firm, but Carrefour was later cautioned by the Chinese government for opening without proper central government permissions in some cases. This rebuke had limited impact and Carrefour by late 2004 was the fifth largest retailer in China overall.

After China changed its policy in preparation for WTO entry in 2000, Carrefour moved its Chinese headquarters from Beijing to Shanghai. It changed the management style of all the 27 stores at the time to joint ventures with the local partners and expanded procurement from domestic suppliers. Carrefour continued to negotiate with the central government to open new stores, and moves towards better integration in China helped smooth relations.

By December 2004, Carrefour operated 56 hypermarkets in China, with 16 opening in 2004 alone. Unlike other global retailers such as Ito-Yokado, Aeon and Wal-Mart, Carrefour chose a distributed store strategy and has stores in several regions of China where other large international retailers have yet to open. It also employs a multi-format strategy, with 164 hard discount stores under its Dia fascia (110 newly opened in 2004), and six supermarkets under the Champion fascia (all opened in 2004). The company is planning to almost double its hypermarket chain to more than 100 stores by the end of 2005.

CARREFOUR AS A MULTI-FORMAT GROUP

Carrefour may be the originator of the hypermarket, but by 2004 it had evolved into a multi-format retailer concentrating on three main formats:

1   hypermarkets
2   supermarkets
3   discount stores.

While it also has other formats within its total portfolio, these three main types are the ones used in its international operations. In 2002 Carrefour was opening 'One Dia discount store a day, one Champion supermarket every three days, and one Carrefour hypermarket a week worldwide' (Annual Report 2002).

Each format is independent from a marketing point of view, but Carrefour uses a common logistic platform in order to achieve scale economies. This multi-format portfolio aims to provide increased flexibility for global expansion, but it also causes more complexity in terms of management. The hypermarket format remains the key, being represented in 29 countries, while the supermarket format is in 11 countries, and the discount format in eight countries.

The hypermarket strategy

The basic pillars of the hypermarket are low prices, one-stop shopping (usually in the region of 80,000 SKUs) and easy access by car. Recent Carrefour hypermarkets have employed an average sales area of more than 10,000 square metres. The hypermarket strategy is based on the idea that, around major cities, consumers seek to do their shopping under one roof, buying food products, clothing, household appliances, cultural products, services such as insurance, travel and financial services, together in the same store.

With hypermarkets, Carrefour aims to take the maximum market share within the commercial area of each store, positioning prices to compete with the lowest available within each local market. Unlike the EDLP (Every Day Low Price) strategy employed by Wal-Mart, most Carrefour stores offer regular promotions, with prices positioned and adjusted to compete with the lowest prices in the local market. Such promotions are further supported by Carrefour own brands and a wide array of services including insurance, travel and financial services. Such additional in-store services were developed largely during the course of Carrefour's internationalization process.

When different markets in different countries are compared, the competitive advantages of Carrefour's hypermarket format change depending on local market conditions. This means an adjustment in the store formula is required. In Taiwan, for example, beside its low price strategy, Carrefour focuses on freshness and cold chain control. In Japan, where the hypermarket was introduced by Carrefour for the first time, it added a shopping centre and restaurant area in each of its stores. In Singapore, the hypermarket forms an anchor tenant role in a larger, independent shopping centre.

Similarly, the competitive advantages of Carrefour's hypermarket format have also changed over time. Large parking lots are now common at other formats, for example, and there are also a number of companies that attempt to offer lower prices in a more cost-based retail format.

In Argentina, from 2000 onwards, Carrefour has further expanded the range of the hypermarket formula. This occurred as a natural response to economic problems.

The formula there is now split into three types of hypermarket depending on the standard of living in local markets:

1   type 1: limited assortment and low prices dedicated to low income populations;
2   type 2: merchandise and service mix targeting the middle class;
3   type 3: merchandise and service mix targeting higher incomes, with an extended assortment particularly health and beauty products and electronic items (Annual Report 2003).

The supermarket strategy

In addition to the standard hypermarket, Carrefour is developing its supermarket networks under the Champion fascia. The main objective for Carrefour supermarkets is to maintain close proximity to customers, with an average of one visit every five days. The selling space of Champion supermarkets is between 1,000 and 2,000 square metres and the proposed assortment makes up around 10,000 SKUs per store. Competition among supermarkets is particularly fierce, however, and Carrefour does not have the degree of competitive advantage in this format that it enjoys for hypermarkets.

The discount stores

The third key format employed by Carrefour in its international operations is the discount store. The three fascias currently employed are Dia, Minipreço and ED. In general, Carrefour's discount stores are a limited assortment food format, concentrating on low prices with a significant share of own labels in a sales space of 300–800 square metres.

In the discount store format, the main worldwide competitors are German retailers such as Aldi and Lidl. In comparison, Carrefour's style of discounting has a softer edge, as the chain does not attempt to cut costs on all aspects of its operations and in every part of the supply chain. In 2003, 4,456 Dia discount stores were operating in eight countries.

CARREFOUR'S GLOBAL VISION

Carrefour's global vision to 2004, as presented by its CEO Daniel Bernard (2002), was based around the following key ideas:

- Retailing is not the last step of the supply chain but the first point of contact with the customer.
- Carrefour aims to be leader in every country it enters in terms of turnover and market share.
- In order to be a leader internationally, Carrefour must also be the leader in its home market.
- Internationalization is a mission for commerce.
- Retailing is the first testimony of sociology.
- Carrefour aims to be a major retail player for environmental, sustainable and social development.
- Retail formats (such as the hypermarket) are a fundamental catalyst for the rise of a worldwide middle class.

From an international point of view, Carrefour defines itself as multicultural, and claims an ability to adapt to local markets. It aims be 'Chinese in China, Brazilian in Brazil', and to adapt locally in terms of culture, assortment, promotion and staff (Bernard 2002). Some of these goals are not easy to achieve in practice. The 'men of Carrefour' have to launch the necessary international subsidiaries and the necessary cultural adaptation is difficult with different conditions and expectations in every market that Carrefour enters. In Japan, Carrefour had to modify its merchandising and assortments policies to meet customer expectations of overseas retailers selling predominantly imported product and, in Carrefour's case, French product. Equally, in South Korea, it moved gradually away from the exclusive use of expatriate managers to employing local retail managers.

MANAGING THE RETAIL INTERNATIONALIZATION PROCESS

The international retail process may be divided into four steps:

1 *Pre-entry*: choosing appropriate markets and countries, conducting market studies, overcoming legal barriers, choosing appropriate modes of entry, finding the right partner where necessary, securing a first location, designing a marketing and strategic plan, recruiting initial staff from the home and the host country. It is necessary to prepare an entry plan that justifies the total means (money, time, people) needed in order to achieve initial entry and success within a new market.

2 *Entry*: opening the first store, facing logistics issues, dealing with local suppliers, adapting the formula.

3 *Growth*: expansion of the network in various cities within a given country.

4 *Consolidation and acculturation*: alternatively, the long-term result may be market exit in case of failure.

In addition to these four stages, certain key concepts are also important in understanding the internationalization of retailers:

1   *Critical size*: minimum size needed to achieve a stable position in the market, to apply in-house logistics facilities, and to control supply chain issues. This is measured in terms of number of stores, turnover, market shares, purchasing power, but the actual size required varies significantly between countries. In general, the less competitive the market, the smaller the critical size becomes.
2   *Challengers and competitors*: these may be local or international and include such problems as local political opposition.
3   *Repositioning*: the operational formula, concept and politics related to a position within an international market. According to Daniel Bernard, the repositioning of Carrefour's retail concepts is considered every three years (2002).

A number of these stages and concepts are considered in greater detail below. Carrefour presents an unusually complete case for the study of internationalization in retailing because it is one of the few current retailers to have not only achieved success, but also to have withdrawn from some markets, so encompassing the full range of the process indicated above.

Pre-entry and entry stages of internationalization

Carrefour has employed a number of different entry modes during its 30-year history of operating in international markets. It has attempted and experimented with organic growth, joint ventures, acquisitions, and, since its merger with Promodès, franchising.

Joint venture agreements, most commonly between an overseas company and a local company, are probably the most common form of market entry mode in retailing. Carrefour has employed this mode on a number of occasions, usually aiming for a majority stake in the venture in order to control overall management and strategy. The main examples of joint venture are Spain (with Pryca), Brazil (with Brepa), Taiwan (with President Group) and Mexico (with Gigante). To date in China, Carrefour has opened stores in joint ventures with various local partners as required under local Chinese law. Joint venture may be a good way to share risk and to benefit from the local experience of a domestic associate.

Following its merger with Promodès, Carrefour inherited a company with a franchising culture. Franchising presents a possible loss of control at the store level, and was not a preferred method of international entry for Carrefour prior to the acquisition.

Sometimes it may be difficult to find a local partner, especially in a highly competitive environment. Alternatively, local business culture may even prohibit joint ventures or only permit conditions under which the overseas partner has a minority share. In such cases, direct entry with a 100 per cent owned operation, followed by organic growth becomes the main alternative. Directly owned operations have been employed by Carrefour in the past, notably in Hong Kong, South Korea, Singapore and Japan.

A final method of entry is by acquisition. Acquisitions have been preferred by Ahold, Tesco and Wal-Mart, but Carrefour has made relatively few international acquisitions. The one key exception is the acquisition of Norte in Argentina, where Carrefour acquired the local company in order to gain a leadership position rapidly.

Critical size

The concept of critical size may vary from one retail format to another. A vital part of attaining this size is the ability to reach a minimum size in order to implement profitable logistics operations. For the hypermarket format Carrefour requires eight to ten stores as the critical size for in-house logistics to be established in most countries. In contrast, it may be necessary to build up to 50 stores in order to achieve a similar critical mass for discount store formats. Equally, in countries such as Japan where physical distribution is difficult due to geographical constraints, a larger chain of stores is required to form a national critical size even for large formats such as hypermarkets. Domestic Japanese retailers have historically concentrated operations on narrow geographical regions for precisely this reason.

Similarly, a critical size is also desired in terms of purchasing power. Given the strategy of Carrefour to be one of the leading firms in each market, critical size can be reached when the company gets at least the same buying conditions as the leading domestic companies. Again, in Japan, Carrefour's smallest direct competitors had 150 to 300 large format superstores, making equal buying power impossible to achieve early on. Despite Wal-Mart's global purchasing strategy, Carrefour still employs a country-by-country or even regional buying strategy, aiming to be a local player within each market that it enters.

Growth and maturity

Having achieved critical size, Carrefour aims for a leadership position. At that stage, it is common for local managers to replace French executives and to share the company global culture. This policy is somewhat different from that of Tesco and Wal-Mart, but such a policy is also an indication of the differing entry strategies.

New challengers may appear from the local or international markets. Increasingly, the key FMCG retailers entering markets in Asia are the same small group of players: Carrefour, Wal-Mart, Tesco, Casino, Ahold and Auchan. Each has the same aim and, particularly in Asia where the local retail development is less advanced than in Europe, there is the possibility that a number of markets will be led by non-domestic retail companies.

Exit stage of internationalization

Carrefour is a case of a major retailer that has not succeeded in every country it entered. Unsurprisingly, most companies are reluctant to discuss cases of withdrawal. While Carrefour will show no pride in exiting a market, experience of unsuccessful ventures or ventures that required extensive readjustment and reconsideration provides the company with the knowledge of potential pitfalls and problems of international expansion. As Wal-Mart discovered in Germany, international operations are often more problematic than simply transplanting a formula from its home market. In Carrefour's case, the experience of market exit may be seen as having the potential to strengthen future market entry decision making and market adaptation strategy. The cases of Carrefour deciding to exit both the Mexican and Japanese market in 2005 have more to do with improving company performance in its home and core markets than with unassailable problems in the overseas markets in question. In Japan especially, the effort made to adapt to the market was considerable and largely successful at store level despite problems with anti-competitive practices in the supply chain. Given the choice of further investment in Japan and using the same funds in China, however, Carrefour logically decided to concentrate on the larger, more attractive market.

THE INTERNATIONAL LEARNING PROCESS

From a methodological point of view the international learning process cannot be seen as a 'black box' where a company's know-how is stored. As in every human organization the learning process is complex and given changes, particularly in the management staff, the difficulties of communication inside the company mean that losses in the learning process are sometimes considerable (Figure 5.1).

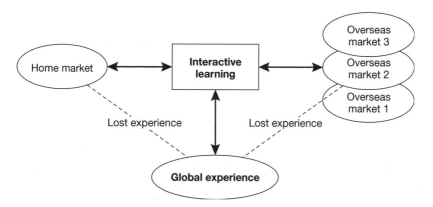

Figure 5.1 *The process of learning and knowledge exchange through international operations*

Carrefour's learning process of expansion and development in its international retail operations is based primarily on the fact that executives are required to undertake various functions at home and overseas. For example, a senior development manager may be asked to start a new network in Brazil, and then be placed in charge of Latin America. By this system of interchanging functions, its managers share values and experiences. Exchange meetings of best practices are organized across the company. But the growing complexity of a multi-country, multi-format organization makes it more difficult to transfer acquired competencies in different markets while maintaining overall context and to avoid loss of know-how.

In the long run, the risk of losing parts of the acquired experience becomes higher, taking into account that staff turnover in a large worldwide organization can be considerable. That having been said, the success of an organization such as Carrefour is clearly related to its experience and ability to successfully facilitate knowledge and learning transfer across international markets. This is at least partly related to the overall structure of the Carrefour organization (see below).

Carrefour's annual reports show tests carried out in a country, a region, or a point of sale may be rolled out to its worldwide network. Every year Carrefour hires 100,000 people around the world, but it makes an effort to maintain central company values no matter where it operates. For example, in 2004 it launched the 'Carrefour Attitude Project' with the aim to disseminate the seven top values of the group to its employees worldwide.

ASPECTS OF COMPANY ORGANIZATION FOR INTERNATIONALIZATION PROCESSES

The centralization/decentralization issue

The corporate culture of Carrefour was originally decentralized. This original organization structure developed in order to operate hypermarket stores. In terms of employee numbers and sales, each hypermarket was the size of a medium-sized firm in itself, employing between 300 and 600 people per store. In addition, in order to serve local markets, the formula called for direct relationships with local suppliers servicing the hypermarket. These were particularly important for fresh produce.

For nearly 30 years, decentralization was one of Carrefour's 'credos'. In 1992, when Daniel Bernard became CEO, this credo changed to become increasingly one of centralization. Daniel Bernard was the former CEO of Metro France, and Metro, a German retail and cash-and-carry group, employs a centralized organizational structure. The reasons why Bernard decided to centralize operations at Carrefour can be summarized as follows:

- High market concentration in retailing reinforces the necessity for strong buying power, and this is best achieved through centralized buying.
- Economies of scale are desirable in order to achieve more efficient and low-cost logistics.
- The perceived threat of the Wal-Mart model was already an issue for French retail managers, suggesting a need to change their fundamental business structure.
- A better coherence of the whole Carrefour network was also desired in order to improve and maintain the image consumers had of the company.

Ducrocq (2003) claimed that Carrefour's centralization of company structure was inspired by the Wal-Mart model. He called this 'the unique thinking' of most of the international retail players and referred to the 'Anglo-Saxon' retailers' model. In comparison, he suggested that the so-called 'Latin model' takes a more flexible and adapted approach to the local needs of consumers. In France, independent groups with a more familiar and more decentralized approach have shown their capability to gain market share on a local basis and to be closer to the consumer. Being both multicultural and multi-format, Carrefour tended to organize its international networks with a matrix combining countries and formats in keeping with the model introduced by Bernard.

A comparison between the leading three retailers, Wal-Mart, Carrefour and Ahold, shows some key differences between their international organizations (see Figure 5.2). While Carrefour adopted a matrix organization of countries and formats in order to gain greater coherence (but also adding more complexity in terms of international management), Ahold took a much more decentralized structure. Ahold aimed to give its various retail fascias the maximum of autonomy in each country. Given the importance of its domestic market, Wal-Mart aims to maintain a centralized international management structure in order to use its key weapon, the control of the supply chain.

The back office

The retail back office includes logistics, information systems and sourcing. The level of control over, for example, product design, quality, price and margins within the supply chain may be considered as strategic in terms of international competitive advantage and profitability. For instance, Zara and IKEA may be seen as having a high level of control over their supply chains given they control the production (Zara) and the design of all their items (IKEA, Zara). Wal-Mart also maintains a high level of control on the relationship with its suppliers, combining a sophisticated logistics and information system with a powerful buying position (Figure 5.3).

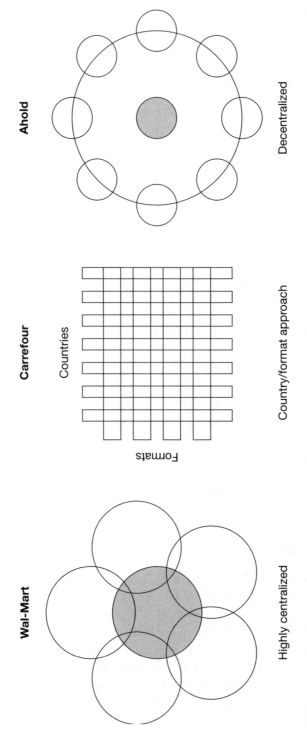

Figure 5.2 Differing organizational models used by leading international retailers

Source: Ducrocq (2003)

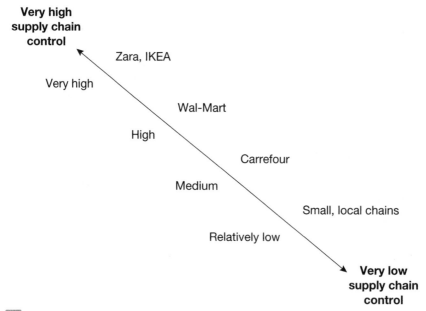

Figure 5.3 *Control over supply chains by company example*

In its early development, Carrefour focused more on its front office, that is, the stores themselves, and only later began to consider logistics and information systems as key components of its global strategy. During the last ten years, however, the group has spent a lot of effort to catch up with global best practices.

Sourcing

Carrefour is organized into business units by country and format, but tends to develop regional strategies for its so called 'premiers prix' and own brand merchandise areas. Negotiations with suppliers are generally in line with the local trading practices, and local procurement accounts for around 85 per cent of the total volume. While buyers purchase products across the group's various formats, marketing teams coordinate the promotional activity for each format. For its 35th birthday Carrefour launched its first worldwide promotion focused on the hypermarket format. In addition, it has set up a number of group-wide structures to coordinate trading practices internationally.

In order to improve product tracking and to trace products back to source, especially for fresh products, Carrefour launched a number of quality programmes in 1992 aimed at its so-called 'quality lines'. Contracts that came under this scheme were based on long-term programmes with producers and have been progressively extended in various countries. At the end of 2001, 300 product lines worldwide were handled under this type of contract.

In February 2000 the Global Net Exchange (GNX) was founded. This exchange includes a number of retailers such as Sears (US), Metro (Germany), and J. Sainsbury (UK), and Carrefour was one of the founding members. The aim of GNX is to rationalize purchasing methods worldwide and to improve supply chain efficiency using Internet technology operated through Oracle. Carrefour aims to achieve significant savings on own labels in both food and non-food lines through participation in GNX.

Logistics and information systems

Carrefour supply chain strategy is to build critical size by opening a key number of hypermarkets in each market in which it operates. As mentioned above, the hypermarket format makes it possible for stores to operate virtually independently, undertaking their own buying activities and managing direct deliveries from suppliers, but once critical operational size is achieved in a particular country, a switch can be made to central distribution facilities. Usually this requires eight or nine hypermarket outlets.

In 1996, Carrefour made the decision to harmonize its information systems globally. It launched the Thalès project which installed management system software on a global scale. The group claims that a return on the investment has already been achieved. One of the key strategy elements of French hypermarket chains has constantly been to get preferred payment terms from its suppliers. For instance, Carrefour will tend to pay its suppliers in 60 days when its inventory turnaround is only 30 days, the difference giving the company cash that may be reinvested for development.

Private labels

Unlike in the case of British retailers, French retailers including Carrefour have not emphasized retail brands and own labels as a key strategic pillar. Nevertheless, Carrefour has offered its own brands for many years. The first of these came in

Table 5.6 *Share of private label in Carrefour total grocery spend by country (%)*

Country	Share
France	23
Spain	16
Argentina	11
South Korea	8

Source: IGD (2002)

1976 when it launched the so-called 'produits libres' or 'free products' along with a major advertising campaign. Over time, Carrefour has increased its interest in own label operations, and now sells as much as 25 per cent from its own assortment. This strategy, which was developed in the French market, is now being progressively extended to the international markets (Table 5.6).

CARREFOUR'S FINANCIAL PERFORMANCE, 2000–2003

After several years of external growth, 2001–2003 was a period of consolidation for Carrefour. Carrefour's debt ratio had risen tremendously between 1998 and 2000 (Table 5.7), most notably due to the acquisition of Promodès (France), GIB (Belgium), Norte (Argentina) and GS (Italy). This was reduced by 1.1 billion euros in 2003 (Bernard 2002).

Carrefour decided in 2001 to focus on its core competencies and to sell off some external businesses such as Picard frozen food. It began to aim for a high turnover to investment ratio as one of its main objectives. Equally, between 2000 and 2003, Carrefour's priority was to gain market share and to improve its worldwide synergies. France remains the core profit source with 66 per cent of Carrefour's operating income as compared with 50 per cent of total consolidated turnover. The economic crisis in Argentina was the reason behind the weak contribution of Latin America in terms of consolidated profitability (Table 5.8).

Table 5.7 Carrefour turnover and profitability, 2000–2003 (€ million)

Year	2000	2001	2002	2003
Turnover	64,800	69,500	68,700	70,500
Operating profit	2,725	2,826	3,025	3,251
Net profit	1,050	1,207	1,389	1,620

Source: Annual Report 2003

Table 5.8 Turnover and operating profit by regions in 2003 (%)

Region	Turnover	Operating profit
France	50	66
Europe (except France)	36	29
Americas	7	1
Asia	7	4

Source: Annual Report 2003

SUMMARY AND CONCLUSION

Carrefour is not only the second largest retailer in the world by turnover, but also one of the most significant and diversified retail companies in terms of international operations. Over the past 30 years it has also been one of the most ambitious and has developed far reaching international operations. Even today, Carrefour operates in some 29 countries, far more than any other large format retail operator. It has found significant success in many of the countries in which it operates and is the leading retailer in many of them today. At the same time, it has one of the most mixed histories of any large retailer, actually withdrawing from several mature markets when it failed to achieve its long-term goals for those markets.

From Carrefour's experience some key strategic points can be highlighted:

- The importance of a strong, stable domestic market cannot be overemphasized as a key criterion for international expansion. Weakness and fluctuations in France are the key reason why Carrefour pulled out of Mexico and Japan. While neither market has been a failure in the absolute sense, such withdrawals release resources for use elsewhere and represent the kind of sacrifice often demanded of public companies by stock analysts.
- For Carrefour, there was relatively little focus in international expansion strategy early on, but it has become more strategically focused and targeted over time and as it became more successful.
- Developing markets are easier to enter than mature markets.
- A critical size needs to be achieved as early as possible in order to make for genuine success in a market. This size is measured by number of outlets, and varies from country to country and between store formats.
- Hypermarkets alone are not enough. Carrefour employs multiple formats in order to access various market segments both within particular countries and across its overall retail network.
- Carrefour shifted from trying to gain economies of scale at store level, and more towards economies at firm and group level.

The chapter illustrates just how much the domestic market must be core and be performing well in order to grow internationally. The degree to which shareholders keep control on the company is also key to internationalization, especially in markets where successful profitability can take a number of years.

REFERENCES

AGSM (2000) Carrefour vs. Wal-Mart, the Battle for Global Retail Dominance, Case study 1–34. Australia

Bernard, D. (2002) Conference at the annual La Rochelle colloquium, France.

Burt, S. (1986) The Carrefour Group, the first 25 years. *International Journal of Retailing*, 1(3): 53–77

Choi, S.C. (2003) Moves into the Korean market by global retailers and the response of local retailers: lessons for the Japanese retailing sector? In: J. Dawson, M. Mukoyama, S.C. Choi and R. Larke (eds) *The internationalisation of retailing in Asia*. (London: RoutledgeCurzon) pp. 49–66

Ducrocq, C. (2003) La nouvelle distribution. (Paris: Dunod)

IGD (2002) Carrefour: a strategic review. www.igd.com

LSA (2003) Argentine, les distributeurs se serrent la ceinture,16 January: 18–19

Chapter 6

The Boots Group PLC

Rethinking the formula

Keri Davies

INTRODUCTION

Boots is an institution in its home market with over 1,400 stores, a strong brand, large sales volume and customer flows second only to the Post Office. In addition, it owns a healthcare business that manufactures, distributes and markets 'over the counter' (OTC) products around the world, including brands such as Clearasil, Nurofen and Strepsils. For those non-British consumers who have not grown up with the brand, it is difficult to explain the attraction, and, possibly as a result, Boots has found it hard to expand outside the UK. In part, this is because of the difficulties involved in transferring the brand and the format overseas, but it is also perhaps because the home retail operations have dwarfed the rest of the organization, monopolizing investment and management attention.

In terms of international activities, originally Boots tried to take their formula overseas by employing a format and formula that resembled that used in the UK market. Over time the formula used overseas has changed significantly, while the company has also had to re-evaluate its formula both in the UK and in international markets. Boots's overseas activities by 2004 most purely reflect the new formula – while, at the same time, not really demonstrating that Boots has overcome its underlying problems. It is not clear whether the new format/formula can succeed in the long term. The most likely response may be a move toward more of a manufacturer-style brand formula, rather than a retail formula.

A SHORT HISTORY OF THE BOOTS COMPANY IN THE UK

The first part of the context for the Boots's story is the lengthy history of the organization in the UK and the heritage it carries from its origins (see, for example, Cook and Walters 1991; Piercy 1999; Whysall 1997). The Boots

Company has its roots in the middle of the nineteenth century, in a small herbalist's shop opened by John Boot in Nottingham, England (still the location of Boots's headquarters and its primary manufacturing site). In 1877 this business was taken over by Jesse Boot, whose business approach was to buy in bulk and sell cheaply, making herbal remedies, medicines and household toiletries affordable for the first time to many working-class people. Over twenty years Boots fought to cut the costs of doctors' prescriptions and the price of medicines, even to the point of manufacturing their own drugs. As the business added new lines over the years, such as fancy goods, stationery, books and picture framing, it also kept its social focus by introducing cheap cafés and Booklovers Libraries in major stores.

Between 1909 and 1930 control of the business passed to an American, Louis K. Liggett, and the United Drug Company. During this period, the company was reorganized to improve internal communications, with a new committee structure and an emphasis on centralization and efficiency. Following Liggett's bankruptcy during the Depression years, in 1933 Jesse's son John Boot led a consortium of British financiers to buy Boots. Milestones in the 1930s and 1940s were the opening of the thousandth shop in 1933, the launch of No. 7 cosmetics in 1935, and a major involvement in chemicals and pharmaceuticals production for the Second World War effort. The 1950s and 1960s saw the death of John Boot and the end of family participation in the business, along with the acquisition of other chemists' chains (Timothy Whites, Taylors) and pharmaceutical brands and producers.

During the 1980s the Boots Group began to expand from medicines and cosmetics/toiletries into a wider range of activities, beginning with the 'Children's World' stores (see Table 6.1):

> The logic underlying this strategy was that as a high street retailer and drugs group, Boots had reached maturity. Conventional portfolio modelling suggested that Boots could move into a new era by using the cash generated from its core drugs and retail businesses to make an acquisition in a rapidly growing sector. Extending its reach into home decorating, home improvement and the automotive field looked an ideal way of leveraging Boots' growth and earnings potential, and establishing the business as more than simply a high street chemist, but staying close to the existing customer base and building synergy in this way.
>
> (Piercy 1999: 263–264)

Between 2000 and 2003 Boots also tried to build on its brand name and to expand into a range of value-added services, most of which were grouped under the heading of 'Wellbeing'. This included services such as dentistry, chiropody and laser eye correction, where it hoped that the Boots name would imply quality and value, as well as more 'New Age' areas such as aromatherapy, reflexology and herbalism.

Table 6.1 Boots's diversification within the UK market, 1986–2004

Concept	Dates of operation	Area of operation	Outcome
Health and beauty operations			
Boots Opticians	Continuing to date	Optician services within stores and standalone units	Standalone units closed but still operating within Boots stores.
Laser eye correction	2000–2004	Laser eye operations	Withdrawn from stores
Boots for Men	2000–2002	Male grooming products	Standalone stores closed
Wellbeing stores	2000–2003	Dentistry, chiropody, opticians and 'lifestyle' services such as aromatherapy and massage	12 parlours closed
handbag.com	2000–2003	Internet business	Closed
Boots Photo.com	2000–2003	Online photo processing business	Closed
Pure Beauty	2000–2003	Upmarket cosmetics stores	6 stores closed
Chiropody	2000–2004	Chiropody services in stores	Withdrawn from stores
Dentistry	2000–2004	Dental services in stores	Withdrawn from stores
Digital *Wellbeing* TV	2001–2002	Digital TV venture with Granada	Closed
Boots at Sainsbury's	2001–2003	Boots pharmacies and Boots product sections within Sainsbury stores	Withdrawn from stores
Non-core operations			
Children's World	1986–1996	Children's products	Sold to Storehouse Group
FADS and Homestyle	1989–1997	Home decorating chains	Sold to Alchemy Partners for £1 and Boots took £180m write-off
Payless	1989–1998	DIY retailing	Merged with WH Smith stores to become Do-It-All chain. Sold to Focus Group for £6.8m
Halfords	1989–2002	Car parts, accessories and servicing, bicycle sales	Sold to CVC Europe for £427m

However, most of this UK diversification turned out to be a drag on the core businesses and the operations were closed down (Table 6.1). In terms of the health and beauty operations, it was soon realized that consumers either weren't ready for such an expansion of niche operations or were not willing to pay sufficiently high prices. In the non-core operations, such as DIY and children's products, it was unclear whether the Boots managers were unable to work in other areas or whether they merely placed it very low on their list of things to do. There appears to have been no synergy between these various businesses and the alternative rationale of spreading risk across different business cycles failed when Boots bought businesses just entering a downturn and a period of increased competition.

By 2004 Boots in the UK had returned to its roots and operated in just the manufacture and retail of pharmaceutical, health and beauty and personal care products. It was the UK's leading pharmacy or drugstore chain, with total sales revenue of just over £5 billion in 2004 and more than 85,000 employees (Table 6.2).

COMPOSITION OF THE GROUP

There are a number of separate businesses making up The Boots Company, each operating largely independently, but they fall under two main headings: Boots Retail and Boots Healthcare International (see Figure 6.1). The various businesses operating in The Boots Group PLC in 2004 are described briefly below.

Boots Retail

The Boots Retail division covers primarily operations in the UK and Ireland. Since 2003 the Boots Retail International division has been pulled back into Boots Retail but its operations will be discussed separately below. With the announcement in September 2004 that the bulk of the remaining *Wellbeing* activities are either to be closed or, as with the opticians' services, brought back into the Boots stores, Boots Retail is concentrating now on the Boots the Chemists brand.

Boots the Chemists (BTC)

Boots the Chemists positions itself as Britain's leading retailer of health and beauty products, operating stores ranging from small community pharmacies to large city centre department stores, as well as health centres. With over 1,400 outlets in the UK and Ireland, it employs almost 64,000 staff and has a massive customer base. In 1999, an estimated 12.5 million people shopped at BTC every week (30 per cent of the UK's adult population) and around 27 million people shopped at BTC every month (59 per cent of the adult population).

Table 6.2 Turnover and operating profit (£m), 2000–2004

	2000	2001	2002	2003	2004
Revenue					
Boots Retail					
Boots The Chemists	3,983.5	3,989.0	4,072.5	4,283.4	4,475.7
Boots Opticians and Dentalcare	198.7	203.6	228.8	258.6	241.6
Halfords	492.6	508.5	528.7	234.9	–
Total – UK and Ireland	4,674.8	4,701.1	4,830.0	4,776.9	4,717.3
Boots Retail International	32.5	42.1	40.3	37.0	43.0
Boots Healthcare International	327.1	362.0	407.3	460.4	504.6
Group and other	180.9	137.0	74.8	79.8	91.5
Group turnover (excluding inter-segmental and joint venture)	5,192.3	5,216.0	5,326.5	5,323.0	5,325.0
Operating profit					
Boots Retail					
Boots The Chemists	557.0	579.8	605.2	568.4	531.1
Boots Opticians & Dentalcare	5.1	(15.0)	(34.4)	(30.9)	(5.1)
Halfords	48.5	41.9	54.3	22.5	–
Total – UK and Ireland	610.6	606.7	625.1	560.0	526.0
Boots Retail International	(33.3)	(43.4)	(24.1)	(22.3)	(10.4)
Boots Healthcare International	32.5	59.6	66.7	70.1	80.6
Group and other	(42.6)	(44.4)	(43.5)	(66.2)	(46.1)
Group operating profit	567.2	578.5	624.2	541.6	550.1

Source: Boots Group PLC Annual Reports

The larger stores stock up to 27,000 product lines but Boots has been withdrawing gradually from leisure areas such as music, video, cookware and greetings cards in order to concentrate on core areas. In 2004 almost 85 per cent of BTC's sales were in the two areas of health and beauty and toiletries, while most BTC stores also have pharmacies. It has also built a reputation for the quality of

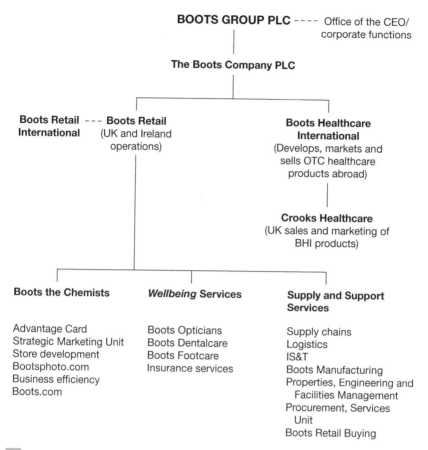

BOOTS GROUP PLC ---- Office of the CEO/ corporate functions

The Boots Company PLC

Boots Retail --- **Boots Retail**
International (UK and Ireland operations)

Boots Healthcare International
(Develops, markets and sells OTC healthcare products abroad)

Crooks Healthcare
(UK sales and marketing of BHI products)

Boots the Chemists

Advantage Card
Strategic Marketing Unit
Store development
Bootsphoto.com
Business efficiency
Boots.com

***Wellbeing* Services**

Boots Opticians
Boots Dentalcare
Boots Footcare
Insurance services

Supply and Support Services

Supply chains
Logistics
IS&T
Boots Manufacturing
Properties, Engineering and Facilities Management
Procurement, Services Unit
Boots Retail Buying

Figure 6.1 *Boots's corporate structure, mid-2004*

Note: The Boots Company PLC is a 100 per cent owned subsidiary of The Boots Group PLC. Boots The Chemists Ltd, Boots Healthcare International, Boots Opticians Ltd, Boots Properties PLC and Crookes Healthcare Ltd are all 100 per cent owned subsidiaries of The Boots Company PLC.

Source: After Boots Group PLC's website, October 2004

its products and the advice of its staff that has placed it high up the list of trusted UK retail brands.

In mid-1997, BTC invested £52 million in the launch of its Advantage loyalty card. Similar in concept to the loyalty schemes launched by UK supermarket retailers, the card was aimed mainly at female Boots shoppers (who make up two-thirds of the customer base) with most of the free offers available on women's products. Although it turned out to be more expensive than expected, the card scheme is judged a success by the company. By the end of 1999 there were 12 million Advantage cards in circulation and 47 per cent of BTC sales were linked to the cards, with 6.8 per cent of holders using their cards regularly (Boots Annual Report 2000).

The underlying significance of the scheme lies in the information collected through the card system. The card contains a microchip instead of a magnetic stripe, allowing instant collection and redemption of points against purchases. Also, the database of transactions enables Boots to manage merchandising better and to communicate more effectively with customers through direct mail and in-store kiosks.

There is always a danger of forgetting that those most likely to take up and use the card were the most loyal of the existing customers but BTC was able to show, for example, that not only did the holders of Advantage cards have a higher average transaction value than non-holders over the first three years of the card but that this value seemed to be increasing at a faster rate than that for all BTC customers.

At the start of 2000, BTC still made up almost 80 per cent of group sales but 90 per cent of Boots's profits (Bahanda 2000), particularly as most of the under-performing non-health and beauty operations had finally been sold off. BTC's overall position in early 2000 was summed up in that year's Annual Report as: 'this reassuring ubiquity, this promise of being "there for you", provides a tremendous foundation for extending the Boots brand.'

In the UK the main product areas were delivering like-for-like sales growth of between 2.5 per cent and 4 per cent. These were very respectable figures in the price-cutting market of the time. This could be taken to be a vindication of the service-led approach, rather than getting involved in price wars with the super-markets and other discounters:

> Blyth . . . attempted to move his managers from thinking about market share and sales per square foot to thinking about value-based strategic planning on a longer time horizon than conventional budgeting. The approach rests on identifying the five or six things which really make a difference to the business, and which of those are most capable of being levered by management. Out of that come alternative courses of action. The overriding principle is that all uses of cash require a return.
>
> (Piercy 1999: 265–266)

Between 2000 and 2004 a number of major changes affected the range of products and services offered by Boots the Chemist. These included the move from film to digital photography, a greater emphasis among consumers on lifestyle issues and products, and significantly increased levels of competition in non-food categories from the main grocery chains, such as Tesco and Asda Wal-Mart. In addition, the late 1990s saw the growth of specialist discount chains in the health and beauty market, such as Superdrug, Semi-Chem and Savers. Together, they ate into the traditional pharmacy and health and beauty markets as well as bringing a stronger focus on price, with BTC being seen by many as a store charging relatively high prices – admittedly while providing a much wider range of products.

Initially, BTC responded by moving upmarket, arguing that price discounting was not the only way to approach the health and beauty market:

> We don't compete on price alone. What marks Boots out from all other retailers is its unique combination of value with quality, range and service. And when asked, health and beauty shoppers say these factors are even more important to them than price.
>
> (Boots Annual Report 2000: 4)

They used research to argue that UK consumers prefer larger, occasional discounts on selected lines (for example, via 3-for-2 offers) and may be alienated by low prices, which they often associate with low status or inferior quality. It was recognized, however, that this position might change and that other ways of reaching and rewarding customers should be explored. Also, over 40 per cent of BTC's counter sales came from Boots own brand products (a total of £1,490 million), including brands such as No. 7, 17 cosmetics, Natural Collection,

Table 6.3 Boots's own brand market shares in UK, 2002 (%)

Cosmetics	Market share 2002	Suncare	Market share 2002	Babycare	Market share 2002
No. 7	11.4	Soltan	18.0	Boots	10.9
17	4.9	Boots No. 7	0.9		
Botanics	0.4				
Total Boots	16.6	Total Boots	18.9	Total Boots	10.9
Avon Cosmetics	11.2	L'Oreal	25.0	Johnson & Johnson	51.4
L'Oréal	10.9	Beiersdorf	20.0	L'Oréal	8.3
Rimmel	9.1	Johnson & Johnson	9.5	Euromark	5.4
Max Factor	8.0	Malibu	2.9	Beiersdorf	4.9
Estee Lauder	4.7	Turstin Uni	2.6	Jackel Int.	0.8
Clinique	4.5	Avon	2.5	Turstin Uni	0.7
Lancome	4.3	Schering Plough	2.5	Eastern Phar	0.6
Top 8	69.3	Top 8	83.9	Top 8	83.0

Sources: Ramzan *et al.* 2004; Boots Group PLC Annual Report 2002

Soltan, Nurofen, Botanics and Tricologie (Table 6.3). Boots also launched brands with partners, such as the Charles Worthington haircare range and Liz Collinge cosmetics.

Second, Boots's research showed that people were increasingly interested in health and fitness. Ageing populations were taking responsibility for their own health and wellbeing. BTC attempted to harness this trend, bringing together a range of existing and new medical services under the *Wellbeing* banner. These high-price, high-margin services included opticians (already a major part of the Boots business), medical and dental services, health insurance, an internet portal aimed primarily at women (handbag.com), and men's stores offering shaving, facials, hair styling, chest waxing, massage and manicures (Table 6.1). Unfortunately, in addition to their direct set-up costs, the *Wellbeing* services took up management time and effectively reduced overall retail space by 1.4 per cent (Davis *et al.* 2002).

Third, in 2001 Boots reached an agreement with the supermarket chain Sainsbury's under which Boots installed small Boots outlets initially inside Sainsbury's stores. This had already been done before with limited success and most of the concessions had been withdrawn. The difference here was that the Boots sales area was to be integrated into the main Sainsbury's sales area but staffed by Boots employees. These Boots departments stocked up to 10,000 health and beauty products over 75–390 square metres in Sainsbury's larger stores (*European Retail Analyst*, 20 July 2001, p. 6).

It looked as though Boots was addressing the threats from the end of the price agreement on drugs in the UK by getting involved in the supermarket sector. Analysts, however, believed that the benefits were probably much greater for Sainsbury's rather than Boots as it was able to expand further into non-food without having to develop its own health and beauty ranges. Boots, on the other hand, was running the risk that it would emphasize to shoppers the gap between the prices charged in its high street shops and those to be found in supermarkets.

The danger for Boots was that growth in the new areas was being bought at the cost of under-investment in its core businesses. 'In our view, BTC does not make operating margins of 15.5% because it is a good retailer, but because it has been under-investing in the business, and crucially, in its customers' (Hawkins 2002). It was beginning to look as though the company needed to make bigger investments in its existing store base, rather than merely looking to cut costs.

Caught between an erosion of its sales in key areas and slow take-up of the new services between 2002 and 2004, Boots was forced to shut down virtually all of the new operations (Table 6.1). The joint venture with Sainsbury's was scrapped and all of the in-store pharmacies and Boots departments were removed from Sainsbury's stores by the end of April 2003. Ironically, this move may have saved from closure a number of the smaller Boots stores that were not doing well and were seen as overlapping with the Sainsbury's stores. In addition, in February and March 2003 Boots announced that both the Chairman and Chief Executive were to leave.

Having entered and then withdrawn from these markets, however, Boots had not solved the problem of how to counter the threat to its traditional markets from the supermarket operators and discounters. Nor had its management impressed in terms of what has been described as a 'yo-yo' strategy. 'I always thought it was not the business that was mature but the managers', Mr McGrath commented (*The Independent*, 28 March 2003).

To this effect, a new Chairman, Sir Nigel Rudd, and a new CEO, Richard Baker, were brought in during 2003. In his comments on the 2003 half-yearly results (6 November 2003), Sir Nigel said: 'The new executive team has been given a clear agenda by me and the board: modernise the business, make it more efficient and focus more effectively on the customer.'

No clearer message could have been given than by not only bringing in an outsider to the role of CEO but also someone from Asda Wal-Mart, one of the main scourges of Boots in the early 2000s.

In interviews with analysts, Baker admitted that BTC had been used as a 'cash cow' by the previous management to fund the investments in the other new businesses, such as *Wellbeing* and BRI. As a result, prices in BTC crept up over time and the value stance was eroded (Bahanda 2004). His aim is to cut back on support functions and to refocus the business on the customer, along with a major investment in price reductions. 'It is not going to be EDLP (Every Day Low Prices), that is not our game. Price is what you pay and value is what you get, and we will offer the best-quality entry-level prices' (Richard Baker, quoted in *Retail Week*, 21 May 2004, p. 1).

In the UK, therefore, Boots is trying to meet the challenge of the grocery retailers (in particular, Tesco, Asda Wal-Mart, and Morrisons) and the discounters. Baker's emphasis is on 'Making Boots more competitive' through the following three criteria:

1 *Expert people.* The aim is to put more staff back onto the shop floor, stressing the knowledge that they can provide to customers across the whole range of products sold in Boots's stores.

2 *Products only at Boots.* Boots is stressing the importance of its own label products and sub-brands, building on its existing market shares in many categories. By stocking as wide a range as possible of unique and exclusive health and beauty products the company believes that it can reduce pressures on prices and margins in a number of product categories. Some of this shift in emphasis can be seen in the change to the sales split between categories between 1999 and 2004 (Table 6.3).

3 *Improving value for money.* Through its 'Lower prices you'll love' promotions Boots is seeking to be competitive in 'everyday beauty and toiletries' which represent 25–30 per cent of sales. And, it has launched a new range of own label products under the 'Boots Basics' label to reinforce the price message.

Analysts responded favourably because they felt that there was, finally, clarity in the direction in which the business was heading (Bahanda 2004). The price message is to be reinforced by a stricter focus on a smaller range of stores, with the company operating from just three distinct formats – convenience, community pharmacies and the larger destination stores.

Boots Retail – supply and support services

In addition to the Boots the Chemists stores, Boots Retail includes a range of other activities. The most important of these are the manufacturing arm and Boots Properties. Boots Contract Manufacturing (BCM) is one of the largest European contract manufacturers in the field of high-quality healthcare, cosmetics and toiletry products for the private label and contract markets. It has several factories in the UK and Europe and a major development laboratory, and around 1,500 of the 2,000 new products launched by Boots each year are developed in-house by BCM.

The majority of its sales are within the Boots group (43 per cent to BTC, including Boots Retail International, and 17 per cent to BHI), but that still leaves almost 40 per cent of sales to third-party customers outside the Boots group. Sales to BTC benefited from the launch of Botanics and Tricologies ranges, higher demand for vitamins and No. 7 cosmetics, and the relaunch of the Soltan suncare range.

Boots Properties is responsible for managing the property needs of The Boots Company's businesses, and it has been involved in developing major shopping centres and multi-tenant retail parks. Boots Properties owns and manages freeholds and leaseholds on over 630 of the group's units and also invests in the property market.

Boots Healthcare International (BHI)

The second major part of the Boots Group in 2004 is Boots Healthcare International. The Boots Group sold its pharmaceutical businesses to BASF in March 1995 for £840 million to focus on core retailing operations, generate funds for investment and reduce debt. It continues to operate in the over-the-counter (OTC) market through Boots Healthcare International.

BHI is a leading developer of consumer healthcare products, in the global self-medication market. It has more than 20 operating businesses based in Europe, Asia/Pacific and Australasia, as well as an extensive export sales operation based at its Nottingham headquarters. Around three-quarters of BHI's business is done outside the UK, with sales in 130 countries, including Australia, Hong Kong, India, Japan, Malaysia and Singapore. BHI's product range spans three core categories, making up about half of the OTC market, with major brands in each, as well as a number of local product ranges developed and marketed in specific countries.

As a result, Boots has a wide range of contacts and market knowledge for countries around the world. Boots brands such as No. 7, Clearasil, Optrex, Strepsils and Nurofen are known all over the world, even though consumers may never have heard of Boots itself.

BOOTS RETAIL'S INTERNATIONAL OPERATIONS

Boots Retail International (BRI)

International retail operations remain one of the smallest parts of the company even in 2004 and one of the most disappointing. Boots's first international activities suggest cultural closeness, if not Commonwealth connections, beginning with New Zealand in the 1930s and continuing with Canada in the 1970s.

Boots opened its first international outlet in New Zealand in 1936, but it still had only 16 stores in the country by the time of its exit in 1990. It had built up a sizeable chain of around 180 pharmacy stores in Canada, beginning in 1977, but the company was forced to withdraw in 1988 after suffering heavy losses. A 17-year attempt to succeed in France with Sephora, a chain of perfume and cosmetics shops, ended in disposal in 1993. This may help to account for the company's decision to move more cautiously in recent years, using pilot stores and seeking the expertise of local partners.

So, by the mid-1990s, Boots had tried to expand in a number of different ways within the UK and in a range of geographical locations around the world but it had ended up withdrawing from all of those markets. In 1996 its management decided to try again, this time establishing a separate trading arm, Boots Retail International (BRI), to be responsible for the development and management of Boots retail stores outside the UK. The activities of BRI can be split into two or three different phases, store-based internationalization, implants and product-led (Figure 6.2), based on the degree of management control of the activities and the increasing importance of the Boots own label brands and sub-brands rather than the Boots (or more precisely, Boots the Chemist) retail brand.

Store-based internationalization

'I said in June that our approach would be prudent, gradual and long-term,' commented Lord Blyth. 'We have undertaken an exhaustive review and identified three countries which we believe offer good prospects for Boots stores. The purpose of opening these pilot stores is to carry out a thorough evaluation of the commercial opportunities and operational issues before considering the scope for further investment in these countries or elsewhere,' he added.

(quoted in *Far East Focus*, October 1996, p. 219)

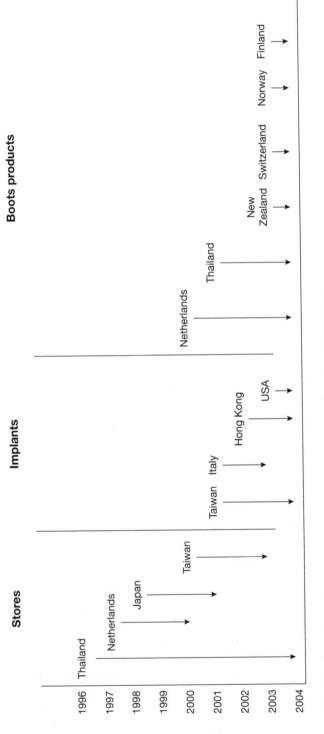

Figure 6.2 *Development of the Boots Retail International strategy, 1996–2004*

Sources: Boots Group PLC Annual Reports and BRI website

The initial strategy was to take the Boots retail brand into new markets, as had been tried in the past. Mirroring one of the smaller UK formats, these stores were to stock international and local brands, including the leading Boots brands – No. 7, 17 cosmetics, Natural Collection and Botanics – and a pharmacy (where allowed by local law). In recognition of some of the problems posed by their previous directly operated businesses, these market entries were to be made with joint venture partners. The three international markets identified initially by Boots were Thailand, the Netherlands and Japan.

Thailand

Thailand has been the odd-one-out for Boots. It was the first market entered in this new phase of expansion and the only one to date in which Boots has maintained its own chain of stores. In late 1996, Boots agreed a joint venture with the Minor Group, a holding company with a range of investments in publicly quoted companies engaged in food manufacture and retailing, fashion and cosmetics marketing, and hotel and retail property management. Minor Group also had a proven track record in the development of Western consumer brands in Thailand, and detailed understanding of the local retail market. Boots took a 51 per cent stake in the joint venture at an initial cost of 19.6 million baht (*Dow Jones Business News*, 14 October 1996).

According to Martin Bell, managing director of Boots Retail (Thailand) Ltd, Boots had chosen Thailand because Thai consumers 'are particularly concerned' about their health and appearance (*Wall Street Journal*, 3 February 1997). The Thai stores were modelled along similar lines to the company's smaller UK stores, with floor space of 150–700 square metres, a pharmacy and a range of OTC medicines, cosmetics, fragrances and toiletries.

As with BTC in the UK, BRI looked to distance itself from competition with supermarkets and department stores, emphasizing its own brand products and promotions rather than general price-cutting (Kittikanya 1999). Indeed, company sources said that Boots products were considered premium brands in Thailand and accounted for 47 per cent of sales at the pilot stores (quoted in Rungfapaisarn 1998). About 40 per cent of the products in the stores were manufactured in, or sourced from, the UK and supply chain management for the new stores was difficult. Boots were importing between three and four 40-foot containers each week and the contents of each container required 30,000 separate labels under the strict Thai customs laws.

For these reasons, Boots began to manufacture some high-volume health and beauty products through local sub-contractors to supply its retail outlets. It was hoped that this could result in a 20 per cent reduction in costs. In some cases, imported Boots brands were cheaper than comparable ones made locally, because of large bulk purchases and Boots's substantial bargaining power. However, it was hoped that manufacturing Boots brands locally would not only save production costs, but also increase flexibility and management efficiency, getting new products into the local market sooner (Jitpleecheep and Nondhanada 1999).

By early 2000, Boots had opened its fiftieth store in Thailand and introduced Medilink into their stores, with the suggestion that a variant of the Advantage card would be introduced in the future. By this stage 13 products were being manufactured locally, with plans to reach 200 products by the end of 2000. In addition to meeting demand in Thailand, the company was considering exporting locally made products to Boots stores in other countries in the region (Rungfapaisarn 2000).

The Netherlands

Boots opened its first Dutch store in Rotterdam in July 1997 under an agreement with Dutch health care group Eerstelijns Voorzieningen Almere (EVA) to provide in-store pharmaceutical services (*Dow Jones Business News*, 10 October 1996). This and the other four pilot stores were around 400 square metres in area. Boots brands accounted for one-third of sales in these stores as it was argued that many Boots own label products were seen as premium brands in the Netherlands. The Boots Company Chairman, Lord Blyth, said:

> Boots combination of cosmetics, fine fragrance, toiletries and healthcare all under one roof has been a completely new concept in the Dutch market and extremely well received. Our customer profile is similar to that of Boots The Chemists in the UK and Boots brands are selling well.
>
> (quoted in Anon. 1999)

By the end of the financial year 1999–2000 Boots had planned to have 36 outlets in the Netherlands (*Het Financieele Dagblad*, 10 June 1999), rising to 45 within a couple of years. These were smaller than in the original trial as further experimentation had shown that the Boots formula could work more profitably in less space (*The Regulatory News Service*, 3 June 1999). In the event, BRI opened only 16 stores in that timeframe. The early shops had a British style that was alien to Dutch shoppers (mixing both pharmacy and drugstore in the same store) but even when this was remedied in subsequent premises the response of the public was still very mixed.

Japan

For a number of years Boots had been keen to enter Japan, where the cosmetics and toiletries market – mainly served by higher priced department stores – was valued at about £16 billion, or four times the size of the UK market. Chemists that sell both prescription medicines and health and beauty care products, common in the US and much of Europe, were still unknown in Japan due to strict regulations on the sale of drugs. Recent reforms had opened the highly lucrative drug market to new competition.

Boots had taken preliminary steps towards expansion in Japan by registering products in the country. Failure to register enough products was one of the problems to hit Body Shop, the cosmetics retailer, when it opened in Japan. Boots also commissioned computer equipment suitable for use in Japan (Abrahams and Wright 1998). After plans to tie up with Jusco were abandoned in 1996, it took more than two years before Boots was able to announce a link up with Mitsubishi Shoji, one of Japan's largest trading houses (Hollinger and Harney 1998). The two companies invested approximately US$13.2 million, 51 per cent from Boots and 49 per cent from Mitsubishi, in a new company, Boots MC Co. Ltd. The director president of the new company came from Boots, while a senior Mitsubishi manager was director vice president.

Boots said that the partnership was based on Mitsubishi providing its knowledge of the market along with its reputable name, and Boots providing its expertise in health and beauty retailing. Mitsubishi had no beauty manufacturing or retailing concerns, although it did operate in other retail sectors (*WWD*, 30 July 1998, p. 14). Both parties to the joint venture suggested that up to 400 stores might be possible over time.

Three pilot outlets were opened in Tokyo in 1999, ranging from 350 to 600 square metres and located at contrasting retail sites – prestige (Ginza), fashionable (Harajuku) and commuter (Kichijoji). Despite the different locations, the format closely resembled the British retailer's flagship Boots the Chemists outlets, stocking OTC medicine, fragrances, toiletries and cosmetics, with brands including local products, international names and Boots lines such as No. 7 cosmetics and Natural Collection toiletries. Initially it was hoping to attract a narrower range of customers than its broad sweep in the UK: 'We are targeting women aged 20 to 35 who have more discretionary spending and are opinion formers. Their preparedness to try new things is much greater than other age groups' (Spence, quoted in Rahman 1999).

Boots could not import all of its private-brand medicines because of the Pharmaceutical Affairs Law and thus had to offer many products similar to those of Japanese companies. Even so, the company reformulated and registered more than 2,000 of its products for Japan. Boots also changed some of its packaging to suit the Japanese penchant for plush wrappings.

What surprised the domestic drugstore industry most was the scale of the joint venture's capitalization of 5 billion yen (US$35 million), which gave it the industry's second-largest capitalization, trailing only the 12.9 billion yen of Matsumotokiyoshi, the largest drugstore operator in Japan (Yoshimura 1998).

It was sufficient to allow for a significant number of store openings within a relatively short timeframe. Boots was even expecting a flood of prime retail sites coming to the market as Japanese banks fled the high street with many of those sites owned by Mitsubishi Bank.

A company spokesman said it was difficult to predict the health and beauty sales split of the Japanese stores, as consumers were different from country to country. For example, in Thailand, pop video screens had been installed because customers had found the original stores too quiet. While there would initially be no such screens in the Japanese store, all assistants would have to stand up while serving customers because Japanese culture dictates that it is rude to serve customers while sitting down, as happened in many of Boots's UK stores (*Cosmetics International*, 25 April 1999, p. 3).

The Boots Annual Report for 2000 stated that, 'our traditional strengths – value, quality, range and service are in demand in much of the developed world' (p. 10). In addition to the direct retail operations, Boots Contract Manufacturing was involved in reformulating and repackaging own brand products for these markets, as well as developing new products, such as a No. 7 branded skin whitener for the Japanese market. The mixed experiences of the test markets did not prevent Boots from opening or planning (to open) in other markets, particularly in Asia:

> It is little more than a year since Boots decided to stake its future on fast overseas expansion, especially in the East. Its ambition is unbounded. In Japan, where it has a powerful partner in the giant Mitsubishi group, Boots foresees a chain of health and beauty chain in the world's second biggest market. Thailand, Taiwan and Malaysia could add a further 200 to 250. Add South Korea, almost certainly Boots's next territorial ambition, and by 2004 the old purveyor of pills and potions could be running 800 Far Eastern stores.
>
> (Nuttal 2000)

Taiwan

Boots opened five stores in Taiwan in 2000 at a cost of £14 million (*AFX (UK)*, 27 January 2000). Taiwan was chosen because of its relatively affluent population of 22 million and a relatively under-developed health and beauty market. As in Japan, BRI planned to test different locations and formats using the experience of staff from Thailand and Japan. While not stated at the time, it is likely that, like other European retailers, Boots saw Taiwan as a test market for future expansion into the larger market of mainland China.

At the time, the Boots's chairman, Lord Blyth, said:

Once again we have thoroughly researched the market and Taiwan represents a great opportunity to extend our international retail business. We
believe that the market has the potential to support a chain of around 100
Boots stores and we hope to build on our success in Thailand.

(Boots press release, 27 January 2000)

Philippines

In early 2000 BRI was reported to be studying whether to establish a network in
the Philippines from the ground up or to buy an existing chain (Cabacungan Jr
2000). Boots was attracted by the signing of the Retail Trade Liberalization Trade
Act that opened the local retail sector to foreign investors and by the dominance
of just one company, Mercury Drug, in the pharmaceutical and OTC markets in
the country.

By early 2000, BRI had 69 overseas stores (50 in Thailand, 16 in the Netherlands
and 3 in Japan), with aggregate sales of £32.5 million. However, an operating loss
of £33.3 million meant that it was difficult to see BRI providing a replacement
profit stream for the Boots Group in the near future (Table 6.2, p. 118). In addition to the problems of establishing the Boots name in these markets, the company
found that competition for drugstores from hypermarkets and supermarkets had
become quite intense on a global scale. As early as 2000, Boots had begun to search
for ways to cut costs in its international operations:

Boots initial intent was to build a network of stores in international
markets. However, it became clear that as a result of an inadequate
customer offer, a high cost base and the difficulty in gaining the critical
mass necessary to drive high volumes to break even, this strategy would
not be successful.

(Whitehead 2002)

The first outcome was the closure of the store networks in the Netherlands
and Japan. In August 2000, Boots announced that it was to withdraw from the
Netherlands altogether, transferring its 17 establishments there, including personnel, to Etos, an Ahold subsidiary (*Het Financieele Dagblad*, 28 August 2000). Boots
wrote off around £14 million of investment with this decision. The provision of
Boots own label products through around 300 Etos stores was to continue (for a
payment of HFL 3.5 million), although only around 100 products were involved,
mainly the No.7, 17 cosmetics and Tricologie ranges.

Then, in July 2001, Boots announced that it was withdrawing from the Japanese
market, closing all four stores. The Boots MC stores lost £12 million on sales
of £10 million in the year before closure (Voyle 2001). Tensions had surfaced

as managers had to decide whether or not to expand the business in order to get economies of scale. Mitsubishi said in a statement that a dispute had surfaced with Boots over market strategies, with the Japanese trading house aiming to sell a wide range of health and beauty products, including health food, and the British partner wanting to focus on cosmetics and maintaining a high-class image (*Kyodo News Service*, 13 July 2001). Voyle (2001) quoted a Mitsubishi representative as saying: 'We decided that the Boots business model would not succeed in Japan.'

The inability to expand its chain rapidly enough, largely due to failure of the joint venture to acquire suitable, viable locations within a reasonable time, meant that the business struggled from very early on. Boots certainly seems to have wanted to sell mainly Boots products but Japanese import restrictions on drug and health foods made it impossible for Boots MC to differentiate its products from those of other operators. Its cosmetics, targeted at women in their 20s and 30s, did not prove as popular. Although cheaper than most similar brands in Japan, the local press claimed this was because they were perceived as being too expensive (*NikkeiWeekly*, 13 July 2001).

The Taiwanese stores continued to operate until 2003 when the new implant policy was deemed to be more profitable (see below).

Only the Thai store network remained in 2004. Having closed 12 stores that were either loss-making or where options to extend a lease would not be taken up, in 2003 Boots began to open stores in a new, smaller format. These had retail space of between 80 and 100 square metres compared with around 200 square metres in its existing stores, and carried about 4,000 lines instead of the previous 10,000. About half of the lines were Boots branded goods, and to improve profitability further, 400–500 of those Boots products were produced locally, accounting for 15 per cent of total sales (*Bangkok Post*, 14 May 2003). With 64 outlets in 2004, the company was increasing its investment with the aim of opening 100 outlets nationwide.

An implant-based model

One of the other underlying reasons cited for withdrawing from Japan was that Boots had been reviewing its international business model with the aim of developing a 'more flexible, less capital intensive approach, based on a simpler, more Boots Brand focused offer in smaller units' (*AFX-Asia*, 13 July 2001). In May 2001, Boots Chief Executive, Steve Russell, referred to these units as 'implants', making a direct comparison with the Boots departments that were being introduced into Sainsbury's stores in the UK. By mid-2001 BRI had eight of these implants in Watsons stores in Taiwan, as well as its stand-alone Boots stores. Watsons is a drugstore format run by A. S. Watson, the retail arm of the Hong Kong conglomerate, Hutchison Whampoa.

The advantages for Boots of the 'implant' approach were said to be:

- access to established footfall and local retail expertise;
- the host retailer had ownership of the stock in the store;
- potential for rapid rollout across each territory;
- minimal infrastructure and management in each country;
- significantly reduced capital and stock investment compared with a conventional store-based approach;
- ability to build brand awareness cost effectively;
- a rapid move to profitability based on reduced investment.

The characteristics of the implant model were:

- 500–2,000 Boots lines in established, high footfall, stores, covering between 20 and 60 square metres;
- investment varying between £500 and £1,000 per square metre, depending upon local purchasing costs;
- sales of products were supported by Boots consultants in a Boots branded environment, allied with brand marketing investment at the country level;
- sales per week of a typical 20-square-metre implant are around £2,000 at manufacturer's selling price;
- the offer was over 80 per cent Boots brand, the balance being brands exclusive to Boots.

This route was seen as low risk, likely to be profitable within two years, and scalable as compared to the original high-cost strategy of expanding via wholly owned stores (Whitehead 2002). BRI's losses were expected to be reduced significantly by this approach. 'The successful trials of this new business model give us the confidence to grow the BRI business in Asia, and to progress partnerships in other markets', said Steve Russell, Boots Chief Executive.

In early 2002, Boots also announced that it was going to restructure its international operations again. BRI was absorbed into BTC, becoming the international arm of the UK operations. In addition to bringing the international operations back under BTC control, it also had the advantage of cutting costs by removing the need for separate property arms and so on. These changes led Steve Russell to comment at the Boots AGM in 2002 that, 'Boots Retail International [is] on track to deliver [its] strategic ambitions'.

This implant model was first introduced into Taiwan but has since been seen as a major plank of BRI's expansion in a variety of different countries.

Taiwan

By 2002 Boots had 14 outlets in Taiwan, 11 of which were stand-alone stores and three were trial implants. Under a new agreement, A. S. Watson began to introduce Boots brand implants in around 100 Watsons stores across the country, while four of the existing Boots stores would close immediately to minimize any overlap with the new venture. Boots's net investment was to be some £2 million. The implants would occupy approximately 10 per cent of Watsons floor space and offer between 800 and 1,200 beauty and personal care products, featuring Boots brands such as No. 7, Botanics and 17, and exclusives such as Toni and Guy hair-care (*Soap, Perfumery and Cosmetics*, February 2002, p. 4).

During 2003 the Taiwan operation was 'simplified' (*Boots website*, 16 March 2004) as all the Boots stand-alone stores were closed and a system of shipping direct to Watsons was introduced in order to serve the implants.

Hong Kong

The implant trial in Taiwan was successful enough for a similar model to be introduced into Hong Kong in 2002. This has proved to be one of Boots's most successful overseas markets, primarily because of the emphasis on pushing exclusive products to younger consumers, particularly young women (the same strategy that hadn't worked in Japan). By mid-2004 Boots had counters in 40 Watsons stores and Watsons said that it was planning to open counters in all of its 150 Hong Kong stores. In addition, in September 2004 Boots opened a concept store in the International Finance Centre Mall to further promote its own brand products (*The Standard (Hong Kong)*, 6 September 2004). Sales in September 2004 were more than 70 per cent up on a year earlier.

According to Watsons, the brand was the best performing unit among the 90 cosmetics brands operating counters in its stores. Indeed, David Boynton, Watsons' Hong Kong Managing Director, said, 'We see Boots as a long term partner possessing the strength to take our health and beauty to a higher level and to capture a much greater share in 2005' (quoted in *The Standard (Hong Kong)*, 6 September 2004).

The performance in Hong Kong may have reawakened a desire for expansion into mainland China. Just a few months after their operations began, the company's then Regional Director for Asia, Martin Waters, said that he saw 'Hong Kong as a potential stepping stone into the booming Chinese market, but that it would be unwise to venture into the mainland for at least twelve months as the company had only five years' experience in international business' (Reported in *SPC Asia*, November 2002, p. 4). With the Closer Economic Partnership Arrangement allowing A. S. Watson to begin opening wholly owned outlets in the People's Republic of China (*South China Morning Post*, 10 November 2003), it seems quite likely that both sides would see this as a major opportunity.

Italy

In 2001 Boots began a trial in Italy with implants in Esselunga grocery stores but this had been shut by 2003.

USA

In November 2003 Boots unveiled implant trials in the US with both Target and CVS. The chains are trialling Boots-branded sections carrying No. 7 and Botanics products around Denver (18 Target stores) and Connecticut (12 CVS stores). If successful, the move will provide a significant entry into the American market as the potential partners control a total of 5,500 stores.

While analysts forecast that the trials would cost less than £10 million, they also attacked the rationale of the move and highlighted the retailer's problems with overseas expansion in the past. 'CSFB analyst Tony Shiret said the venture was a "rubbish idea". "What is it about Boots's products that Target can't get some bloke to do in America a lot cheaper?"' he asked (quoted in *Retail Week*, 14 November 2003, p. 1).

Peter Jones, of KBC Peel Hunt, said that the American trial appeared to be relatively cheap and free of risk. But he added: 'Almost everywhere Boots has failed overseas. In this case, I can't see within the context of the group (that) this is going to deliver much.' Another analyst added:

> Boots has got more important issues than wondering whether it can sell lipsticks to Target. This is just a sideshow. Boots's grand designs to become a global retail brand have effectively been reduced to trying to get a global presence *but not as a retailer*.
>
> (*Financial Times*, 15 November 2003, p. 60 – our emphasis)

Product-based expansion

In addition to the implant strategy, Boots is expanding its efforts to sell Boots own brands and sub-brands. A range of Boots's products has been available to retailers for years through the activities of Boots Healthcare International. BRI, however, has entered into agreements to widen the sale of its brands in specific markets. First, the retention of Boots brands in ETOS stores was a specific element of the withdrawal from the Netherlands. Then, in Thailand, the company also began to offer its products through outlets belonging to Central Department Store, Big C, Carrefour, Robinson Department Store, A. S. Watson and Tesco Lotus. The aim was said to be to reach a wider range of consumer groups through a variety of distribution channels. But, while these outlets yielded equally satisfactory turnover, Richard Morgan, managing director of Boots (Thailand) said in mid-2004 that, 'we see more opportunities in our own stores' (*Bangkok Post*, 3 July 2004).

In 2004, BRI also set up a variety of agreements in other countries (Figure 6.2, p. 126). A range of Boots brand products were offered through Migros (Switzerland), Sokos Department Stores (Finland), Spar Kjop (Norway) and Unichem Store (New Zealand), while the No. 7 brand was available through the Clicks Health, Home and Beauty Stores (South Africa) and independent pharmacies in Ireland. These were not 'full' implants but were being treated as BRI efforts and as significantly different from any pre-existing export activities. While they expand still further the international activities, there must be a danger for Boots that they further blur the line between retailer and manufacturer. There is no explanation as to the expected outcome of this strategy, nor is it clear when selling product to a significant retail partner becomes an implant (as currently defined) and what effect this has on efforts to establish Boots's own overseas chains, as in Thailand.

THE FUTURE

Looking forward from 2004, Boots Group PLC would appear to have two inter-related concerns when considering the internationalization of its retail operations. First, there is the requirement for management to focus on, and get a grip on, the home market and the BTC operations. This focus is needed not just for the benefit of those operations but also in order to convince retail analysts and shareholders of management's intent. '"[Internationalization] is really a sideshow," said Tony Shiret, retail analyst at Credit Suisse First Boston. "The real focus is the UK, where Tesco has parked its tanks on Boots' lawn"' (quoted in Anon. 2002).

Second, the company has already moved away from internationalizing its retail format and appears to be on the verge of abandoning the internationalization of its retail formula, in favour of something more akin to a manufacturer brand formula. Or, as Richard Baker put it in Boots's 2004 Annual Report (May 2004):

> We are starting to see if there's real demand all over the world for Boots own brand products, and our expert customer care. This was the year when Boots Retail International (BRI) began to make real progress towards meeting that demand, profitably . . . Our long term vision is to help consumers throughout the world to look and feel their best. Originally, we aimed to achieve this by opening stores; but we have since developed a new implant strategy based upon taking the very best Boots own brand products – currently, around 600–800 of them – and offering them to shoppers in a Boots-branded environment, within a host-retailer's store . . . We are gaining confidence in the strategy for BRI. We are starting to find that customers around the world like Boots products, and that our retail partners are seeing an enhanced offering with a Boots presence in their store.

At the moment, it is a stripped-down version of the new retail formula devised for the UK, incorporating two of the pillars of the 'Making Boots more competitive' initiative. The main part of this international formula has become the Boots own label and its related sub-brands, while Boots still feels that it can add to the customer experience through its staff training within each implant. In this way, it is offering something closer to the operations of the major cosmetics manufacturers than a general health and beauty retailer, and this relieves it of at least some of the pressure to deliver improved value for money.

If BRI is seen as more of an own-brand export operation than a retail operation then this can also be seen as decoupling it from many of the problems at home (indeed, linking it more closely with BHI and its existing overseas networks), while reducing the amount of attention required from the retail management in the UK. In 2003, the then Chairman, Mr McGrath, said of BRI, 'It should be an export business, not a retail business. We don't need regional managers and country managers' (quoted in Finch 2003) and it appears that he is about to get his wish.

The pressures on BRI to move further towards becoming very much a niche retail brand or even a manufacturer brand in overseas markets look set to increase in the near future. Thailand is currently the only international market in which Boots is running a significant number of stand-alone, Boots-branded stores. Boots Thailand was listed as the 413th largest retailer in the Asia-Pacific region in 2003 (*Retail Asia*, April 2004), yet this operation was smaller than that of its major competitor, Central Watson. While there are synergies in using this retail chain to pump-prime the local manufacturing activities, at what point will the attractiveness of the A. S. Watson store network in Southeast Asia make it more appropriate for Boots to aim to run implants in all of A. S. Watson's country operations?

Acquisitions by A. S. Watson in Europe now make it one of the largest drug-store chains in the world, with 3,442 stores in mid-2004 (*M+M Planet Retail* 2004). In the UK alone its Superdrug and Savers discount chain have a total of over 1,000 stores making it one of the more powerful threats to Boots in its domestic market-place. There is a powerful incentive for Boots to keep the Asian contracts in place but it is the strength of the Boots product brand that is now of more importance from A. S. Watson's point of view.

In effect, Boots found that its formula was far more important than its format, just at the time when that formula came under severe attack from other health and beauty retailers, grocery retailers and discounters. It has amended both the formula in the UK and that used internationally, to a large degree decoupling the latter from the UK format. The UK formula is strong among only part of its traditional UK market, younger female shoppers who value the quality of the product at a lower price, and the formula does not travel.

The pressures on the international format are only likely to grow as Boots strives to keep control of its international formula, building acceptance of the Boots brand overseas. It seems that any hopes that Boots had of transferring both its UK retail format and formula overseas have truly missed their opportunity. It remains to be seen whether it can do much, as a retailer, with its new formula.

REFERENCES

Abrahams, P. and Wright, R. (1998) Boots poised to announce Japanese joint venture. *Financial Times*, 25 July, p. 19

Anon. (1999) Boots plans major Dutch expansion. *International Retail Review*, 1 March

Anon. (2002) Boots seeks to grow overseas with local link-ups. *Reuters*, 25 February

Bahanda, S. (2000) *Boots Company PLC*. Deutsche Bank, 26 July (via Investext)

Bahanda, S. (2004) *Boots Group PLC*. Deutsche Bank, 25 February (via Investext)

Cabacungan Jr, G. C. (2000) British retailer eyes local outlet. *Philippine Daily Inquirer*, 12 June 2000, p. 3

Cook, D. and Walters, D. (1991) Case Study 9: Boots Company PLC – Retail Division. In: Cook, D. and Walters, D. (eds) *Retail marketing: theory and practice*, (London: Prentice-Hall) pp. 378–410

Davis, R. *et al.* (2002) *Boots Company*. Morgan Stanley, Dean Witter, 26 July (via Investext)

Finch, J. (2003) Boots u-turn takes it back to basics. *The Guardian*, 28 March, p. 23

Hawkins, N. (2002) *Boots Company*. Merrill Lynch Capital Markets, 1 February (via Investext)

Hollinger, P. and Harney, A. (1998) Boots to enter Japanese market. *Financial Times*, 29 July, p. 30

Jitpleecheep, S. and Nondhanada, I. (1999) Local manufacturing studied as way for Boots to reduce costs. Chain will have 40 stores by year-end. *Bangkok Post*, 6 May

Kittikanya, C. (1999) Boots aims for 150 shops. *Bangkok Post*, 29 July, p. 3

M+M Planet Retail (2004) AS Watson acquires again. *M+M Planet Retail Global Bulletin 124*, 22 July: 8–10

Nuttal, R. (2000) Now Boots takes Taiwan in its stride. *The Express*, 28 January, p. 74

Piercy, N. (1999) Boots the Chemists. Vanity, value and vision. In: N. Piercy (ed.) *Tales from the marketplace*. (Oxford: Butterworth Heinemann)

Rahman, B. (1999) Boots throws down the gauntlet in land of the rising sun. UK cosmetics group wants a foothold in the £16.bn market. *Financial Times*, 14 August, p. 20

Ramzan, F. *et al.* (2004) *Boots Group Plc*. Lehaman Brothers, 2 March, London

Rungfapaisarn, K. (1998) Boots big on Thailand despite economy. *The Nation,* 14 May

Rungfapaisarn, K. (2000) Boots Retail eyes Thailand as export hub. *The Nation* (Thailand), 6 April

Voyle, S. (2001) Blow to Boots' global aims from Japanese exit. *Financial Times,* 13 July

Whitehead, R. (2002) *Boots Company PLC.* Deutsche Bank Alex Brown – Europe, 31 January (via Investext)

Whysall, P. (1997) Interwar retail internationalization: Boots under American ownership. *International Review of Retail, Distribution and Consumer Research,* 7(2): 157–169

Yoshimura, S. (1998) U.K. retailer's venture has drugstores reaching for aspirin. Boots, Mitsubishi plan large investment to enter market domestic companies dominate. *The Nikkei Weekly,* 31 August, p. 8

Chapter 7

Royal Ahold

Multinational, multi-channel, multi-format food provider

Steve Burt, John Dawson and Roy Larke

INTRODUCTION

With more than 30 million customers per week through over 8,000 stores across four continents Royal Ahold was, in 2003, one of the world's leading retailers. Royal Ahold developed as a major international presence relatively recently and relatively quickly since its first international move in 1976. In 2002 it had over 85 per cent of group sales outside its original home country of the Netherlands.

This chapter considers the development of Royal Ahold as it expanded its international presence and considers the implications for the wider retail internationalization process. The development until late 2002 is reviewed. At this point accounting discrepancies were discovered in the operations in the US and Ahold entered a period of considerable strategic and operational turmoil with a major divestment of international activities in order to re-establish financial control over the firm. The full story of post-2002 events has yet to be revealed. In November 2003 a 'Road to Recovery' plan was announced. This involved a substantial sale of operations in Asia and South America and lesser disposals in the US and Europe, to raise €2,500 million. By 2005 it was claimed that the finances had been stabilized and a new period of expansion was to begin based on a more focused and more transparent approach to growth.

HISTORICAL BACKGROUND

Ahold's origins reside in the mid-nineteenth century in the Netherlands with the Heijn family grocery store at Oostzaan, near Zaandaam. In 1887 responsibility for the store passed from father to son when Albert Heijn Snr took control. Over the following decade branch stores were opened in surrounding communities and by 1897 there were ten shops in the emerging firm. The following decades were ones of steady expansion. As was common in the early twentieth century, grocers branded some of their own products, buying in bulk from wholesalers and packaging the products in the store. The packaging carried the name of the retailer and so these items were, in effect, branded by the retailer with the brand signifying a level of quality control over the contents. By 1911 the Albert Heijn stores had, for example, their own brands of coffee and biscuits and were making their own bread.

Expansion of the chain continued through the first half of the twentieth century with some modest acquisitions of other small family firms. The additional shops enabled moves into new regions, and organic growth resulted in the firm being the largest grocer in the Netherlands by 1939. Growth began again in the postwar years with further acquisitions, for example, the Van Amerongen regional chain in 1951, and also with innovations starting in 1952 with self-service in small stores, newly introduced from the US (Henksmeier 1960). The first Albert Heijn self-service supermarket opened in Rotterdam in 1955. This provided the basis for expansion over the next decade which saw an increase in average size of supermarket and a steady growth of domestic market share through the 1960s.

By 1971 the first store of over 2,500 square metres opened. This included non-food ranges and a restaurant. In the early 1970s other new formats were developed including a specialist wine and spirits chain (initially called Alberto) and a health and beauty chain (Etos). There was some growth by acquisition during the 1970s with the Albert Heijn company leading the consolidation that was occurring in the Dutch retail grocery sector. Knowledge on article numbering and scanning was gathered, with Albert Heijn personally being an active member of the technical committee of the European Article Numbering Association and a frequent visitor to North America and other European countries to observe new developments.

To reflect the broader base to the firm the name was changed from Albert Heijn to Ahold in 1973. By this time the firm was dominant in the food retailing sector in the Netherlands and it was clear that future growth would either be through substantial diversification or entry into foreign markets. Vroom and Dreesman in the department store sector in the the Netherlands faced a similar dilemma. While Vroom and Dreesman chose diversification into an ever-wider range of consumer and business services, Ahold chose the international retail route. The subsequent 30 years shows the contrast of the two approaches. Initially, it appeared that the Vroom and Dreesman diversification strategy had been more successful but this foundered and the Ahold approach appeared to be a more sustainable long-term strategy. The events of 2003 may result in re-evaluation.

DEVELOPMENT OF THE INTERNATIONAL RETAIL STRATEGY

Multi-format growth through acquisition

Investigation of international opportunities in the mid-1970s led Ahold to enter Spain in 1976. Many retailers believed they saw opportunities in Spain around this time – the market had a substantial population in several large cities, the retail market was highly fragmented, it seemed likely that many of the tight controls of the Franco regime would gradually be relaxed and entry into the common market was likely when regime change was effected. While the potential was viewed as positive the actual conditions in the mid-1970s were far from ideal for new entrants as many of the old commercial and political practices lingered. The entry into Spain by Ahold was by organic growth because there was no reasonably sized firm to purchase. There was also an attempt to take the Ahold brand into the new market, thus the firm was faced with not only having to inform consumers about a new brand but also having to come to terms with mismatches between existing systems and local trading practices. The contrast between the Ahold store systems and the prevailing business conditions, together with the difficulty of responding to Spanish consumer needs, made expansion very difficult and Ahold withdrew from Spain after less than ten years, selling its Cadadia chain to Dee Corporation of the UK. Ahold was not alone in failing with a foreign venture in Spain at this time.

Alongside the Spanish expansion Ahold purchased BI-LO in the US in 1977. Market entry through acquisition made the American expansion very different from that in Spain. An existing set of systems and management was purchased together with the physical assets. A customer base existed and could be retained if the name was not changed. While some practices could be transferred from Ahold to BI-LO there was also reverse transfer of ideas and expertise. This was certainly in contrast with the Spanish activity. The contrast between success of internationalization by acquisition and the opportunities in the developed market of the US compared with the problems of organic growth into an evolving market seems to have been a critical influence on all the subsequent internationalization strategy of Ahold.

The decision around 1980 to focus on the Netherlands and the US seems to have been the result of the recession in mainland Europe and the international experiences to that time. The results were further investment in food retailing in the Netherlands in order to consolidate the domestic core through the 1980s. Notable were improvements in operational efficiencies and developments in retail branding. Also in 1988 there was the acquisition of Schuitema in the Netherlands with its wholesale and voluntary chain activities. In the US, Grand Carlisle was acquired in 1981 and the First National supermarket chain in 1988. A critical mass was being established in the eastern states of the US but with the retention of trading names of the acquired firms.

In common with other major European retailers the events in Central Europe in 1989 opened new strategic opportunities for Ahold. The difficulty for Ahold, however, was that Central Europe offered no acquisition targets in the normal sense. In order to enter Czechoslovakia in 1991 a wholly owned subsidiary, Euronova, was established, while for Poland in 1996 a joint-venture with Allkauf was used. Euronova succeeded, although the dynamics of the Czech market has meant major changes to format operations, but the Polish joint-venture failed and Ahold took full ownership of the operations in 1999.

A joint-venture approach was also used to enter Portugal. Ahold took 49 per cent of Jeronimo Martins' Portuguese operations in 1992. The Portuguese operations were subsequently strengthened by several acquisitions by the joint-venture vehicle. This venture was successful for a few years but joint ventures are inherently unstable (Inkpen and Beamish 1997; Palmer and Owens 2005) and difficulties in Jeronimo Martins' operations outside Portugal in the late 1990s caused friction in the joint-venture, particularly in relation to the strategic direction to be taken.

The acquisition approach proved by far the most effective mechanism for expanding Ahold's international operations in the early 1990s with further purchases in the US – Tops Markets in 1991, Red Food Stores in 1994, Mayfair in 1995 and Stop & Shop in 1996. The strategy of the early 1990s was to build on the growing strength in the east of the US and to cross-fertilize knowledge across the various acquired companies while building scale. Operating fascias, with a few exceptions, were left unchanged although systems and practices were made more effective. Over 50 per cent of sales of Ahold were derived from the US in the early 1990s, with the acquisition of Tops Markets in 1991 raising the American share of Ahold sales to 52 per cent.

By early 1995 Ahold had a very strong domestic operation, a substantial portfolio of store chains in the east of the US, and an emerging presence in the Czech Republic. From this base a programme of extensive expansion was launched into Asia and South America, a return to Spain, and further acquisition in North America. With the exception of North America, where Stop & Shop was acquired in 1996 and Giant Landover in 1999, joint-ventures were the favoured entry mechanism with, in many cases, either full ownership or withdrawal occurring within three or four years. The mid-1990s were a turning point in Ahold's strategy with moves to build on the solid foundations in the Netherlands and the US by expansion into higher risk markets.

The continued acquisitions in North America provided both scale and knowledge that could be used to underpin expansion elsewhere. The Chief Executive Officer, Van der Hoven (1999), stated that as a result of the acquisitions in the late 1990s:

The economies of scale are yielding significant synergy effects in distribution and production, store operation, and information technology. A major factor is the savings coming from synergies in buying and merchandising. . . . We also see Giant-Landover giving Ahold a pool of talented retail professionals to populate other sister companies in the U.S. and abroad. That helps our globalization process.

(p. 78)

Elsewhere, where Ahold's presence was less well established, a different approach was evident.

In 1995 and 1996 joint-ventures were established in Poland (full ownership in 1999), Spain (failed but full ownership of some stores in 1998), Malaysia (full ownership 2000), Singapore (withdrew 1999), China (withdrew 1999), Thailand (full ownership 1999), and Brazil (full ownership in 2000). In 1998 and 1999 further joint-ventures were established in eight Central and South American countries with partial withdrawal from Ecuador in 1999, and later after a forced move into full ownership, from Chile (2003). In cases where the joint-venture hit problems withdrawal took place. In China, for example, the joint-venture with Zhonghui Supermarkets China, with 40 supermarkets in the Shanghai region, came into operation in 1996. The stores were converted to the imported TOPS formula and a further 22 stores in Shanghai were acquired from Yaohan Group in 1998. The joint-venture did not work well and the stores were sold to the local partner in October 1999.

In countries where full ownership was taken, usually, there was an attempt to expand rapidly by acquisition.[1] For example, in Spain, following full ownership being taken in the 15 stores after the failure of the joint-venture, seven supermarket groups were acquired in 1999 and a further two in 2000 representing over 550 stores. Similarly in Poland, Thailand and Malaysia, acquisitions and strong organic growth followed the assumption of full control.

In countries where joint-ventures have been retained, growth was slower as knowledge was gained about the market. The important exception to this 'model' was the joint-venture undertaken in 1999 with ICA in Sweden. The size of this joint-venture, with ICA having sales of €6.6 billion through 3,100 shops in Sweden and Norway and the nature of the original ICA organization as a retailer cooperative made this international move of a different nature to the previous joint-ventures. Because of the large market share held by ICA in Sweden (35 per cent share) further expansion was difficult. Consequently, ICA-Ahold targeted the Baltic States with acquisitions in Latvia and initial joint-ventures in Estonia (subsequently fully owned) and Lithuania. In addition, a joint-venture was entered with a small Danish supermarket chain and more importantly with Statoil, Scandinavia's leading petrol distributor, to enable moves out of supermarkets into convenience stores.

By 2000, therefore, the outputs of the post-1995 internationalization strategy were evident as:

- a focus on food and grocery retailing;
- a solid base in the food sector in the domestic market of the Netherlands;
- the attainment of market share through acquisitions and later by organic growth in the US and Spain;
- the establishment of joint-ventures in emergent markets (Central Europe, South and Central America, Asia) with subsequent acquisition of partner or withdrawal;
- the utilization of the ICA-Ahold joint-venture to build a multi-format presence in Scandinavia and the Baltic States.

The contributions of these various parts of the corporate structure were considerably different. In 2001 in terms of sales, the US accounted for 59 per cent, Europe 33 per cent, Latin America 7 per cent and Asia slightly less than 1 per cent. It is important to point out, however, that the sales of a number of joint-ventures were not consolidated into the group level accounts so Latin America and Asia may be slightly under-reported in these shares with other joint-ventures being fully consolidated and so over-reported, particularly in Scandinavia.

Development of the multi-channel strategy

In 1999 a significant shift in strategy was announced and the implementation of this became evident in the early years of the twenty-first century. This was diversification in respect of the channels used to reach the market. Although the same product categories were retailed there was a strategic move into foodservice and also into e-channels of distribution. This move is illustrated by the change in the mission statement of Royal Ahold. In 1998 the mission statement was:

To become the best and most successful food retailer in the world

In 1999 the mission statement had changed to:

To become the best and most successful food provider in the world

By 2001 the mission statement had become even more explicit as:

To become the best and most successful food retailer and foodservice operator in the world

Ahold, thus, was using its established strength in the Netherlands and the US and emerging strength in Scandinavia to underpin both retail expansion into high-risk emergent markets and diversification into two other channels. This change of strategy to diversify into foodservice perhaps may be seen in retrospect as the turning point in the fortunes of Ahold, although at the time there were very positive responses from sector and financial analysts and from investors.

At the end of the 2001 financial year Royal Ahold reported sales of €66.593 billion. Store-based retailing accounted for 77 per cent of sales, foodservice for 22 per cent and e-commerce for 1 per cent. The shift over the previous year was substantial with foodservice increasing from a 15 per cent contribution in 2000. The regional division of sales activity was US – 59 per cent, Europe – 33 per cent, Latin America – 7 per cent, Asia – 1 per cent.

Store-based channel

Stores were operated in 27 countries with 8,842 stores operating at the start of 2002. In several of the countries – the Netherlands, Sweden, Czech Republic, Costa Rica, Guatemala and Latvia – Ahold was the largest food retailer, although in some of these markets the structure was very fragmented. Of more importance, is that in larger markets Ahold was the largest retailer in a substantial region, for example eastern US and north-east Brazil, although only fifth largest in the US and third largest in Brazil. By concentrating activities spatially, cost efficiencies in operation were achieved.

Table 7.1 shows the ownership pattern of stores. This includes company-operated stores, franchised operations and associated stores with their operation being under contract with the store owner. Stores within joint-ventures are classified as being company operated.

The non-supermarket formats included some specialist stores mainly in the Netherlands, hypermarkets in Portugal, Brazil, Spain, Central Europe and

Table 7.1 Stores operated by type of ownership, financial year end 2001

	Company-operated super-markets	Franchised super-markets	Associated super-markets	Company-operated other formats	Franchised other formats	Total
US	1,223			378	9	1,610
Europe	1,902	638	2,625	849	506	6,520
Latin America	379			229		608
Asia Pacific	104					104
Total	3,608	638	2,625	1,456	515	8,842

Source: Ahold corporate data

Scandinavia, and local convenience stores/superettes in the US and Brazil. The operations in the US were almost totally operated within company. Stores in the US accounted for 39 per cent of retail sales of Ahold but represented less than 20 per cent of the store portfolio. Within Europe there was more variety of ownership with the ICA-Ahold stores in Scandinavia operating under contract to Ahold and franchising being important in the Netherlands with 30 per cent of the Albert Heijn supermarkets and chains belonging to Schuitema operating under franchise. The Albert Heijn franchise arrangement comprised a five-year contract that defined the ranges to be operated in the store subject to the franchisee adjusting this by 5 per cent to meet local conditions. Typically locations were in the smaller communities and franchised supermarkets tended to be smaller than company-operated ones. Franchisees agreed to source products from Ahold, paid a franchise fee and received a range of support services including marketing, logistics and staff development.

Foodservice channel

Although since 1970 there had been a small foodservice operation in the Netherlands the substantive change in scale and performance in these activities in 1999 made foodservice into a major channel for the firm in its two major markets of the Netherlands and the US. In 1999, Gaastronoom, a Dutch foodservice company with sales of €353 million, was purchased, more than doubling the level of activity in the Netherlands and making Ahold the largest foodservice company in the Netherlands. Even more significantly, during 2000–01 five foodservice companies were purchased in the US with a combined sales of over €11,000 million, taking the Ahold operating unit, US Foodservice, to be the second largest firm in, the albeit fragmented, foodservice sector in the US.

Foodservice operations were in five national markets. The market position was number one in the Netherlands and Belgium and second largest elsewhere, in the US, Sweden and Norway. Table 7.2 shows the markets in which foodservice operated and the scale of operations. Foodservice USA dominated this part of Ahold. DeliXL had two divisions, one targeting the institutional food market and the other the hospitality sector. ICA Menyföretagen also operated through two divisions, one operating foodservice and the other providing a specialist service to Statoil convenience stores. Foodservice in the US had become a major component of Ahold's business following the acquisition of US Foodservice in 2000. Coverage was nationwide. Acquisitions had strengthened regional presences with PYA/Monarch, Parkway Food Service and Mutual Distributors all strengthening market shares in south-east USA. The healthcare and hospital sector had been identified as a specific target market because it is less cyclical than hospitality. Nonetheless, hotels and restaurants made up three-quarters of the customer accounts with a mix of small firms and large chain hotels, including Marriott.

Table 7.2 Foodservice operations by major market

Company	Country	Sales 2000 (million)	Sales 2001 (million)
DeliXL	Netherlands and Belgium	€761	€884
ICA Menyföretagen/ Hakon Meny	Sweden Norway	€338	€441 €94
US Foodservice	US	$5,952	$12,134
Total		€7,754	€14,888

Integration of Alliant, acquired in November 2001 was expected to be complete by mid-2003 with integration of the logistics operation reducing by 25 per cent (to 76 across the US) the number of distribution centres to be operated in the fully integrated firm. The downturn in the American economy from mid-2001 and the negative effects on business and leisure travel caused by terrorist activity resulted in a decline in the foodservice sector generally and this impacted Ahold's foodservice operations severely.

E-commerce channel

The moves into e-commerce were smaller in scale but followed a similar pattern to foodservice with major initiatives in the Netherlands and the US and lesser ones in other countries. Internet ordering was introduced in the Netherlands in 1999 and the effective purchase of Peapod (51 per cent of a joint-venture) in the US in 2000 became the basis of the e-commerce retail service. ICA-Ahold in Sweden and Ahold retailers in several other countries also offered a small internet ordering service. The foodservice units were similarly developing e-commerce channels at this time.

E-commerce was a very small part of the trading activity by 2003 but it had been given the status of a strategic unit within Ahold. Several of the retail operations and the US Foodservice operated internet-based ordering services. Sales accounted for less than 1 per cent of total sales in Ahold. In the Netherlands www.albert.nl had consolidated the individual websites of five retail chains with customers able to access each of the chains through the one portal and make a single payment. The consolidation of the provision enabled the operation of three dedicated distribution centres from which orders were serviced. In the US, Ahold acquired Peapod through a rescue programme in April 2000. The service in several markets was suspended as it was consolidated into six major East Coast markets where Ahold had existing market coverage. The service was directly linked to retail chains, for example with Peapod by Stop & Shop. While some of the markets were profitable Peapod was continuing to record losses overall and had failed to reach critical mass. Even smaller sales were recorded in Brazil, Argentina, Central America and Portugal with a slightly better performance in Scandinavia. The Asian e-commerce sites were at a very early stage in their development with only the Bangkok market having sufficient internet users in the population to make a service feasible, but not profitable.

Inter-channel synergies

The three main areas of activity had some interconnections with attempts to gain benefits from each other. The objective was to provide cycles of mutual support around the three activities as shown in Figure 7.1. In late 2002 these various

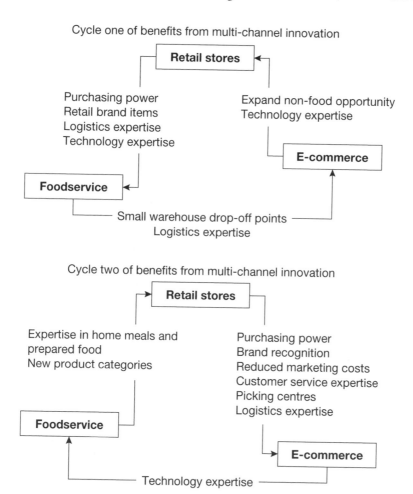

Figure 7.1 *The potential interrelationships between the three areas of major channels of commercial activity*

benefits were at an early stage of being obtained. The strategy that had put the three channels in place was only three years old and the balance between the three channels was uneven. E-commerce was very small and at a very early stage of its life cycle while retailing was much larger and more mature. Foodservice was a recent activity of substance for Ahold and had yet to prove its sustainability.

Throughout this change in strategy to be multi-channel, the core markets remained food and grocery. The concept of a limited number of core national/regional markets was retained and acquisition remained the favoured method of entry into new channels.

The problems begin: 2002

The position at the start of 2002 was:

- In the retail sector there was consolidation in the mature European markets and the US, a search for growth opportunities in the emergent markets in Asia and Central Europe and a somewhat fragmented and dynamic situation in South and Central America.
- Ahold's retailing operated though a large number of locally known trading names and through a range of different ownership structures with a resulting comparatively high level of transaction costs being offset by the added value of a higher level of identity by consumers and the better local market knowledge of owner manager or franchisee. In theory this high level of transaction costs poses problems for the exploitation of knowledge resources in the firm (Conner and Prahalad 1996) but in managerial terms there is an opportunity to reduce the cost base of the overall group by a targeted reduction in these costs.
- There was a general shift towards foodservice with attempts to focus on non-cyclical institutional markets and with the foodservice in the US being a major part of the overall business.
- E-commerce was a relatively small activity at a very early stage of development with knowledge acquisition appearing to be more important than sales contribution.
- The firm's financial structure depended heavily on its retail base in the Netherlands and the US to provide the income to pay debt resulting from acquisitions in retailing and foodservice and to cover losses in the e-channel activities.

The evolution of Royal Ahold, through over a century, showed some consistent features of its strategy:

- Operation in the food and grocery sector – when moves outside have been made they have generally been short-lived and not successful.

- New market entry through acquisition or joint-venture, with organic growth and acquisition then used as mechanisms for growth in market share – this was evident in new country entry, in new channel entry and even in the early moves into new regions of the Netherlands.
- Operations in new markets were provided with the managerial flexibility to respond to the local market and not constrained by imposition of standards from head office – the lessons learnt from the initial false move into Spain were instrumental in this approach which frequently resulted in local trading names being retained.
- The market was accessed by spatial expansion of networks of stores, structural expansion of channels and functional expansion of operating formats.

There were many managerial implications for the implementation of this strategy. Major implications were:

- a willingness to allow a high level of local responsiveness to the dynamics of supply and demand in the food and grocery market;
- a capacity to gain competitive advantage through increased scale but without standardization;
- a willingness to embrace innovation across channels and formats;
- a required ability to integrate acquisitions into the firm;
- an ability to operate in a highly decentralized way with local operational decision making managed centrally;
- a capability to work with the ambiguity inherent in joint-ventures;
- a capability to obtain synergies from multi-channel, multinational, multi-format and multi-brand operation;
- a high level of debt resulting from rapid, multiple acquisitions;
- an ability to control finances across several different accounting systems.

The problems faced by Ahold subsequent to 2002 suggest that while management had some competencies to manage these implications of their strategy they fell short on some of the key ones.

The strategy began to unravel during 2002 with a reorientation evident by November 2002 in response to problems in Argentina and the general slowdown in American and European economies. This can be seen as a sign of the unwinding of the multi-channel strategy. A new plan for the 2003–05 period was announced that contained four strands:

1   increased organic growth in the core food businesses;
2   cost reduction in operations and in channel relationships;
3   capital efficiency in order to reduce debt levels that had risen following acquisitions;

4   portfolio review both to identify and divest non-core activities and under-performing core activities that could not be turned around and to identify gaps that could be filled by smaller acquisitions.

This plan was never implemented because of the emerging accounting crisis. A 'Road to Recovery' plan was introduced in November 2003 to address the crisis.

STRATEGIC IMPLEMENTATION

In the implementation of Ahold's strategy prior to 2003 several key operational features can be discerned. These key issues are:

■   identification of potential markets;
■   identification of acquisitions and subsequent integration;
■   knowledge transfer as part of integration;
■   operational innovation aimed at organic growth;
■   matching of formats and formulae to markets;
■   marketing and merchandising within and across the markets;
■   sourcing and supply chain efficiencies.

Identification of potential markets

With the broadly based approach to the food market Ahold's strategy was to expand into markets where their expertise in supermarket operation could gain them a foothold. Other than in their domestic market there had been few moves into the highly competitive, heavily stored and low growth markets in Western Europe. In addition, in several of these markets the levels of concentration were high and entry barriers were correspondingly high. Major acquisitions or joint-ventures have become the only way to enter these markets. Ahold thus ultimately entered Sweden with a large-scale joint-venture that gave an immediate large market share. In the late 1980s, Ahold explored entry to the UK and France with a buying alliance and joint share investment involving Safeway and Casino (Bailey et al. 1995; Robinson and Clarke-Hill 1995). The alliance originally involved Asko from Germany but Asko's secretive buying of substantially more shares in Ahold resulted in Asko's expulsion from the alliance. There was a widespread view that this alliance would develop into a closer joint-venture as the three remaining firms worked together on cooperative buying and exchanged ideas on merchandising. The strong support for this alliance by the three chief executives in the early 1990s eventually waned, partly as personnel changed but also as opportunities in Central Europe offered a perceived faster payback.[2] While there were initial benefits from the alliance no second phase of benefits appeared and Ahold remains absent from the UK and France, although they are major markets that are physically close and relatively close culturally to the Netherlands.

Spain, with a more fragmented structure and strong growth in the 1980s, was one of the few options for international expansion within Western Europe. Spain was identified as an opportunity quite early in the internationalization process but the initial entry mode was not successful.

The potential that exists in the US attracted Ahold because of the regional structure of the grocery market there, the large size of some of these relatively compact markets and the familiarity of consumers with the supermarket concept. The US provided the potential to enter large regional markets, each of which could be considered individually, at least for initial entry purposes. As market mass was obtained so it became possible, within the US, to move into adjacent markets. This is also seen in the moves in the foodservice sector that gave regional presence and then through a larger acquisition to give national coverage.

The opportunities in the emergent markets in Central Europe after 1989 caught many West European retailers unprepared for expansion into these markets. German retailers with experiences in the eastern Länder were better prepared. The low levels of growth in the grocery market in Western Europe through the 1980s made Central Europe appear particularly attractive despite the high risks due to economic uncertainty in the years immediately after 1989. Additionally, the lack of consumer familiarity with West European formats resulted in consumers being attracted particularly to low-priced discount stores and large-range hypermarkets. Only as the market has evolved have the mainstream supermarkets come into their own as a key part of the network of stores. Ahold, therefore, was somewhat slow to enter the major markets and focused on the smaller market in Czechoslovakia taking some existing stores and developing hypermarkets, a relatively new format for them, and supermarkets. With the split into the Czech Republic and Slovakia most of the development had been in the Czech Republic. Slovakia was entered in 2001 with hypermarkets. The joint-venture in hypermarkets and supermarkets in Poland made little progress for several years but after Ahold took full control the supermarket activity developed in a more substantial way and hypermarkets were purchased from other operators who decided to exit the market, notably the six Jumbo stores purchased from Jeronimo Martins. Development in the Baltic States had to wait for the Ahold-ICA platform to become fully operational and the target was a 25 per cent market share in the three Baltic States. The countries of South Central Europe remain outside the operational ambit of Ahold. Although competition has increased and there has been a slowdown in economic growth since 2001, Central Europe therefore continued to be viewed as having substantial market potential.

The opportunities in South America derived from a perception of markets that were underprovided with supermarket provision and where consolidation was possible (Wrigley and Currah 2003). The joint-venture with Disco in Argentina provided entry into other national markets but the financial crisis in 2002 in Argentina forced Ahold into taking full ownership and assuming a substantial debt from their joint-venture. The scale of the operation in Argentina, within the totality of Ahold, was not great but the debt and losses resulted in excessive investment in managerial time and effort and little potential market growth. Operations in Brazil, where activity was heavily concentrated in the north-east region had more market potential both within the region and also using the regional strength as a springboard for regional extension. There was thought to be a parallel with the US in the intention to build regional market strength in a very large national market. The Central American situation mirrored to an extent that of the Baltic States where small, essentially emergent, markets were served through a joint-venture and where there was the possibility of building a dominant market presence.

Substantial market potential exists in Asia but the political difficulties make realizing the potential more difficult than in Central Europe and North America. The entry and withdrawal from China illustrated how the presence of a potential market does not mean that it is accessible. The potential of some of the East Asian markets had been addressed with joint-ventures in Malaysia and Thailand both of which were brought into full ownership, but activity was still small scale and at an early stage.

There had been a presence in foodservice in the Netherlands for many years but the potential of this market was not tapped until the market in the US was addressed. Regional acquisitions were followed by a major acquisition, similar to the pattern of development seen in a number of the retail markets. Subsequently, smaller regional acquisitions were made to build strength in specific regions and to fill gaps in market coverage. Such an approach goes back to the early development of Ahold's retailing in the Netherlands.

Although the accessing of potential markets has an element of serendipity, it is interesting to note that the most opportunistic moves, notably into South America, have proved to be the most difficult to manage. The opportunism in Central Europe was notable in Poland (Dawson 2001b) and again development here was more difficult than in Slovakia where a much clearer strategy was implemented.

Identification of acquisitions and subsequent integration

Acquisition activity exhibits some distinct patterns. It was the preferred mode of market entry into lower-risk markets. For the higher-risk markets joint-ventures followed either by a buy-out of the partner or withdrawal were preferred. Acquisitions have been used to build market presence in a region of a large national market or in a smaller national market, first through a series of small acquisitions and then by a substantial one.

Because of the substantial number of acquisitions, 40 in eight years, through the 1990s and particularly between 1995 and 2000, the integration process was well established. With each new acquisition, integration first occurred with the other operations in the regions or national market. At a later stage there was integration into the centralized services but the main aim was to gain integration with the other operations in the same market. The process of integration that is aimed for is shown in Table 7.3. The objective was to follow this model but this was not always achieved.

Examples of the operation of this integration process were:

- Ahold-USA Financial Services provided accounting services for six Ahold companies in the US.
- Category-specific purchasing groups sourced product for the retail chains in the US. The categories included health and beauty, general merchandise and produce. This enabled a single distribution centre to be used for Tops and Stop & Shop in respect of health and beauty and general merchandise.
- Tops and Giant Carlisle in the US shared a service structure with a single functional office for logistics, property, security and construction. In this office

Table 7.3 *The integration process for new acquisitions*

Timing	Activity
Pre-announcement	Research on target firm Identify medium-term benefits on sourcing Identify benefits that can be achieved quickly
Post announcement 0–6 months	Action to obtain quickly achievable benefits with 'hit squad' of 10–15 experienced Ahold executives Establishment of functional teams to undertake integration
2–12 months	Generate sourcing benefits with: Consolidation of ordering and purchasing Rationalization of suppliers Integration of promotions
6–18 months	Integration of support systems using best practice from across the organization, especially in: IT systems Logistics Store replenishment Employee development and training
8 months onwards	Joint retail brand product development with other units in the organization
Final stage of integration	Shared support services and platform of finance, property, IT, logistics

the two operating units had a single Chief Financial Officer, Logistics Manager, IT Manager and Property Manager. The impact of this integration was the elimination of 200 duplicate jobs in the two units during the integration process.

■ There were four regional support centres that acted as reviewers of best practice in their region and then passed this knowledge to firms in the integration process. These centres were in Zaandam (the Netherlands), Chantilly, Virginia (US), Buenos Aires (Argentina) and Bangkok (Thailand).

■ La Fragua in Central America had 250 Tops (US) retail-brand items in frozen and grocery categories.

Insights into the acquisition and integration process can be seen in the establishment of the joint-venture with ICA (Hunt 2001). In late 1998 ICA announced plans to float on the Swedish stock market. This was necessary to provide the capital to facilitate continued expansion. About a year after the announcement that ICA would seek a public listing, Ahold approached ICA. The choice for ICA was to hope to make a placement in the market or to join with Ahold. The deal with Ahold ensured that ICA members received a firm offer rather than waiting for an uncertain market valuation. The retail members of ICA retained 50 per cent of the investment company that owned ICA-Ahold. The deal gave Ahold entry into Scandinavia through an organization with a substantial existing market share and also was able to retain some of the decentralized, federal, structure of ICA. This acceptance of a decentralized operating structure was central to the culture of ICA and Ahold. Initial integration benefits came through improved sourcing arrangements for ICA stores who obtained access to the Ahold regional buying power particularly with the multinational supplier companies.

Knowledge transfer as part of integration

Within the structure of the international operations there is considerable emphasis placed on knowledge transfer. This involves the transfer of best practice among the operating units, the transfer through the organization of knowledge gained through acquisitions and also the collection and distribution of knowledge from the marketplace outside the firm. The knowledge base has been categorized into 15 areas of expertise that are used in a company intranet to transfer knowledge. Most of the areas are of direct operational relevance. The 15 areas are:

1 business development
2 category management
3 communication
4 customer marketing
5 e-commerce

6   finance and administration
7   foodservice
8   general management and strategy
9   general merchandise/non-foods
10   human resources
11   information technology
12   logistics and supply chain
13   real estate
14   store operations
15   technical development and sourcing.

Another form of knowledge transfer was the planned interactions between business areas. Figure 7.1 (p. 149) shows the planned interactions between the three business areas in Ahold. E-commerce remains very small and Foodservice was present in only the US and the Netherlands/Belgium. The sharing of innovations in technology and logistics is important in achieving synergies between the channels. These functional benefits are more likely to be achieved than benefits in sensorial aspects of the activities, for example branding and positioning. While it is feasible to obtain synergies between the channels, the operational reality is difficult to implement.

Operational innovation aimed at organic growth

Innovation has been a central aspect of the managerial approach in Ahold. The early moves into developing retail brand products and later moves into self-service illustrate the continuing commitment to innovation. The search for innovation extended across all the functional areas. This involved new format development, local ranging, and in-store operations that introduced individuality at local operating level. There was also innovation that generated benefits to scale across the organization with innovations in retailer branding and in multi-regional/national promotions. It is worth considering two different areas of innovation that require individual but different mixes of technology and managerial knowledge to generate innovative activity: moves into financial services and the introduction of loyalty cards.

The introduction of financial services illustrates innovation in store operations. In January 2001 an easy to use customer savings account was launched in Albert Heijn in the Netherlands. The account enabled customers to bank discounts on products they buy, via a loyalty card scheme, to save the proceeds from bottle recycling and to round up their shopping bill by placing the extra money into the savings account. There were around 250,000 active users of this savings account by 2003. A similar banking service is provided in ICA-Ahold. Bompreco in Brazil operated a customer credit card that was widely accepted in the north-east of

Brazil. Managerial decisions to design financial services positioned for supermarket users were combined with the technology to support the communications network and security on financial transactions.

Although a number of the acquired companies had loyalty cards at the time of acquisition the main innovations in this respect have been with the BI-LO card that was launched following Ahold's acquisition. This card had 2.5 million regular users out of the total card ownership of 7 million. The card was linked to several customer clubs that allow customers to register their interests and so receive targeted promotions. Local charities were also linked so that the rewards could be directed to charities of the customers' choice. The information that was accumulated was used for location-specific ranging in BI-LO stores, particularly facilitating specialist ranges to be introduced into areas with different ethnic mixes of consumers in the neighbourhood. This expertise was transferred to the Albert Heijn supermarkets in the Netherlands. A loyalty programme developed in Poland in 2000 allowed customers who made a purchase above a specified amount to purchase an additional book of coupons redeemable on gifts, special instore discounts and discounts at restaurants. The scheme was transferred to Tops Thailand in 2002. Again there was a combination of the managerial ideas on local marketing and merchandising with the technology support required to provide the appropriate replenishment system.

Matching format and formulae to markets

In considering Ahold's store operations it is essential to distinguish between the formats that are used and the branded formulae that Ahold create. Ahold operates many different store formats. While the supermarket is the dominant format, the companies acquired by Ahold developed hypermarkets, discount stores, convenience stores, superstores, drugstores, specialist food stores and department stores. The range of branded formulae of these formats is very large. Across the total of stores, the three formats of supermarkets, food superstores and discount supermarkets accounted in 2003 for approximately 7,000 of the 8,600 stores. There were approximately 140 hypermarkets and approximately 400 convenience stores, including forecourt stores, with most of the remainder being specialist formats, particularly in the Netherlands.

Within individual markets the format and formulae are the result, in most cases, of the operations of acquisitions and joint-ventures. With most of the acquisitions there has been a presumption that the trading formulae, and names, of the acquired stores are retained initially, and in some cases for an extended period. In Spain, for example, the acquired retailers, often with strong local brands, retained their brand names and most of their formulae characteristics until 2001 when a decision was made to consolidate under the single name and formula of SuperSol. By 2001 it was believed that the Spanish operation had achieved sufficient scale to enable unified marketing and to obtain a return on national marketing programmes, for example in promotional activity and logo awareness. In Central America and Brazil the acquisitions continued to trade with their pre-acquisition formulae.

In Asia the approach was different and acquired stores were converted quickly to a single Tops formula, which although responsive in its ranges to local markets, had common characteristics in Thailand, Malaysia and Indonesia. A similar approach was adopted in Poland and Czechoslovakia. The reason for this standardization of formulae is twofold. First, there was a belief that these markets are emergent markets and consumers have few traditions associated with the supermarket format and so pre-acquisition names have little scope for expanding the network. Second, it was expected that, in emergent markets post-acquisition, substantial changes to the formula would be needed to improve efficiency and productivity in the acquired stores, so formula standardization results.

The formulae that are operated in the markets, however, are not a static legacy of the acquisitions. The formula is a dynamic concept. The operating formula evolves with market changes and also has been changed as innovations and knowledge are applied. The importance of the Ahold innovation network, therefore, is evident in the ways that the formulae evolve. So, for example, although the ICA formulae in Sweden had a strong relationship with the local market before the joint-venture, changes in retail brand and in back-office systems have meant that the formulae have evolved using Ahold knowledge post-acquisition.

Alongside the changes to inherited formulae Ahold undertook three major new developments of formulae. One is in supermarkets, one in hypermarkets and one in convenience stores. All three are in the Netherlands. The World of Worlds formula for a large supermarket was initiated in 1997 and five were developed over the following four years. The concept was for product offerings to radiate from a central space (L'Avonture) that contained a café, various delicatessen ranges, fresh juices, patisserie and prepared meals, that can be eaten in the café or taken away. Several service counters surround this central space. From this central area sections focusing on convenience, discount and dry grocery radiate so allowing the customer to 'mix and match' across different needs including discount, congruent priced and premium products. The grocery section is organized by meal type rather than by more traditional categories. The discount section was only included in the first experimental store and was then dropped in later versions of the formula. There was a strong branding of Albert Heijn across the 25,000 items in the overall range. A specialist wine shop was provided within the store. A range of customer services were provided including self-scanning and demonstrations of food and meal preparation.

The second new formula was the Albert Heijn XL hypermarket. This opened in February 2002 as a conversion of an older hypermarket in Kronenburg Centre in Arnhem. The store covered 4,000 square metres and, as with the new supermarket, involved an innovative layout. The store was divided into six zones termed:

escape, indulge, well-being, fresh, eat and inspire. In each zone there was a focal point, for example a fresh juice bar in the fresh zone, internet café in the escape zone, a health and beauty adviser in the well-being zone. The aim was to allow some customers to shop quickly, for example groceries are merchandised by meal type and a meal solutions offer and other quick service counters close to the entrance, while other customers could browse in the non-food areas without feeling pressured by those who wish to shop more quickly.

The third formula was 'AH to go' which is a convenience store formula designed to be located at petrol filling stations, in hospitals, at railway stations and in town centres. A joint-venture with Shell in 1996 had the potential for convenience stores across the 300 Shell petrol stations in the Netherlands but development was slow and the joint-venture failed in 2000 with Shell wishing to develop its own Shell Select formula. This also allowed Ahold to develop a convenience store format with over 30 stores in operation by early 2003. The AH to go stores at petrol filling stations are in a new joint-venture with Esso who have 350 sites across the Netherlands. Stores are between 100 and 250 square metres in area. Two main ranges are provided. One is termed 'Nice for now' and the second 'Nice for later'.

The World of Worlds supermarket formula has been influential in changes made to the standard Albert Heijn supermarket and in the concept of the XL hypermarket but it has not been widely used. The XL hypermarket was initially more successful and there were plans to develop up to 50 of these in the Dutch market by 2006. The AH to go formula was planned for rapid development with over 50 per year being planned initially. The three new innovative formulae were all developed in the Netherlands drawing on knowledge gained from across the organization. Formula development in the foreign operations tended to be incremental rather than the radical approach of these three Dutch formulae. Thus, in Thailand, the City Market store in Bangkok was a store targeting office workers and located in a city office block, and Jiffy Kitchen was a convenience store linked to a petrol forecourt and had the potential to be developed in a joint-venture with Conoco.

Marketing and merchandising within and across markets

The marketing activities involve local implementation of centrally defined policies. Two areas will be used to illustrate this approach: the areas of retail brand items and promotional activity.

There was a central policy of developing retailer branded products and the execution of this was the responsibility of local operations. Retail brand penetration was strongest in the Netherlands accounting for approximately 40 per cent of sales. In the South American operations it was a much smaller percentage of share being well under 10 per cent. The central policy was one of having two market positions: one congruent in quality but at a lower price than the main manufacturer brand and the second a discount position. Ranges were developed for both positions. For example, in the Czech Republic Albert was the standard brand and Koruna was the discount brand. In some markets where the positioning of the supermarket was towards the higher end of the market, then a premium range of items was produced. This was the position in Chile prior to the sale of Santa Isabel. Local markets also had their own brands for specific specialist categories, for example Selský Dvur (Farm Yard) for organics in the Czech Republic, Gold Medal for meat in Tops Thailand. In the hypermarkets the non-food categories were locally branded according to the situation in the local market, for example Track & Field was used for sports goods in Hypernova hypermarkets in Central Europe. Across the retail formulae in the US there were a large number of names used to brand Ahold produced items. There was, however, an expectation that the local operations would use group-wide or regional expertise in the development of these products although in different countries they may carry different brand names.

The retail branding activities were related to local markets but often lacked real authority because of the small share of these items. While strongest in the Netherlands even here there were only about 4,000 in the Albert Heijn range and while for some categories Albert Heijn branded items were very strong (most notably coffee where it was linked to an Ahold production unit – Ahold Coffee Company) this strength was not sustained across all the categories. The main innovations in the branding of merchandise were seen in the Netherlands with the development of new ready-to-cook microwave meals and in the production of single serve coffee-bags. Elsewhere the retail branded items were generally copies of manufacturer branded items or basic commodities.

In promotional activity it was again local-level decisions that affect the main decisions on promotional campaigns, items promoted, media used and extent of the use of promotion. Local in-store magazines were widely used. Some chains, for example Albert Heijn in the Netherlands, operated high-low pricing backed by price promotions, some others used EDLP (Every Day Low Price), for example BI-LO in the US, while some operated a very local pricing and promotion policy related to competition in the immediate market, for example Tops in the US. There was, however, one major group-wide promotion per year. This was coordinated from the head office in Zaandam. The first was in Autumn 1999 with a promotion termed 'World Champions' that was undertaken in 17 countries and involved 19 multinational suppliers. Table 7.4 shows the subsequent promotions of this type.

Across the marketing area Ahold attempted to respond to local conditions and so front-of-store marketing activities were decided by the local chain and in some cases by local store management. This approach resulted in high levels of transaction costs for marketing activities and few returns to scale. It also resulted in a high level of locally based tacit knowledge that was difficult to transfer within the organization.

Table 7.4 Multinational promotions

	World Champions 1999	Best in your Home 2000	Festival of Food & Fun 2001
Number of participating stores	3,000	6,000	8,000
Number of participating countries	17	23	25
Number of participating multinational suppliers	19	36	48
Potential customer base	20 million	30 million	40 million
Estimated promotional compliance	75%	80%	85%

Sourcing and supply chain efficiencies

Returns to scale in retailing generally are greatest in respect of sourcing activities. By 2002 Ahold was making major attempts to move from local sourcing to regional sourcing with some items being sourced on a global basis. The shift to more centralized sourcing was aimed to generate scale economies that were lacking across the whole group. While there was wide variation across individual items, the different operating units were sourcing between 70 per cent and 90 per cent of their merchandise locally. Moves into regional sourcing were under way and Ahold had given these moves strong support. Regional sourcing was seen as a first step and one that would give benefits quickly. The reason for the two-stage approach, first with regional sourcing and then global sourcing rested on four arguments:

1 The value of most grocery products is low and they do not carry large transport costs.
2 Replenishment rates are high and the replenishment cycle needs to be kept short. This affects not only short shelf-life merchandise but all items in order to reduce inventory costs.
3 The capabilities of many suppliers are such that they are only able to provide a regional sourcing response.
4 Consumer cultures can be accommodated more effectively through a regional response.

Regional sourcing was based around four groups: Europe (Zandaam), Asia (Bangkok), Latin America (Buenos Aires) and the US (Chantilly, Buffalo and Boston). The Latin American and Asian groups were small and new. A non-food showroom had been developed for Latin America; La Fragua's economy brand had been adopted across the region as the economy retail brand (less than 20 items comprised the range in 2002); Asia had been using internet buying to source some items centrally. The US group was more advanced having begun in 1994. General merchandise, health and beauty, and perishable categories, and retail branded items were purchased centrally, amounting for over 30 per cent of sales volumes. In Europe, a number of sub-regional buying 'desks' operated. The chains in the Netherlands bought through one such buying desk which, in 2001, was the first to begin operations, and others operated for Central Europe, Scandinavia and Southern Europe. A few dry grocery products and some retailer branded items were bought through a European-wide buying desk. Other than in the US the moves to regional sourcing were still at an early stage of development and only a few benefits had been delivered by 2003.

In respect of the operational features, the position of Ahold in early 2003 can be characterized in the following ways:

- Expansion of the network and access to new markets had been rapid and substantial. The increase in sales points over a short period had been considerable. This growth had been driven by a centrally directed strategy of acquisition and joint-ventures. The objective had been to obtain sales by additional sales space.
- Acquisitions and joint-ventures resulted in a store portfolio that had a variety of different formats and a large number of formulae. Rationalization of this large number of formats had begun but was at a very early stage.
- There were few signs of the synergies that were expected from the three strategic divisions of retailing, foodservice and e-commerce.
- The acquisition process has enabled knowledge transfer across the group and the formal mechanisms in place facilitated this transfer of ideas. What is surprising is that the large number of acquisitions had generated relatively few new formulae that have been transferred out of their local market.
- Innovation generally was concentrated in the the Netherlands. The gradual evolution of practice was typical of operations in other countries. This was very evident in formulae development and retail brand merchandise. Brand building had been slow and there had been minimal transfer of brands.
- Branding was decentralized with store and merchandise branding being locally determined. A slow shift to regional level coordination was evident but this was at an early stage of development.
- Scale-related benefits from regional and global sourcing had yet to be obtained.

The transition of Ahold from a national Netherlands-based supermarket firm to a bi-national firm with supermarkets in the eastern region of the US was successfully achieved with coordination in the US and integration of acquisitions in the

163

US. The initial moves to a transformation into a multi-format, multinational firm had generated a plethora of chains, brands and operational practices in need of rationalization and coordination in order to achieve success. The further transformation into a multi-channel firm was at a very early stage of development.

THE IMPLICATIONS OF THE STRATEGY

This review of the strategy and operations of Ahold enables some conclusions to be drawn but also raises questions that are of relevance to any large FMCG retailer that pursues a substantive programme of internationalization.

Ahold exhibited rapid growth in sales. This was achieved, outside the Netherlands, mainly by acquisition and joint-ventures that extended the operational floorspace rather than through organic growth using innovation. Rapid international growth can only be achieved through acquisition or joint-venture but the question that has to be answered for any international retailer is:

- What balance is sustainable between sales growth by acquisition, sales growth by direct investment in new space and sales growth from greater productivity from existing assets, including but not exclusively floor-space?

Organic growth, outside the Netherlands, in Ahold was small compared with the acquisition-based growth and the imbalance may have created some instability. The transition to organic growth being sought in the change of strategy in 2002 is difficult when the culture has been one of growth by acquisition.

In any acquisition the speed and processes of integration are critical to the degree to which the acquisition contributes to the overall growth of the company. In the case of Ahold the processes of acquisition had been formalized to enable benefits to be achieved rapidly. But as the size of the acquisition or joint-venture got larger so the speed of obtaining benefit, other than through an increase in recorded sales, decreased, so that with the ICA joint-venture the integration benefits were slow to appear. The speed with which benefits are needed also rises related to the price paid and the method of funding the acquisition. The increase in debt in Ahold was considerable, as a result of acquisitions made at the height of the 1980s economic boom with these acquisitions, in retrospect, appearing to be relatively highly priced. The slow generation of benefits from the acquisitions increased the effective debt burden. For retailer internationalization, the general questions raised from this experience are:

- How can the retail firm obtain benefits from integration quickly?
- What, in a retail context, should the balance be between multiple small acquisitions and a few large ones?

Ahold moved into a large number of foreign markets. In some cases with a relatively small presence that then remained small for several years. In other cases there was a substantive building of market share. This large number of markets resulted in relatively high transaction costs in markets where there was limited presence. Decisions about which markets should provide growth and which should be exited appear to have been slow. For international retailing the general questions this raises are:

- What is the critical mass necessary in order to remain in a market (national or regional) and build a potentially profitably presence?
- How quickly should this critical mass be achieved before decisions on market exit are made?

Operating a multi-format strategy is becoming widespread in international retailing (Dawson 2001a). Operating a multi-formula strategy within a format or operating a multi-channel strategy is less common. While the synergies in a multi-format strategy are obtainable across many business functions (marketing, buying, logistics, human resources, etc.) the cost economies of scale and scope in these functions become less obvious and also more difficult to obtain with a multi-formula strategy and/or a multi-channel strategy. The questions in a multi-formula strategy are:

- How is the balance between back of store standardization for scale economies and front of store localization for scope economies obtained in the different regional or national markets?
- Is there a point (critical mass of market share in a market) at which standardization can be implemented at the front of the store across the several formula in a format?
- What are the characteristics that allow a formula to be transferred into other markets?

The issues with a multi-channel strategy are different. A fundamental question is:

- What are the realizable synergies in a multi-channel strategy?

It would seem that Ahold did not gain competitive advantage from a multi-channel strategy and it is notable that a problem in one of the channels can have major implications on operations in other channels. So while it is difficult to obtain benefits the risks are high.

The continuum between the poles of localization and standardization that is widely discussed in respect of internationalization is particularly complex in respect of retailing. The continuum has to be considered in respect of functions, processes and item ranges. In addition there is the question of whether all markets are considered in the same way. Different positions are required for different functions. Ahold generally localized store operating practices but standardized some functional processes, for example sourcing. Ahold also had to grapple with the issue of the level at which standardization is applied – a national market, a regional collection of markets or at the level of the total organization. The speed at which acquisitions were made resulted in some confusion in this issue. There was also an apparent confusion in the position of processes on this continuum. Thus, for example, processes of retail brand development were different in different countries, logistics processes were dealt with in different ways with a different split between localization and standardization even among the different operating units in the US. The large number of items that are sourced and resold means that for the different products there may be differences in the extent to which adaptation to the local market occurs. Again, this was apparent in Ahold. Thus, for Ahold the result was an eclectic variety of situations with no clearly articulated rules. The generic question that this raises is:

- What are the dimensions that define the optimal balance between local responsiveness and centralized standardization?

The dimensions are not the same in retailing as they are for manufacturing (Dawson and Mukoyama 2003).

A GLOBAL RETAILER?

Aspirations to be called a global company are evident from a number of retailers including Ahold. It is not clear in retailing what constitutes a global company. A global company will have global structures and global processes. In developing a global structure the firm will move away from country-based structures to integrated format (or channel) structures within business divisions that are the main decision makers. The role of the centre coordinates the divisions and implementation is at national level. Regions, defined as groups of countries have a support role only. Such an approach to structure then allows global sourcing from firms who have global account management systems in place. In generating global processes, then, there will be clearly defined responsibilities with two-way communication between the centre and implementing units. There will be rationalization and standardization of processes, but importantly not implementation, worldwide, for example with global branding or global promotions. The processes then have the potential to create a global corporate culture. With this perspective, then, Ahold in 2003 came close to being an emerging global company. Several of these structures were being put in place but the global processes were still at an early stage of development. Whether they will ever now be created is doubtful. The generic question in this context is:

■ Is this perspective of a global company applicable in a retail context?

To be termed global a retailer needs more than a global structure; it also needs global aspects to its retail operation. Expanding the work of Zou and Cavusgil (2002) global retail operation can be construed as:

■ Product standardization – the degree to which format (the retailer's product) concepts, not necessarily the detailed design (formula), is standardized across country markets.

■ Formula design – the extent to which the principles of design of the retailer's formula are applied in operations in different countries.

■ Promotion standardization – the extent to which the same approach to the promotional mix is executed across country markets.

■ Standardized channel structure – the degree to which the retailer uses the same philosophy of channel structure across different country markets.

■ Standardized price positions – the extent to which the retailer uses the same price position across country markets.

■ Standardized branding – the extent to which the retailer has a common branding policy for the firm, its stores and items across country markets.

■ Concentration of marketing activities – the extent to which a retailer's marketing activities, including development of promotional campaign, pricing decisions, distribution activities, and customer services, are deliberately performed at head office, at a regional office or at country locations.

■ Coordination of marketing activities – the extent to which a retailer's marketing activities in different country locations, including development of promotional campaign, pricing decisions, distribution activities, and customer services, are planned and executed interdependently on a global scale.

■ Global market participation – the extent to which a retailer has operations in all the major markets of the world.

■ Integration of competitive moves – the extent to which a retailer's actions in competitive marketing in different countries are interdependent.

■ Global marketing values – the extent to which a retailer's corporate values can be interpreted globally and a common positioning strategy exists in different countries.

■ Global sourcing – the extent to which the retailer's relationships with suppliers include suppliers providing items for distribution throughout the retailer and negotiations with suppliers involve principles of global account management.

Ahold in January 2003 was starting to develop many of these characteristics albeit in a small way. On some of them, however, it was certainly not moving towards a global view. Undoubtedly, Ahold had aspirations to be a global firm.

Before the financial crisis was made public there were signs that the strategy of being multi-format, multinational and multi-channel was starting to disintegrate. It would seem that Ahold lost focus in the second half of the 1990s when it embarked on a 'collecting countries' approach to expansion. A strong basis in the Netherlands and the US had been established on which to build international expansion but the decision was made to acquire sales rather than to innovate to grow sales. More acquisitions were then required in order to service the debt that resulted from the acquisitions. This snowball effect was exacerbated by the buoyant valuation of companies and the consequential high prices paid for acquisitions. Despite the frantic growth of the late 1990s Ahold never became a truly global business. This raises a question of whether or not the idea of a global retailer is, indeed, a valid one.

NOTES

1   The notable exception is Argentina where Ahold was required to take full ownership because of the failure of the domestic company during the economic crisis of 2002. The taking of full ownership in Argentina triggered a legal requirement to take full ownership in Chile in 2003.

2   It is interesting to note that the other partners in the alliance followed different strategies. Safeway in the UK remained a domestic operation but failed to grow and was later acquired. Casino strengthened its position in France, expanded internationally into markets similar to those addressed by Ahold, and also acquired the poorly performing Lauraus in the Netherlands. Casino had more modest aspirations for growth than Ahold but now faces the problem of achieving a critical mass in its foreign markets.

REFERENCES

Bailey, J., Clarke-Hill, C. M. and Robinson, T. M. (1995) Towards a taxonomy of international retail alliances. *Service Industries Journal*, 15(4): 25–41

Conner, K. R. and Prahalad, C. K. (1996) A resource based theory of the firm: knowledge versus opportunism. *Organization Science*, 7(5): 477–501

Dawson, J. (2001a) Is there a new commerce in Europe? *International Review of Retail, Distribution and Consumer Research*, 11(3): 287–299

Dawson, J. (2001b). Strategy and opportunism in European retail internationalization. *British Journal of Management*, 12(4): 253–266

Dawson, J. and Mukoyama, M. (2003) Concepts, dimensions and measurement of the retail internationlisation process. Paper to SARD workshop, UMDS, Kobe, April 2003

Henksmeier, K. H. (1960) *The Economic Performance of Self Service in Europe*. (Paris: OEEC)

Hunt, J. (2001) Going Dutch. *The Grocer*, 21 April: 24–26

Inkpen, A. C. and Beamish, P. W. (1997) Knowledge, bargaining power and the instability of international Joint-ventures. *Academy of Management Review*, 22: 177–202

Palmer, M. and Owens, M. (2005) Internationalizing retail: new directions for joint venture research. Paper to EAERCD conference, Lund University, June 2005

Robinson, T. and Clarke-Hill, C. M. (1995) International alliances in European retailing. *International Review of Retail, Distribution and Consumer Research*, 5(2): 167–184

Van der Hoven, C. (1999) Royal Ahold: a global strategy based on local independence. *International Trends in Retailing*, 16(1): 73–80

Wrigley, N. and Currah, A. (2003) The stresses of retail internationalisation: lessons from Royal Ahold's experience in Latin America. *International Review of Retail, Distribution and Consumer Research*, 13(3): 221–243

Zou Shaoming and Cavusgil, T. (2002) The GMS: a broad conceptualization of global marketing strategy and its effect on firm performance. *Journal of Marketing*, 66(4): 40–56

Chapter 8

Tesco

Transferring marketing success factors internationally

John Dawson, Roy Larke and Sang Chul Choi

INTRODUCTION

In 1919, Jack Cohen used his £30 ex-serviceman payment to establish a market stall selling groceries in East London. By 2004–2005, 85 years later, Tesco, the company Jack Cohen founded, had profits of £2,064 million from 1,780 stores in 14 countries. The origins of present-day Tesco lie in strongly opportunistic behaviour that determined the culture of the firm for several decades. The adoption of a strategic approach and the intense focus on marketing date from the last three decades. The development of the international presence, which by 2005 accounts for almost 50 per cent of the sales space of Tesco, has a very recent origin with substantive activity being less than a decade old. The core strategy has been to develop a strong domestic base as a launch-pad for internationalization with the transfer of marketing concepts into non-domestic markets. Throughout this development over 85 years, an entrepreneurial culture has permeated all activities, initially in an opportunistic way and more recently in a strategic framework.

Table 8.1 summarizes the position of Tesco over the five years to 2005. Overall sales remain strongly UK based but the rapid growth in the rest of Europe and Asia is evident with these international markets contributing over 20 per cent to total retail sales in 2004–2005. Profit contribution from international activity lags sales due to the young age of the store portfolio in the foreign markets and development costs in these markets. Nonetheless, international operations were contributing profits of £370 million in 2004–2005. This is considerably more than the domestic profits of all but a handful of European food retailers. The UK store portfolio increased substantially in 2002–2003 due to acquisitions of convenience stores, making Tesco a significant operator of small food stores in the UK. Internationally, there is a focus on hypermarkets with more than half of the international portfolio being in this format and considerably more hypermarkets being operated

Table 8.1 *Tesco sales and stores operations, 2001–2005*

Financial year ending:	2001	2002	2003	2004	2005
Group sales £m	22,585	25,401	28,280	33,557	37,070
of which: sales turnover (exc. tax) £m	20,800	23,400	26,004	30,814	33,974
of which: UK	18,203	19,821	21,309	24,760	27,146
Rest of Europe	1,737	2,181	2,664	3,385	3,818
Asia	860	1,398	2,031	2,669	3,010
Underlying operating profit £m	1,174	1,322	1,509	1,832	2,064
of which: UK	1,100	1,213	1,297	1,526	1,694
Rest of Europe	70	90	141	184	218
Asia	4	29	71	122	152
Number of stores UK	692	729	1,982	1,878	1,780
of which: hypermarkets	23	41	62	83	100
non-UK (inc. joint ventures)	215	250	309	440	554
of which: hypermarkets	68	102	152	194	273
Total sales area ('000 sq ft) UK	17,965	18,822	21,829	23,291	24,207
non-UK (inc. joint ventures)	10,397	13,669	18,115	22,111	24,928

outside the UK than within the UK. This different balance of format within and outside the UK, together with the rapid growth of new stores internationally, has pushed, by 2005, the share of floor-space operated internationally to over 50 per cent of the total.

This chapter explores the evolution of Tesco to the position shown in Table 8.1. The creation of the strong domestic base has been of fundamental importance to international expansion and to diversification in the UK. The critical success factors and the important non-failure factors of this domestic growth are considered as economies of scale and scope have been exploited. The current extent of international activity is reviewed with evaluation of what has been transferred from the domestic operation to the foreign ones. The experience of Tesco in building its presence in Poland, Korea and China are used to illustrate the nature of development. Finally, the criteria for international success are considered for the continuing internationalization of Tesco.

HISTORY

After the early years at a market stall, by the early 1920s Jack Cohen was trading from stores in London. The Tesco name, later to become the brand, was used first in 1929 being derived from a combination of the initials of T. E. Stockwell, a supplier of tea, and the CO of Cohen's own name (Powell 1991; Seth and Randall 1999). Growth and trading practices were opportunistic and deal-based in these early years with short-term profit being high on the agenda. A small chain store organization had developed by the mid-1930s but there was relatively little store discipline in the operations. A critical event was the visit to the US in 1935 by Cohen and a further one in the late 1940s. On these visits he saw self-service stores in operation, coming back with the idea firmly established that this was the direction that food retailing would go. The labour shortages during the Second World War added to the pressure to reduce labour input and so to pass store functions to consumers. By the second half of the 1940s there was widespread experimentation with self-service methods in the UK. While the consumer cooperative societies were early innovators Tesco and other small chains were also having trials of this new form of operation (Fulop 1964). By 1950 Tesco had around 20 stores operating through self-service. The transfer of the ideas from the US had taken more than a decade but the impact on Tesco was fundamental. This new technology involved the introduction of new operating procedures and increased the need for adherence to store systems. The systems enabled control to be exerted over a larger network of stores and so Cohen began the acquisition of medium-sized chains through the 1960s, building up a chain of 800 shops by the end of the 1960s. This period can be characterized as one of entrepreneurial opportunism.

The removal of resale price maintenance on foods in UK in 1964 changed the sales environment for retailers. Price competition became much stronger and decisions on pricing and promotions became more the preserve of retailers than had formerly been the case (Pickering 1974). In order to sell at low prices and make a profit it was necessary to buy at low prices. The importance of scale economies in the buying process increased substantially from the mid-1960s. Therefore, having a large chain of stores with steadily increasing sales increased the retailer's bargaining power (Dawson 2004). This suited the Tesco style and culture of opportunism and entrepreneurship. Managing the pricing was an art-form perfected by Tesco through the activity of Daisy Hyams, a long-time associate of Cohen. A strongly led central management team imposed authority on the growing store network, but as it got bigger so the difficulty of this form of control became more apparent. Low prices and high volume was the Tesco mantra through much of the 1970s. Store location, ambience, stock availability and even quality had lower priority than pursuing low prices and high volume.

While the focus of Tesco was on price, other retailers explored non-price issues that were gradually gaining in significance in the minds of consumers. The Tesco focus on price had generated a perception of low quality in the minds of consumers just as their aspirations were starting to move upwards. The strong, and very evident to consumers, corporate culture of opportunistic operations was starting to have a negative impact on the performance of the firm. The moves to address this issue and to begin to move to a more strategic approach to management started in the late 1970s but the existing culture was too strong for a strategic approach to take strong hold. In 1977 Tesco withdrew from a longstanding pseudo-loyalty scheme that provided shoppers with 'Green Shield' stamps that were redeemable for gifts. The number of stamps provided to a shopper was related to the amount spent. At the same time Tesco launched an aggressive price campaign, called 'Operation Checkout' which increased their market share but did not generate a substantial increase in profit (Akehurst 1984). The focus was on increasing volume sales. The major increase in volume resulting from the campaign put serious pressure on logistics and operations and Tesco came close to commercial collapse. Partly to alleviate these problems there were closures of several hundred small shops over the following five years and a move towards opening large stores. Survival was high on the agenda so the opportunity for strategic growth and development was limited.

Following various boardroom tussles deciding the way forward, by the early 1980s it was clear that any change in strategy had to be accompanied by a change in corporate culture. A corporate strategy to move Tesco away from the low-price–low-quality market position was coupled with a more strategic and less opportunistic approach to management. This shift in strategy was only possible because of the high level of consumer awareness that had been generated from the substantial network of stores in place. That the awareness was of an image of a 'cheap and cheerful' posed problems but the extensive network and large scale of buying provided a sound platform. The move up-market was orchestrated by Ian (later Lord) MacLaurin who as CEO and, from 1986, Chairman, pushed investment in large supermarkets (superstores) often close to suburban residential areas. These stores provided one-stop shopping facilities for food and grocery purchasing by the increasing number of time-pressured women who were entering the formal workforce. The large stores enabled wider ranges to include higher quality items that gradually displaced the lower quality ones. Tesco branded products were introduced that were priced lower than manufacturer brands but were of significantly higher quality than the previous retail branded items. The target was the development of stores that 'conformed' to a corporate model, with 'conforming' stores having centralized disciplines in terms of systems, logistics (Smith and Sparks 1993), new technologies, ranges, merchandising and employee practices. Thus a centralized, marketing-driven, strategic view was imposed on the new stores, but much of the network, although being rationalized, was still a legacy of the previous 30 years of opportunistic acquisitions.

By the early 1990s the rationalization of the store network and the focused marketing strategy were resulting in moves in Tesco's market position such that it was no longer seen by consumers as a low-quality supermarket. Quality had improved, price points had crept higher, volumes had increased and margins had improved to over 5 per cent, to be the envy of food retailers across Europe. The level of investment in new, large supermarkets had been huge.

In the early to mid-1990s firms operating from a limited line discount store format believed a market opportunity had been created in the UK with the move up-market of Tesco. Aldi, Lidl, Netto and others began to build a market presence. Tesco adopted a strategic reaction to this threat by introducing a discount brand, termed Value lines, within their stores. The number of items, initially 70, was limited to those in direct competition with Aldi and the like. Prices on these lines were largely matched with these limited line discount stores. The large superstore format of Tesco allowed these Value lines to exist alongside the usual ranges with little detriment to the move up-market that was core strategy.

The success of the Value lines served to reinforce the importance of marketing being the central plank of the overall strategy of Tesco. By placing marketing in this position the ground was prepared for moving Tesco to become a brand in its own right (Wileman and Jary 1997). Not only were product ranges segmented to provide discount, congruent, premium and specialist ranges in store but also stores were segmented, using different formats for different locations with convenience stores, local supermarkets, superstores and hypermarkets all being developed. The Tesco brand was used for the different ranges and was used to change the formats into the Tesco store formulae of Tesco Express, Tesco Metro, Tesco Extra and so on. The marketing-based strategy was implemented also by the improvement of communications with the customer through the establishment of a loyalty card that rewarded frequent and heavy shoppers. The appointment as CEO in 1997 of Terry Leahy, previously Deputy Managing Director and a very strong advocate of a marketing approach, sealed the change in strategy and paved the way for the domestic market domination and international moves that have subsequently developed.

The changes in Tesco over the last half century have involved a major change of corporate culture and the adoption of a strategic approach to management. The strategic shift first involved the use of a buying-driven strategy to exploit the scale derived from the extensive store network. This enabled centralized cost control of operations. From this platform it was then possible for Tesco to rationalize the store network and, in parallel, introduce a marketing-driven strategy. The development of the marketing strategy has enabled exploitation of economies of scope, alongside those of scale, through the use of segmentation and branding of items and store operations. Embedded in the strategic shift has been a change in corporate culture from inward looking entrepreneurial to outward looking customer responsiveness and, logically from this outward looking culture, to a more international perspective.

THE BASIS OF STRENGTH IN THE DOMESTIC MARKET

Depending on the detail of the definition of the market and of the criteria of measurement of market share, Tesco, in 2005, had between 26 per cent and 30 per cent of the UK food and grocery market. This is more than double the market share of 1995. The growth in sales is shown in Figure 8.1 and it is clear that the sales in the UK, although declining as a share of all sales, continue to dominate the performance. The strength of the domestic base is key to understanding the international activity of Tesco.

The development of Tesco in 2005 had four components:

1   Maintenance of a strong core business in food and grocery items in the UK with continuing growth of market share.
2   Growth in non-foods with a goal of being equally strong in food and non-food sectors. This is particularly relevant in the UK through expansion into clothing and household goods ranges.
3   Expansion of consumer services, particularly financial services. Financial services are in a joint venture with Royal Bank of Scotland and include a range of insurance, loans and general banking services.
4   International expansion into a limited number of foreign markets where, for several of them, market leadership is a feasible objective within approximately ten years. This will involve transfer of knowledge from the UK to foreign markets and also transfer back to the UK, particularly of sourcing information.

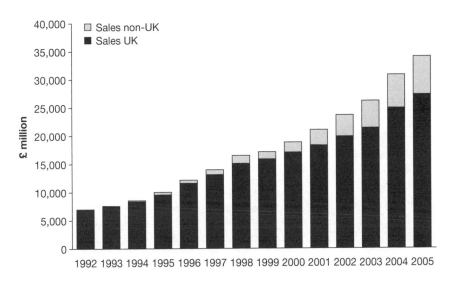

Figure 8.1 *Sales volume of Tesco, 1992–2005*

Key to implementation in the UK of the components of the strategy are:

- operation of a multi-format approach to market access;
- building Tesco as a brand;
- use of a coordinated business planning system;
- simplification of in-store systems;
- collection and use of customer information;
- reducing the time of the supply cycle for replenishment.

Operation of a multi-format approach

In the UK Tesco operates store formulae related to five formats. Each formula is a Tesco branded version of a major format as shown in Table 8.2. The aim of this multi-format approach is to provide stores for different types of shopping occasion and for different types of markets. The stores provide a means of bringing Tesco brand values to consumers in a wide variety of situations. Table 8.3 shows the change in store numbers of the various formulae since 2000.

Table 8.2 The multi-format approach of Tesco

Format	Formula	Number in UK 2005	Comments
Hypermarket	Tesco Extra	100	First store 1996 Average size 62,000 sq ft 15–20 new stores or conversions per year
Superstore	Tesco Superstore	446	Specialist food stores with some non-foods Size ranges from 20,000 sq ft to 45,000 sq ft 15–20 opened per year
City super-market	Tesco Metro	160	First store 1992 Food specialists with extensive ranges of convenience foods 6–10 opened per year
Convenience store	Tesco Express T&S One Stop[1]	546 527	First store 1995 Substantial growth through acquisition
e-retailing	Tesco.com	Potential coverage of 96 per cent of UK population	Effective from 1999 Store-based picking and delivery model Delivered 150,000 orders per week in 2004/5 Sales of £719 million in 2004/5

1 T&S was acquired in 2002 and stores are being transferred to the Express formula. Some stores are being sold to other firms

Table 8.3 *The evolution of the formula network in the UK*

	2000	2001	2002	2003	2004	2005		
	Number of stores					Number of stores	Million sq ft	% of total sq ft
Extra	9	23	41	62	83	100	6.6	27.2
Superstore	358	370	444	441	446	446	13.9	57.4
Metro/high street store	41	38	168	167	61	160	1.9	7.8
Express	27	45	75	109	277	546	1.1	4.5
T&S	0	0	0	1,202	910	527	0.7	3.1
Other[1]	224	215						
Total	659	691	728	1,981	1,877	1,779	24.2	100

1 Stores that were not allocated to one of the format groups

The development of hypermarkets in the Tesco Extra formula began slowly and relatively late. Asda had several years of experience in the UK before Tesco developed their formula. The formula has become a major part of the Tesco network within ten years and accounted for over 25 per cent of floor-space by 2005. Tesco Extra stores are developed as new units and also as conversions and extensions of Tesco superstores. The formula contains a full range of food and grocery, including serve-over counters for specialist foods, and ranges of household goods, electrical products and clothing. Limited ranges of toys, gifts, DIY items and motor accessories are also provided.

Tesco superstores are the main formula of Tesco in the UK with over 50 per cent of floor-space. It provides the cash-generators for Tesco. A programme of openings and refits maintains this formula at the core of the Tesco network with new stores replacing those that are converted to the Extra formula. The Tesco superstore is a large food and grocery supermarket with limited non-food ranges focused on household items. A small number of stores below 20,000 square feet are developed for small town markets. These focus on food and grocery only and have limited ranges of products such as wines and serve-over counters.

Tesco Metro, typically with a sales space under 12,000 square feet stocking 6,000 items, is an urban supermarket that caters mainly for basket shoppers. Full ranges of health and beauty and dry goods are not provided and the emphasis is on convenience foods. Specific ranges are adapted to the local market.

Tesco Express is a convenience store typically less than 3,000 square feet. Some are developed in alliance with major oil companies but more are developed as stand-alone stores. There is a high proportion of Tesco branded items in these stores. Store numbers doubled to over 500 during 2004–2005 with acquired stores, mainly from T&S group and Adminstore, being converted to the Tesco Express formula. While comprising less than 5 per cent of overall Tesco UK floor-space, the formula is important in expanding the store network not only into local markets in cities and but also into small communities in rural areas.

Tesco.com provides online shopping facilities accessible from home, office and other venues. By the end of 2000, with modest investment of £56 million (little more than the investment needed for two superstores) the service was available to 90 per cent of the UK population through links to, and delivery from, 300 stores. By 2005 sales were £719 million and profits £36 million. This is by far the smallest format in sales volume being used but sales increases are substantial, at 24 per cent from 2003/4 to 2004/5 with little additional investment and none of the problems associated with building stores, such as obtaining permissions for additional floor-space.

Building Tesco as a brand

The concepts of branding by Tesco are advanced. Branding is at three levels; branding items and services for sale, branding the store formulae, and branding corporate culture of the Tesco Group.

Branding items and services is an important area through which Tesco maintains control over the ranges in-store, including the merchandising of ranges. By developing new retail brand items it can fill gaps in ranges and provide customers with wide choice, and by on-shelf promotions and communications of Tesco brand items there is constant brand reinforcement throughout the store. In respect of price–quality positioning in the food sector, Tesco uses three brands:

1   Tesco Value – this was initially launched in 1993 as a low-price competitive response to limited range discount stores in UK. It was expanded considerably in 1999 and was then relaunched in 2003 with the number of SKUs being increased from 2,000 to 4,000. Packaging is distinctive with the 5 blue stripes above the Tesco logo, making the items clearly visible in merchandising displays.

2   Tesco – this is positioned to compete directly with the main manufacturer brand and in some products has become the effective market leader. There are 8,000 SKUs in UK with a steady introduction of new products.

3   Tesco Finest – this was launched in 1998 as a premium retail brand and by 2004 contained 1,900 SKUs. There are frequent new product introductions and withdrawals. Packaging quality reflects the premium positioning. The brand has been extended to non-food areas including cosmetics, toiletries and glassware. It is also used in branding some financial services.

In addition to the three price-quality positions, there are also four retail branded specialist ranges for food products:

1   Organic – this comprises approximately 1,200 products. All the store formulae carry some products with a full range present in Tesco Extra. There are targets to expand sales to £1 billion by 2006.

2   Healthy Living – these products are targeted at the consumer trend towards a more active and healthy lifestyle. This was formerly branded 'Healthy Eating'. The rebranding is enabling extension of the brand into some non-foods areas, for example, sports equipment.

3   Free From – developed from the Healthy Living range, this is a range of 150 items that are suitable for consumers who have various types of allergy or medical condition. The range contains products that are free of wheat, gluten or cow's milk.

4   Tesco Kids – this range was launched in 2002 with 50 items aimed at children aged 5–11. These are 'fun foods' to encourage children to eat healthily. There is minimal use of artificial ingredients.

In addition to those brands in food and grocery, brands have been developed in the non-food area, particularly in clothing. Tesco obtained the rights to use the US brand Cherokee and this has been used since 2002 for middle-market leisure clothes. Florence and Fred is a Tesco developed brand for semi-formal wear. Back to School has been developed as a range of items for children. Tesco Value has been transferred to clothing for deep discounting of standard items, for example denim jeans. The Tesco name is used to brand other standard price clothing.

Use of a coordinated business planning system

An important factor in the implementation of the four components of strategy is a business planning approach that uses the 'Tesco Steering Wheel'. This is shown in Figure 8.2. The wheel is divided into four quadrants: operations, people, financial and customer. Each quadrant is further subdivided into goals for business planning. Each quadrant has a rolling five-year plan that implements the goals. Progress towards the goals is monitored using a simple red, amber, green scorecard in which red indicates a problem and green indicates that everything is on plan. Each department and store has its one specific steering wheel of detailed objectives within the general structure of the corporate wheel. This is made visible on staff noticeboards to motivate all employees even at store level. The importance of this tool has been in the integration of activities across functions with the firm.

Simplification of in-store systems

Although product and service ranges have increased substantially and the number of stores has also increased, Tesco has tried hard to simplify operations systems in stores. Technology has played a big role but other approaches have also been used to simplify operations.

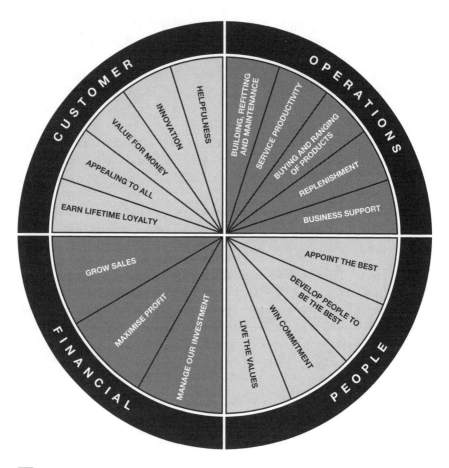

Figure 8.2 *The Tesco Steering Wheel for business planning*

Technology applications include advanced planogram software that provides store-specific ranging. The planogram for each store is derived by incorporating the sales in the store, space availability, product cubic volume and a factor that equalizes the shelf-stock run-down. This additional factor makes shelf replenishment easier because the whole fixture will require replenishment at the same time. This system can incorporate local demand factors. Tesco TV was introduced in March 2003 with in-store screens providing information about promotions. Suppliers are able to purchase advertising time on the screens. The pilot in eight stores was extended to 100 and the aim is to have the system in operation in 300 stores by summer 2005.

Merchandising systems have also been simplified. Shelves have been made deeper so that more stock can be held on the shop floor. Display racks for magazines and stationery contain low-level drawers for easier replenishment. Merchandising units have been redesigned to be mobile and to allow them to be supplier filled before delivery. Space is being provided in aisles for shelf fillers to place stock before shelves are replenished. This moves the un-shelved stock away from customers and eases their access to the shelves. The use of shelf-ready packaging, both of reusable secondary packaging and single-use packaging, has been increased. In 2005 there is planned to be a substantial increase of cases handled by shelf-ready packaging.

Collection and use of customer information

Tesco tries to obtain long-term loyalty from customers. The Tesco Clubcard is the basis for the loyalty programme. It also serves as an important market research vehicle (Humby *et al.* 2003). Information is collected on shopping patterns and this allows the localization of product ranges for stores. In the UK there are 11 million active members of the programme.

The Tesco loyalty programme allows particular groups to be identified and form specific 'clubs'. For example, the Healthy Living club and the Kids club are linked to the retail brand product ranges. The Baby and Toddler club has been particularly successful in building loyalty among families with new babies and small children. Cardholders can also register as vegetarian or following specific dietary regimes. The loyalty scheme has several functions:

- Rewards customers on the basis of the amount spent with 1 or 2 points awarded for each £ spent. Points are transferred into cash discounts each quarter. Cardholders also receive various promotional discounts and coupons for extra points linked to particular products. These promotions reflect the spending pattern of the cardholder and the registered 'club' memberships.
- Provides detailed customer information for the market research activity of Tesco. Information is available on purchasing patterns that can be used to influence product ranges generally and regionally. There is the opportunity also to sell data on purchasing patterns to suppliers.
- Provides an opportunity to extend customer purchasing into financial and other services, for example by giving discounts for first time buyers of specific financial products.

Reducing the time of the supply cycle for replenishment

The number of days stockholding by Tesco has fallen from 14.5 in 1998 to 9.4 in 2004. This has been achieved despite the addition of substantial non-food ranges that sell more slowly. For its UK stores Tesco operates 26 distribution centres in the UK and 23 consolidation centres of which 18 are in the UK and five elsewhere in Europe. The consolidation centres allow small loads from regional suppliers to be consolidated for transfer to the distribution centres. Of the distribution centres 11 are temperature-controlled, five distribute nationally and the remainder service stores regionally.

A move, since 1999, to continuous replenishment from batch replenishment has resulted in a reduction in lead-time and an increase in delivery frequency. This has underpinned the reduction in stockholding in the firm. Table 8.4 shows lead-times and frequency. There is a strong seasonal element in some of the frequencies of product groups, for example 'Beers, wines and spirits' at Christmas. The figures in Table 8.4 are averages. They show reductions in the order lead-times between supplier and distribution centre but little change in the lead-time of store orders on the distribution centre. The overall reduction is particularly notable in fast moving lines and in short-life items where the average lead-time in 2004 was the same as the lowest in 2000. Deliveries have become more frequent in large stores but have been rationalized for the smaller stores. With the larger network of small stores this rationalization of deliveries has been essential to keeping costs at an acceptable level.

Continuous replenishment involves orders being placed on suppliers on the basis of the previous day's sales and forecasts for the next day's sales. Multiple daily orders can be sent to suppliers enabling multiple deliveries to the distribution centre. The average is two orders per day per supplier but this varies widely with product groups. Products are then cross-docked directly onto the vehicle designated to transport to store. Many products are then moved from vehicle to shop floor.

Tesco's strength in the domestic market of UK has provided an important foundation for international expansion. The strategic components implemented in the domestic market have been mutually reinforcing in generating continuing growth. The domestic position has provided a financial safety net for foreign growth and also has provided systems of operation that can be transferred to foreign markets. Possibly most importantly, however, the growth process has created a consumer-orientated corporate culture that has been the vehicle for international activity. Also central to an understanding of Tesco's internationalization is the appreciation of the time-lag of around eight years that was involved between initiating the domestic strategy and Tesco securing its strong position. For several years the strategy appeared to have minimal impact but became effective as synergies among its operational aspects began to be mutually supportive.

TESCO'S INTERNATIONAL EXPANSION

In 2005 Tesco was operating shops in 14 countries including the UK. Table 8.5 shows the extent of the foreign operations. There has been a major expansion of international operations since 2000. This has involved entry into new countries,

Table 8.4 Order lead-times and delivery frequency in 2000 and 2004

	Fast moving goods		Slow moving goods		Frozen		Beer, wine and spirits		Non-foods		Produce		Chilled and meat	
	2000	2004	2000	2004	2000	2004	2000	2004	2000	2004	2000	2004	2000	2004
Lead-times (hours)														
Supplier to DC	48–72	24–48	48–96	48–72	48–72	48	48–1,440	24–168	48	24–180 days	24–48	24	24–48	24
DC to store	18	18	48	36–48	18	18–22	24–48	24–48	48	48	12–24	12–24	12–24	12–24
Deliveries per store per week														
Extra	21	40		6		14		6		6		27		27
Superstore	21	30	7	6	7	12	14	6	21	6	21	21	21	21
Metro	14	12	7	5	7	6	7	4	14	5	14	6	14	6
Express	7	5	7	3	7	4	7	3	7	3	7	7	7	7

Table 8.5 International store operations

Country	Year of entry	31 December 2000		2000/1	31 December 2004				2004/5
		Number of stores	Floor-space '000 sq ft	Sales £m	Stores			Floor-space '000 sq ft	Sales £m
					Total	Of which: hyper-marketts	Planned to open in 2005		
Ireland	1997 (re-entry)	76	1,652	859	85	1	6	2,046	1,336
France		1	16		1		0	16	n.a.
Czech Republic	1996	12	1,191	236	25	19	8	2,145	386
Hungary	1994	45	1,646	296	69	42	14	3,515	933
Poland	1995	40	1,432	223	78	47	20	4,212	691
Slovakia	1996	10	833	142	30	25	6	2,053	326
Turkey	2003				5	5	3	406	146
China	2004				31	31	15	2,637	n.a.
Japan	2003				104	0	15	385	266
Malaysia	2001				6	6	5	584	83
Taiwan	2000	1	107	3	5	5	1	452	108
Thailand	1998	24	2,847	532	107	61	83	5,920	969
South Korea	1999	7	689	326	38	31	31	3,211	1,585
Total		216	10,413		586	273	300	27,581	7,600

Sales converted to £ sterling at average exchange rate for the year and substantial increases in the network and of sales in several markets. Planned expansion for 2005 will increase by more than 50 per cent the number of stores in these foreign markets. This will generate a further 6.8 million square feet of floor-space, 69 per cent of which will be in the hypermarket format.

The preferred format for international operations is the hypermarket although in several countries initial entry used a different format and multi-format operation is the plan for substantive market penetration. The original entry into Ireland was through discount stores and this failed. Subsequent re-entry was through acquisition of supermarkets with hypermarkets being developed in 2004. The original entry into France in 1992 through acquisition of mainly super-markets failed and led to exit in 1997. A nominal presence in France continues with a beer, wine and spirits store targeting day-tripping international shoppers. Entry into Poland was through a majority investment in a small chain of small stores. In the Czech Republic and Slovakia entry was through the purchase from Kmart of large variety and discount department stores. In Japan entry was through the purchase of small local supermarkets. Formats operated by the entry vehicles have been used as a mechanism to gain market knowledge and to gain a modest presence in the market. Even in countries where entry has been through acquisition or joint venture with a large format operator, as in Hungary, Turkey and South Korea, entry was on a modest scale with the chosen entry firm having a generally small market presence. Only in Thailand was a major retailer purchased with the acquisition of 75 per cent of Lotus, Thailand's second largest retailer (Yahagi 2003).

Development subsequent to entry often has involved a change of format. Hypermarkets were developed in Poland and Hungary before they became well established in the UK. To some extent the experience of hypermarket development and operation in Central Europe was used to inform the development of Tesco Extra in the UK. Feedback was provided on how hypermarkets operate on lower costs but also lower sales per square foot and so a different return on investment. In the mid-1990s, particularly in Poland, the leading French and German retailers, with a long experience of hypermarkets, were developing state-of-the-art hypermarkets and these were seen as role models for Tesco, which at that time was relatively inexperienced in hypermarket operation (Dawson and Henley 2002). Hypermarkets have become the main format for development in Slovakia and the Czech Republic but with increased knowledge of the market a compact hypermarket has been developed that is more suited to smaller markets in these countries. In most cases development has been through new store development because potential acquisitions were unavailable. Acquisition does occur, when suitable firms are available (Dawson 2001), as in Poland with HIT, a German-based hypermarket firm that in 2002 wished to sell its Polish operation. Also in Poland, nine supermarkets were acquired in 2005 for Julius Meinl as part of the Tesco development of its multi-format approach. In Japan, after initial entry through acquisition of C2 Network in 2003, the opportunity arose in 2004 to purchase Fre'c out of effective bankruptcy.

After the initial failures in Ireland and France, although in both cases valuable knowledge was obtained, a more considered approach to internationalization has been evident in Tesco since 1994. In general, organic growth or small acquisitions have been the favoured development mechanism. This is slow, at least initially until an understanding of the market is obtained. The pattern has been one of slow growth and only after several years has growth quickened. This is seen in the pattern of new opening planned for 2005 (Table 8.5) as related to length of time in the country. With the exception of Taiwan the rapid growth is in countries entered before 2000. Tesco is able to accommodate slow initial growth and a relatively long initial payback on investment because of the strength in the domestic market.

Table 8.6 shows the typical timetable for development in a country in which entry is through organic growth or through organic growth following a small acquisition. By 2005 only the earliest entered countries were providing a return on investment that fitted with Tesco long-term expectations.

Table 8.6 Timescale for development through small acquisition or organic growth

Activity	Typical time in years
Market research and knowledge assimilation	Indeterminate but seldom less than 2.5
Decision in principle to proceed with entry or acquisition – entry team established to propose mechanisms for entry	0.2
Identify target acquisition or find first substantive site	1–1.5
Undertake acquisition or gain permissions to construct	0.5
Build and fit out new store	0.5
Time to first new store opening from initial reviews	3.5–4.5 years
Post-entry period to achieving development to growth of about 6 stores per year	Variable but seldom less than 4
Maturity of store to provide 20% return	3
Total time for return on investment to achieve acceptable level	8–9

Knowledge transfers in Tesco's internationalization

There are several major areas where transferring UK knowledge to the international operations has been undertaken. The international operations are viewed as an important aspect of the overall strategy of Tesco and so knowledge transfer is a major activity both from UK to foreign markets and back to the UK from the international operations (Palmer 2005; Palmer and Quinn 2005).

Increased regional sourcing capability. This is allowing country operations to source locally. Using experience in the UK, this activity is most advanced in Central Europe where links have been established with small- and medium-sized suppliers. The experience from Central Europe is now to be transferred to Asia. This is important in enabling Tesco to adapt its operations to local conditions and, particularly, to local consumer demand. It also provides for transfer of knowledge on suppliers from the foreign countries back to the domestic operations. This is particularly important in non-food items and has helped the expansion of non-food ranges in the UK.

Extend data sharing with major multinational suppliers. This is part of Tesco's global sourcing initiative to enable volume purchasing in long-term relationships with suppliers. Multinational suppliers are given access to information from Tesco's international operations and this enables cost benefits on product development, scheduling and logistics to both Tesco and the supplier.

Transfer of the multi-format approach. The multi-format approach when trading in the foreign market has become stable and established. The markets where experience is greatest, therefore, have more new format development. Express stores are being introduced slowly into foreign markets, for example, South Korea and Thailand. In Thailand a low price formula has been developed that includes a traditional wet market within the formula. In Central European markets a 'compact' hypermarket formula has been developed to complement the full size Tesco hypermarket formula. Supermarkets of around 10,000 square feet began to be developed from 2004 in several Central European markets. These stores are targeted at the medium-sized towns that are not large enough to sustain a full-size hypermarket. Although the principle of a multi-format approach is transferred, the detail of the formula in use is strongly influenced by local market conditions. The increase in store numbers in many markets that is planned for 2005, as shown in Table 8.5, reflects the development of Tesco Express and supermarkets in several countries. The Tesco model of internet-based shopping has been transferred to Ireland and to parts of South Korea.

Transfer of retail branding. In most markets Tesco is used as the branding for the store but this can be in association with a strong local brand when entry and early development was by acquisition. Thus, for example, in South Korea, Homeplus is used, in Thailand Tesco Lotus, and Tsurukame has been retained in Japan. The UK product branding strategy has been transferred to most international operations. The three price-quality positions retail the Tesco names. Value lines have been introduced into Central European and Asian stores, for example, 500 items in Hungary where the Value brand was launched in 1988 and 600 in Poland. In Thailand the brand initially was Super Save in 1999 but was relaunched as Khum Kha, in 2002, but its price position is similar to Value. Tesco products are also available in foreign stores with a much smaller number of items, typically 600–800 but with over 1,000 in Hungary. The Finest range has had minimal transfer to international markets with some items on sale in long-established markets, for example 20 items in Hungary. The specialist brands from the UK have been adapted to local conditions. For example, Healthy Living was launched in Hungary in 2003 with 60 items under the name Fitt.

Centralize supply chains. In the UK central distribution resulted in increased efficiency of the supply chain. This expertise is now being transferred to international markets. Examples include a large central distribution centre of 1.5 million square feet at Mokdong to serve South Korea, and in Hungary a centre with automated warehouse that was opened in 2002 and expanded in 2003 and a fresh food distribution centre at Gyál that opened in 2004. In 2004 in Poland the first central distribution centre for ambient items, of 400,000 square feet, was opened at Teresin, near Warsaw, and later in the year a 160,000-square-feet centre for fresh items was opened in the same logistics park.

Move Every Day Low Pricing (EDLP) policy to international markets. The consumer cultures in several of the non-UK markets in which Tesco operates appear to prefer promotions and High-Low pricing. The success of EDLP in the UK allows Tesco to transfer EDLP to its international markets and so be different from other retailers, emphasizing low prices as the normal situation. This is a slow process of transfer involving changes in consumer attitudes. Some price policies are across several countries, for example a price cut on 50 key Value lines was undertaken across the Czech Republic, Hungary and Slovakia in December 2004.

Transferring retailing services to the international markets. This includes, for example, the transfer of customer loyalty schemes to international markets. Clubcard has been introduced in Thailand and South Korea. These services related options were not introduced initially but as development becomes established so service aspects are introduced as part of the overall establishment of the Tesco culture in the foreign market.

Types of knowledge transferred. The knowledge used in the internationalization of retailing may be categorized in a variety of ways. Experiential knowledge, which is implicit knowledge gained through operations in the domestic market, is often situation specific. This type of knowledge arises as development in the foreign country occurs and is used to localize the operations in a country. There is some experiential knowledge that can be transferred from one foreign entry to another. Thus, the experience gained in Hungary was useful for entry to Poland and meetings to exchange information between the country managers of the Central European markets took place. This knowledge comes from practical experience. Routine knowledge comes from learning about the way things work, for example knowledge about how to operate a distribution depot for Tesco, and this becomes transferred to operating the distribution centres in the foreign markets. Often the routine knowledge is changed into more explicit systematic knowledge that is codified into operating manuals. Thus, Tesco have codified the operating procedures for a country manager into a development programme and documentation that provides the procedures for establishing operations in a country. Conceptual knowledge is also explicit and results from the design and use of the symbols of the firm – what can and cannot be done with brands, for example. The Tesco Steering Wheel for planning and budgeting (Figure 8.2) is widely used across all the international operations and provides an explicit statement of the framework of processes. The knowledge that is required to produce actual plans and budgets in each country draws on other forms of knowledge, particularly experiential knowledge.

TESCO POLSKA, SAMSUNG TESCO AND TING CAO

As illustration of the extent of international development and the relationship with the domestic operation it is useful to consider the ways Tesco has entered and grown in Poland, South Korea and China. The three cases illustrate some differences as knowledge has been gained.

Tesco Polska Sp. Zo.o

Tesco entered Poland in 1995 through acquisition of a minority stake in a small chain of 36 stores, some selling groceries and some selling homewares and furniture. The attraction of the firm as an acquisition target was less the store network and more the senior Polish managers who had shown ability to manage successfully in the complex environment in Poland in the early 1990s. The initial stake was increased such that Tesco owns 98 per cent.

Although initial plans were for the development of discount stores this was changed when Tesco management saw the activities of French and German retailers in the Polish market. The first Tesco hypermarket was opened in 1998 and this marked a period of focus on developing and adapting a Tesco hypermarket formula. Development was relatively slow because of difficulty in obtaining sites such that by 2001 only ten stores had been developed with a further five in the pipeline. The decision in 2002 of Dohle, an early entrant into hypermarket retailing in Poland, to refocus on Germany, provided Tesco with the opportunity to make a small acquisition that doubled its hypermarket network and paved the way for a viable central distribution system. The Dohle acquisition comprised 13 HIT hypermarkets, two stores under construction and several sites for future development. Changing the HIT formula to the Tesco formula was completed in 2003 using systems transferred from existing stores and from the UK. With the additional stores under construction and the new sites, Tesco was able to open five new stores in 2003. By the end of 2004 there were 44 Tesco superstores in operation.

By 2004 the development of a multi-format approach was becoming apparent. Alongside the core Tesco hypermarket formula of 70–90,000 square feet a compact formula of around 50,000 square feet was being developed. This is a Tesco formula that has been developed for introduction into several Central European markets and particularly for the smaller regional cities. Additionally, in October 2004, the first of a new supermarket formula was opened. This is about 20,000 square feet with a very limited non-food range. By summer 2005, four were operational with six more under construction. The acquisition of nine supermarkets from Julius Meinl in 2005 will add to this supermarket network.

The step growth provided by Dohle reinforced the need for central distribution. The first centre, of 400,000 square feet, was opened in 2004 at Teresin near Warsaw, Poland, but initially served all the hypermarkets. A second centre has been built close to the first for fresh produce. These centres, by 2005, were handling 95 per cent of the volume passing into stores. There are plans for two more, one in Silesia to serve the south of Poland and one in the west at Poznan. These four centres will service the total store network as it grows through to 2009.

Tesco brand products in 2004 accounted for approximately 14 per cent of sales. The range is limited but increasing with approximately 600 items in the standard range and the same number in the Value range. By 2006 it is planned to double the number of items in the Tesco branded ranges.

After initial slow development in Poland, not only in developing the store network but also transferring knowledge in the areas of logistics and brand development, the pace has quickened since 2003. This follows the somewhat opportunistic acquisition of Dohle's HIT hypermarkets. Other firms were also targeting this acquisition. The success by Tesco provided the step change need to propel development to the next stage of multi-format network development. By 2007 Tesco will have added 2 million square feet of new space in the four years since its acquisition of Dohle and be trading from close to 5 million square feet in total. The possibility of more acquisitions as the Polish market structure concentrates could increase the network even more.

Samsung Tesco Co. Ltd

In South Korea, Tesco bought 51 per cent of the distribution operations of Samsung Corporation in May 1999 for $250 million (Choi 2003). The assets comprised two trading Homeplus hypermarkets and three sites for development. Tesco has steadily increased its ownership to 81 per cent in June 1999 and 89 per cent in February 2004. Although a joint venture agreement has been signed until 2011, when Tesco will own 99 per cent, effective ownership is through Tesco. In January 2005 acquisition of 12 stores from Aram Mart in Pusan was agreed.

By the start of 2001 a total of seven stores were operating. During 2001, seven more hypermarkets were opened and a further eight in 2002 and six in 2003. This rapid growth triggered the need for the new distribution centre at Mokdong, opened in 2003, which serves all South Korea and is capable of expansion. By the autumn of 2005, 35 hypermarkets were in operation. The early hypermarkets were in excess of 100,000 square feet but developments since 2003 have tended to be around 80,000 square feet with sites for this size of store easier to obtain. Around 75,000 SKUs are present in the product file. In 2003 the development of Tesco Express was announced with the first store opened in April 2004, followed by a further six during the year. These stores range in size from 1,850 square feet to over 10,000 square feet but the target size is 4,500–5,000 square feet. In the acquisition of Aram were six stores suitable for conversion to Tesco Express. During 2005, 24 new Express stores were planned. This acquisition also has made possible the creation of a compact hypermarket or large supermarket formula. By Autumn 2005, three of these had been developed with 30–40,000 square feet. Development of more of these stores is anticipated.

Considerable efforts have been made to adapt Homeplus stores to respond to Korean consumer tastes. Stores are often in shopping centre complexes that include a food court and some small shop units. Culture centres have been introduced into many stores as places where educational and craft skills classes can be attended. The Tesco loyalty card was introduced in 2002 and this was linked to a Tesco Homeplus credit card. Homeplus brands are increasing with around 500 items and the Value brand has been added in a small number of food ranges. These Tesco brands, however, account for less than 5 per cent of sales. In non-food there are a large number of labels, particularly in clothing, but these are not always clearly targeted. The Tesco internet shopping system is available, www.homeplus.co.kr, for customers linked to ten stores.

One of the difficulties that had to be overcome was the lack of recognition of the Tesco name. This has been overcome by using Homeplus as the formula name and by retaining the name Samsung in the name of the firm. Extensive PR has been undertaken to build brand recognition and links have been built with governmental agencies and suppliers. Samsung Tesco was awarded the title as Most Ethical Firm in 2003. It is claimed that 95 per cent of items are sourced from South Korea through 3,500 suppliers but increasing amounts of the non-food ranges are sourced in China so this percentage is likely to fall. Most of the food items are sourced from within South Korea.

On current growth trends and from announcements by Tesco, by the end of 2008 it is expected that there will be at least 60 hypermarkets, ten compact hypermarkets/large supermarkets and 160 Tesco Express. Growth could be even greater if opportunities arise for small scale acquisitions similar to Aram Mart. This network, of probably about 5 million square feet, will represent a decade of involvement in the South Korean market.

Ting Cao

Tesco's entry into China was in 2004 through a 50/50 joint venture with Ting Cao for operation of Hymall stores. The investment by Tesco was £140 million. Stores operated by Ting Cao are also present in Taiwan where they compete with Tesco Taiwan but the Taiwanese stores were not included in the agreement. In 2004 there were 26 hypermarkets in China, including 11 in Shanghai, operated as per the Hymall formula and an additional ten under development. At the time of the joint venture Hymall did not have central distribution. There is also no retail brand development of items.

The new stores developed under the Hymall formula are typically 80–100,000 square feet. The opening plans are ambitious with 15 actively planned to be opened during 2005. By 2005, the focus on Shanghai will generate a critical mass large enough to warrant the development of central distribution facilities and potentially retail brand product development. The speed of new store development is much greater than in Tesco's previous international activities. Transfer of expertise will have to take place at a much faster pace than in previous international ventures. On expected developments almost 2 million square feet of additional space will have been added in the two years 2004 and 2005. The 5 million-square-foot watershed is likely to be achieved within three years of Tesco becoming a joint venture partner. This very rapid development is likely to test the processes that Tesco have in place for the international transfer of expertise and knowledge and may require new processes to be created.

CONCLUSIONS AND FUTURE DEVELOPMENTS

In evaluating Tesco's international retail approach some conclusions can be drawn that both provide a framework for understanding developments so far and indicate possible future issues. Several of these issues are ones that are relevant to understanding retail internationalization as a process and Tesco serves as an illustration of these general points.

In general, developing economies have been the target markets but Japan and the use of e-retail expertise in the US are the exceptions. Given the general proclivity to developing economies the expansion of activity in China and Turkey is likely to be an important development over the next few years. In all cases there is extensive evaluation of markets, usually for at least two years, before a decision is made. On this basis future targets are likely to include large markets, for example, European Russia and main island Indonesia with some smaller markets also likely to be of interest, for example, Vietnam, Slovenia, Croatia, Bulgaria and Romania. In all of Tesco's entry activities there is an element of adventitious activity in respect of timing and vehicle for entry.

The strong business in the UK has been an essential prerequisite for international expansion. Success in international moves only occurred after the changes of the early 1990s secured a sufficiently strong UK position. Growth in the UK has provided a strong cash flow and the negative working capital, resulting particularly from moves into non-foods in the UK, have been important as underpinnings of international expansion where returns are slow. Expansion in the UK in Express and Extra formulae will continue to provide the necessary security for funding.

Entry into foreign markets has generally been by a small acquisition or joint venture followed by organic growth or further small acquisitions. This has occurred in most markets with the search for a joint venture partner in Taiwan eventually being abandoned in favour of organic growth. The use of a joint venture partner or small acquisition speeds up the learning process by two to three years. This is a low risk approach and contrasts strongly with Wal-Mart's entry mechanisms into Europe and Japan. The Tesco approach requires the collection of considerable local knowledge on the firms in the market. By targeting developing markets and the fragmented market of Japan so it will be possible to continue to expand by a mixture of small acquisitions and organic growth.

Development after entry has drawn heavily on the multi-format concept with the format being adjusted to a formula for the local market. There has been use of a common format with adjustments by country. Thus, the hypermarket format has been developed in most of the markets but with significant local adjustments, for example, to respond to the nature of the built environment in South Korea where stores can be multi-level, and in Central Europe where the addition of a small number of additional specialist stores creates a French-style focused shopping centre with the Tesco formula hypermarket as anchor. Similarly, there are adaptions to the Express formula to adapt it to Thailand and South Korea. This adaption process may create new formulae, for example, with the discount formula in Thailand and the compact hypermarket in Central Europe. These new forms come when the common format has become established. It can be expected that more new formulae will emerge as operations become established and learning increases.

By having a common format but varied formulae the speed of growth is quickened because core systems can be transferred quite easily. Quickly achieving a critical scale in the market is important to support central distribution and the management of relationships with local suppliers. The focus on a few countries and a few formats potentially allows relatively rapid growth to the critical level of 20–25 hypermarkets, at which point centralized logistics becomes economical, and promotional activity, Tesco branded items and staff development start to respond to scale economies. In all the countries these scale economies will become more important over the next stages of international development.

The presence of common back office systems enables the international operation to be effective quickly and provides the potential for transfer of key success factors from the UK, for example, the use of Clubcard in South Korea and the transfer of established internal communication systems. A further central and common facility is the use of centralized buying systems for stores. By providing common core systems there is then the scope to adapt shop-floor operations to the local consumer culture (Rogers et al. 2005). The implication of this combination of standardized and localized features is that Tesco is able to transfer its retail capability into the new market. The transfer from the domestic to the international operations will continue and, in addition, in the future there are likely to be more transfers between foreign markets, particularly those within the same culture realm. Thus, ideas for operations are likely to be transferred around Asian countries, for example, with aspects of the discount formulae in Thailand being transferred to other Asian countries.

Management systems in the foreign markets are built around a small number of Tesco managers and recruitment and development of local managers. The initial research is carried out by a small team of five or six managers. The implementation team is similarly small, usually of five or six which is then gradually reduced to key managers comprising the local Chief Operating Officer, Finance Director and Director with responsibility for property/site evaluation. Local managers are important for their local knowledge of consumer and employee practices, and of relationships with suppliers and government agencies. The use of the Tesco Steering Wheel and balanced scorecard for planning and budgeting is an important part of the development of the local management. The gradual passing of responsibilities to locally recruited managers is likely to continue in the future.

A final factor evident in the success of the internationalization activity of any retail firm is the need for stakeholder communication. In the case of Tesco this has been present in the explanations to shareholder investors of what to expect from the international growth. The slow build up and the delay in returns has been explained to investors who generally expect more rapid returns from investment. It has been necessary to explain the difference between domestic and international operations. Similarly important is communication to government agencies as another stakeholder in the foreign firm. In the retailing context the ultimate stakeholder is the customer. Communication to the customer through branding, through all aspects of store operations, and through the corporate culture is vital such that the consumer, who initially is unlikely to have any knowledge of the foreign firms, can quickly gain understanding of what the foreign retailer is offering that is new, different and of value.

REFERENCES

Akehurst, G. (1984) 'Checkout': the analysis of oligopolistic behaviour in the UK grocery retail market. *Service Industries Journal*, 3: 161–179

Choi, S. C. (2003) Moves into the Korean market by global retailers and the response of local retailers: lessons for the Japanese retailing sector? In: J. Dawson, M. Mukoyama, S. C. Choi and R. Larke (eds) *The internationalisation of retailing in Asia*. (London: RoutledgeCurzon) pp. 49–66

Dawson, J. (2001) Strategy and opportunism in European retail internationalization. *British Journal of Management*, 12(4): 253–266

Dawson, J. (2004) Retail change in Britain during 30 years: the strategic use of economies of scale and scope. Paper to BAM Conference, 1 September

Dawson, J. and Henley, J. (2002) The internationalization of grocery retailing in Poland after 1989. In: M. A. Marinov (ed.) *Internationalization in Central and Eastern Europe*. (Burlington: Ashgate) pp. 169–180

Fulop, C. (1964) *Competition for consumers*. (London: George Allen & Unwin)

Humby, C., Hunt, T. and Phillips, T. (2003) *Scoring points: how Tesco is winning customer loyalty*. (London: Kogan Page)

Palmer, M. (2005) Retail multinational learning: a case study of Tesco. *International Journal of Retail and Distribution Management*, 33(1): 23–48

Palmer, M. and Quinn, B. (2005) An exploratory framework for analysing international retail learning. *International Review of Retail, Distribution and Consumer Research*, 14(1): 27–52

Pickering, J. F. (1974) The retail trades without RPM. In: D. Thorpe (ed.) *Research into retailing and distribution*. (Farnborough: Saxon House) pp. 23–41

Powell, D. (1991) *Counter revolution: the Tesco story*. (London: Grafton Books)

Rogers, H., Ghauri, P. N. and George, K. L. (2005) The impact of market orientation on the internationalization of retailing firms: Tesco in Eastern Europe. *International Review of Retail, Distribution and Consumer Research*, 14(1): 53–74

Seth, A. and Randall, G. (1999) *The grocers: the rise and rise of the supermarket chains*. (London: Kogan Page)

Smith, D. L. G. and Sparks, L. (1993) The transformation of physical distribution in retailing: the example of Tesco stores. *International Review of Retail, Distribution and Consumer Research*, 3(1): 35–64

Wileman, A. and Jary, M. (1997) *Retail power plays*. (London: Macmillan)

Yahagi, T. (2003) The internationalisation process of Tesco in Asia. In: Proceedings of the Asia Pacific Retail Conference 2002 (Oxford: Templeton College) pp. 36–53

Chapter 9

The international transfer of key success factors

John Dawson and Masao Mukoyama

INTRODUCTION

The internationalization of Wal-Mart stores since November 1991 has raised awareness of the international activities of retailers. Over 1,000 stores outside the US were operated by Wal-Mart within a decade of their first international move. Similarly, the substantial development of Tesco, Zara and many other major European firms has occurred since the early 1990s and highlighted the opportunities and impacts of international retailing. Mintel (2003) identified 2,588 intra-European cross-border retailers operating 74,160 stores in 2002. Many of these had been initiated in the previous decade although a few have a longer history. These intra-European developments represent approximately two-thirds of all cross-border retail operations by European-based retailers. The international operations of large Asian retailers are even more recent with foreign sales being only a few per cent of total sales in the major Japanese firms even in 2004. There are a few exceptions with a longer history among the food and grocery-based retailers; Carrefour, Auchan, Ahold, Delhaize le Lion, Metro from Europe, and Dairy Farm and A. S. Watson in Asia, have a somewhat longer history but even with these firms the major expansion of international activity is relatively recent, dating from the mid-1990s. Specialized retailers, for example, Laura Ashley, Benetton, Body Shop, have operated internationally for longer but again it is since the early 1990s that retailers have expanded their international networks of stores and more specialist retailers have moved into operating internationally.

It is not only the amount of international activity that has changed since the early 1990s there has also been a major shift in the pattern of markets addressed. Until the end of the 1990s and while there are some exceptions, American-based retailers generally explored international opportunities in Canada or, to a lesser extent, moved into Mexico. European retailers for the most part remained within the Western European market although some explored Central Europe from the mid-1990s. Historically, there have been some high-profile failures when European retailers moved to the US or Asia and when American retailers have moved to Europe. These failures appeared to serve as warnings to retailers considering intercontinental developments. The international aspirations of Wal-Mart have changed this pattern. International activity outside their home continent has become, since about 2000, a significant strategic trend for the major retailers. Major retailers from Europe and the US have become established in South America and Asia, such that for the first time substantive competition is occurring between American-style and European-style retail management (see Chapter 2).

In this final chapter we consider come of the key success factors of European retailers during the period of increased internationalization starting in the late twentieth century. The success or otherwise of internationalization for many firms will depend on the extent to which these factors are transferable internationally within Europe and from a European managerial environment to an Asian or American environment. We conclude the chapter with some considerations on the current and likely future impacts that international retailers may have on the societies into which they move.

THE EMERGENCE OF CRITICAL FACTORS FOR THE SUCCESS OF RETAILING

Davies (1998) has argued cogently for an evolutionary view of retailing development. Retailing is not a new industry, unlike the electronics or the aero-space industries. The retail sector of today results from a continuous process of structural change and adjustment within a very varied base of resources across the constituent firms. Some retail networks, buildings, management practices, and many companies of 2005 were in operation in 1950. Other features of retailing are of very recent origin. In order to understand the nature of the sector, and its success factors, in 2005 it is important to see these in historical perspective.

It is now widely recognized that the balance of power in consumer goods markets in Europe moved steadily in favour of retailers in the post-1945 era. The move was gradual for several decades but has quickened since the 1980s. This shift in power in the economic system has had consequences for the management and operation of retailers across Europe. A European retail managerial style has emerged that results from the changing structure of the retail sector since the middle of the twentieth century. This changing structure can be seen to comprise three major phases, each characterized by a particularly potent managerial innovation. First, there was self-service, second the concept of marketing and third the convergence of information and communication technologies (Dawson 1999). The pattern of change that has resulted from these successive innovations has created the managerial environment on which the internationalization process has been based.

For about two decades after 1945 there was a period of rebuilding and reconstruction of infrastructure and the establishment of a sound base to consumer demand. Jefferys and Knee (1962), in their classic account, describe the state of retailing at this time. Store size was being steadily increased with the advent of self-service (Bauman 1956; Henksmeier 1960; Thygesen 1951). The Chambers of Commerce in France and Italy were already exhibiting a powerful role protecting smaller firms, and ideas were emerging of stimulating growth and reconstruction through growth poles linked to new towns with shopping centres at their core. Dickinson's (1951) study of the history of the West European city pointed to the importance of retailing in sustaining city centres. Relationships between retailers and suppliers were hotly debated within a public policy framework as pressures grew for the abolition of Resale Price Maintenance (Boggis 1966). Although some of today's issues were present there were two major differences that made retailing in the 1950s and 1960s radically different, namely a legacy of recent product shortages and rationing and Resale Price Maintenance. Not only was there not a surfeit of product but also there was little price competition possible by retailers. Manufacturers controlled the channel. Retailers, therefore, focused on making profits from store operation rather than from sourcing. The innovation of self-service that swept through Europe in the 1950s and 1960s, therefore, was a fundamental innovation that changed the way retailers managed their stores. Self-service and supermarkets had a profound impact on retailers and consumers in changing methods of merchandising, changing the systems of stock management and passing to consumers some of the costs previously carried by the retailer.

In the 1970s and 1980s the strong moves to European integration with the consolidation of the idea of the European Common Market generated substantial economic growth and an increase in demand for goods and services. Retailers at this time were influenced by the second major innovation, namely, the idea and philosophy of marketing. Until this period retailers had been mainly concerned with shop-level sales, not with marketing. Consumers had been content to buy more products from displays in-store but by the 1970s the consumers were seeking different and better products, not simply more. Retailers had to respond to new demands from consumers and also to increased competition from other retailers who were being freed from the controlling influences of manufacturers. Marketing as a managerial concept provided a way for retailers to begin to change the profit balance in the distribution chain, moving profit from manufacturer and supplier to retailers. Managerial practice in retailing began to consider the vertical value chain as well as the shop-floor efficiencies.

With the acceptance of marketing ideas so retailers began to segment the market and focus the stores on different groups of consumers, using techniques of store design, merchandising, promotion, new pricing tactics and service-related activities. Retailers began the serious development of retail branded products, taking control of aspects of product development previously undertaken by suppliers and manufacturers. As market segmentation developed, so many types of retailer explored new formats. For example, the large self-service, single-level superstore format, often located on the edge or out-of-town, was developed through the 1970s and early 1980s in several sectors, notably the hypermarket for general merchandise (Dawson 1984), and superstores for food, DIY, toys, electrical goods, furniture, etc. Much of the innovation at this time was internal to Europe as the large firms consolidated in their national markets. Although there were some influences from North America, a distinctly European style of retail management was emerging.

The third phase of evolution is one of restructuring operations into a network structure and is particularly associated with the convergence of information and communication technologies. This has resulted in new approaches to retail competition with global sourcing and the efficient operation of network firms, some with over 5,000 stores. Firm structures have been able to be changed to be networked so enabling a more widely spatially dispersed structure of sourcing and operations. Economies of scale have been obtained with the larger spatial networks. The retail sector, in consequence, is passing through a period of substantial restructuring with the closure of many thousands of retailers each year and the consolidation of operations into fewer, often larger firms. This is generating substantial market concentration. Now we see the transfer of ideas within Europe and also to and from countries outside Europe. It is as part of this third phase that the substantial internationalization has taken place.

The European retail management style, therefore, has developed through these three phases, each marked by a major innovation. Over the same period the retail sector has taken on a new role within the European economy. Retailers and distributors have become more powerful in their relationships with other groups in the economy. Distribution has become more influential in the macro economy becoming an economic sector comparable in size and complexity to manufacturing. When comparison is made among Europe, the US and Japan there are contrasts, therefore, in retail management style and in the role and influence on the economy of the distribution sector. Within each of the three economic cultures the evolution, development and innovatory path of retailing has been different. In considering the internationalization process, therefore, it is necessary to understand the origins of the firms involved and the economic realms in which they are rooted.

In establishing the new distinctive role for retailing, the leading firms have developed a distinctive European model of management in retailing and distribution (Costa *et al.* 1997; Dawson 2005; Eurostat 2000, 2002). This European model is:

- Internationalist in outlook, not domestic; compare, for example, Metro and Tesco from Europe with Kroger and Target rooted in the US or Aeon and Ito Yokado from Japan. The initiative of the Single European Market in 1992 was influential in widening the horizons of the domestic operators in Europe and encouraging them to explore markets beyond their immediate milieu. The opening of Central Europe to investment from West European retailers was a further major stimulus to the development of the more internationalist view. Reinforcement occurred with the launch of the single European currency.

- Structured around a consumer-driven integrated demand chain, not a supplier-driven supply chain. This is evident in firms in many sectors, for example, Zara, IKEA and Lidl. This means that the retail firm is making profits at several points in the channel not only at the point of sale to the final customer. The relationship between stock-turn and supplier payment period is different in the European model from the American or Japanese model. This is also seen in differences in apparent productivity, particularly labour productivity, which has risen sharply in America when measured for firms focusing only on the final stage of the channel and increases have been less for, often more profitable, European firms having a greater involvement in more channel functions (Reynolds et al. 2005).

- Built around a core of market innovation, not copying. The adoption of retail marketing in the large firms from the 1970s has spread through the whole sector to become a widespread feature of European retailing. This has increased the emphasis on innovation and competing by being different rather than benchmarking against standard approaches of competitors. Benchmarking and copying across Europe have also been rejected in many cases because the considerable variety in consumers and cultures that exist in Europe reduces the value of these comparisons. Innovation and adaption, therefore, have become a core aspect of the European approach to retail management.

- Using network structures to create the management controls. Relationships between retailers and suppliers have involved a major shift in power towards retailers but also the nature of the relationship has changed to it being less transactional and more cooperative. This does not necessarily lessen the competitive aspects but the nature of the relationship has changed to one of achieving joint objectives and greater use of concepts of trust (Nooteboom and Six 2003). This has resulted in the European retail management model becoming less transactional in style and culture. The network style has been evident also in the ways that horizontal structures among firms and shops have been operated. For corporate chain store operations the size of the network that can be managed has increased, due in large part to changes in technology, and for alliance chain store operations, for example Leclerc, Intersport, Euromadi, Edeka and the like, the network form has proved to be successful.

- Adaptability. The considerable variety of long-established national, regional and even local cultures in Europe has forced retailers to eschew standardized approaches and required them to be locally adaptive in their operations. This has resulted in a management style more sympathetic to the need for local adaptions.

A distinctive European retail management style has emerged that reflects the variety of societies and cultures within Europe and the historical evolution of the sector. The key factors of the success of European retailing relate to the emergence and increasingly strong presence of a particular managerial style. An important consideration for the future intercontinental spread of international retailing is whether or not the European approach is transferable to other culture realms. This is particularly relevant to moves into Asia where cultural values and even ways of thinking contrast strongly with those in Europe and North America (Nisbett 2003).

CHARACTERISTICS OF THE EXPANDING INTERNATIONAL RETAILERS

In considering the reasons behind the domestic successes of European retail firms, both large and small, it is possible to identify five factors. All the successful firms have an emphasis on *innovation* – innovation in formats, processes and items for sale. In addition, the firms have one or more of other success factors that are attributable to them. Most of them have *taken control of branding* and the retailer now controls branding, not the manufacturer. Most have *entered and adapted to new markets*. These are new market places in their own country and elsewhere in Europe. In addition several have entered new service markets, for example, financial services. Most have sought *economies of scale and scope* in respect particularly of sourcing and marketing. Most have tried to find ways to *increase the speed of response*, notably the speed at which managerial processes operate and the speed at which managerial decisions are made. In terms of the future development of international retailing a key question is the extent to which these success factors can be transferred beyond Europe.

Innovation

Innovation in a retailing context is apparent in three important areas. Innovation can be applied to format and formula development. Innovation can be applied to the processes that operate within the retail firm. Innovation can also be applied to the items (goods and services) that are sold by the retailer. To some extent there is overlap in the ways that the innovations have effect (LSA 2004) but it is useful to consider innovation in these ways when viewing the transferability of this key factor.

Examples of innovation applied to formats are changes that provide faster, easier and better customer service. Electronic pricing and customer self-scanning are specific examples that are now becoming more widespread. Technology is critical in these examples and is relatively easy to transfer from domestic to international operations. Developments in shelf-ready packaging (see Chapter 8) are of this type. Innovation can also be seen in many aspects of store design and layout, for example the experimental stores developed by Ahold (see Chapter 7).

The development of totally new formulae provides further examples of innovation at this level. The Tesco decision to develop a Tesco Express formula for the convenience store format involved an innovatory approach to rapid store development and conversion. The operation of these stores required new ways of thinking about providing logistics services to small stores.

Format innovation is a major part of retail innovation. It is transferable across borders in Europe and transferable from Europe to Asia. This is clearly evident in the ways that ideas about formulae development in the domestic markets of Carrefour, Tesco and Zara are transferred to formulae in Asian markets. Also new formats emerge in the new markets as is seen in the new Value format of Tesco in Thailand and in the compact hypermarkets in Central Europe.

In addition to format innovation, there is innovation in the processes within the firm. Important here are innovations to remove costs from the supply chain with retailers taking control of logistics and operating through central distribution depots. Similarly, innovation can occur in the design and development systems for products and their distribution to stores. The new systems devised by Zara are examples of this type of innovation (see Chapter 4). The international transfer of the systems associated with operational process involves the production of manuals and documents that make explicit the tacit knowledge involved. This is a broad managerial issue (Augier and Vendolø 1999; Bennett 1998) but is particularly relevant in highly networked retail firms.

The third area of innovation is in the items for sale. Ready-to-eat meals, or meal solutions, are good examples of innovation at the item level. This is a rapidly expanding product category in all the successful food retailers and has become an important means of inter-firm competition. A further food category where item-level innovation is extensive is in organic products. This initially was in fresh products but has been extended to processed foods and even to non-food so that organic clothing is now available as a specialist product category. A variety of more exotic and ethnic food items have also been added to the ranges of retailers to increase their competitiveness. There is also widespread innovation in non-food areas, for example, in furniture, home furnishings and fashion.

Innovation by retailers, therefore, can be seen as transferable but there is a combination of managerial practice and consumer acceptability that is necessary before the innovation becomes successful for the retailer. Innovation is the essence of being able to compete in a highly competitive market. Consistent innovation is the way that retailers have been able to compete with established and new competitors.

Innovative stores, systems and products are able to be transferred internationally. But being innovative in the domestic market does not automatically mean that international success will follow (see Chapter 6). While innovation is necessary for success in international retailing it is not a determinant of automatic success. Innovation as an aspect of management and the results of innovation are transferable internationally.

Control of the brand

The second key approach of European retailers in becoming competitively successful has been through taking control of the brand. The brand concept in retailing is complex. The brand operates at three levels: that of the company, the store and the item for sale. Each is different but when retailers align their brand activities across all three levels then they become significant brands. Thus, the retail firm becomes a brand. In some cases the power of the retailer and the strength of their brand have become so dominant that the activities of the manufacturer can be seen as complementing the activities of the retailer rather than the more traditional reverse of this situation.

In non-food categories retailing brands have long been a major aspect of competition by retailers. IKEA, Marks & Spencer, Benetton and many others have shown that it is possible to have shops that are single-brand shops with the brand owned and controlled by the retailer. Only since the mid-1980s have the major food retailers realized the power of branding. Tesco (Chapter 8) has moved strongly in this area since the mid-1990s moving from branding the items for sale to branding their store formats. Similarly, Inditex (Chapter 4) is operating a portfolio of brands each targeting a different consumer group.

Alongside the branding of the stores there is strong branding of items for sale in the stores. Retail branding of items has been present for a considerable time but it has reached new levels of sophistication in recent years. Across many product categories in the food area it is not unusual for retailer branded items to be accounting for 40 per cent or more of sales volume. In the large discount food retailers, brands owned by the retailer can account for over 75 per cent of sales volume. This control by retailers of brands on sale in the store is present across all of the successful retailers, irrespective of retail sector, in all of the European countries.

The transferability of a brand to another cultural market is complex but can be successful as we see with some specialist retailers, particularly in non-foods. Louis Vuitton very clearly is successful in transferring their brand into Asian markets. When store, brand and item are very closely related, as with many specialist non-food retailers, transfer of the brand may be achieved with minimal adaption, but unless it meets consumer expectations success may be limited. For food and grocery retailers with a complex product portfolio of their own brand items and those of their suppliers, transfer is less straightforward. In transferring the brand to a new market it is often necessary to build the brand rather than expect it to obtain an immediate response from consumers. This may involve adaption of some of the peripheral brand values to allow the brand to engage with consumers. It will also involve a substantial programme of communication to consumers as was undertaken by Tesco in South Korea.

Few European retailers have so far been able to take control of all aspects of their brand when operating in another culture realm in the way that they have done in their home European markets. In general, retailers can more easily transfer their brands to culturally similar markets than to culturally distant ones.

Adaption to the market

Alongside the focus on innovation and on control of branding, the third of the five key success factors has been adaptability and adaption to new markets. This has occurred in several ways.

Existing formulae in home markets have been adapted to the changes in the customer base. Boots have adapted their formula in the UK to respond to consumer changes and also in response to competition from retailers in the food and grocery sector. Carrefour have changed their hypermarket formula in France with new concept stores being developed on a regular basis. Tesco moved away from the conforming store concept to more rapid formula evolution.

New formats have been developed in existing markets, for example, super-market retailers launching hypermarkets, and retailers launching Internet formats. Ahold and Tesco have both moved into convenience store formats within their domestic markets. Inditex has developed Zara Home in Spain to address the home-furnishings market. These developments have allowed retailers to become multi-format operators in domestic markets and so broaden their portfolio of target consumer groups.

Retailers have also entered new sectors in their domestic market. A major example is the expansion into banking that has been undertaken by several of the large firms, including Tesco. There has also been an expansion into food services, for example, with Ahold (see Chapter 7). Successful retailers have shown an ability to adapt their operations and even brands to address these new sector markets. Clearly in this exercise of adaption, innovation is an important activity.

Adaption is a fundamental prerequisite for entry by retailers into non-domestic markets. The major retailers are not global in their operation in the same way as major manufactures, for example, Sony, Microsoft, Shell, Coca-Cola, Unilever and the like. Retailers operate in local markets with local customers and so adaption to all aspects of local economy, society and politics is necessary. This not only involves adaption for entry but also continuing adaption as the market changes.

This requirement on the international retailer for continuous adaption to the local market is very strong. It sets international retailing apart from international production.

Thus the transferability of the ability to adapt is an essential part of international retail management. Adaptability in the home market is a key success factor for domestic operation. Not all firms are able to transfer to foreign markets this ability to adapt. While the core concepts of the firm are often relatively easily transferable, the responsiveness to local markets is much more difficult. The capability to adapt depends on the extent to which local managerial control is released by the head office of the retailer to enable decisions to be made locally. But, success also depends on consumers accepting the foreign firm's way of doing business and their approach to adaption.

Exploitation of economies of scale and scope

The fourth of the five success factors is the exploitation of the economies of scale and scope. The scale economies of the organization are much greater than the scale economies associated with shop size. Thus 7–11 in Japan, for example, gains great economies of scale although operating only small shops. The moves into convenience stores by Tesco results in an increase in organizational scale and consequent scale economies. It is not necessary to have large shops in order to gain scale economies if managerial processes are centralized. The scale economies for the large organization result from the consolidation of sourcing, benefits of replication of a store formula across many outlets and considerable scale-related benefits in marketing. Although organizational scale economies are more important there are scale economies to be gained, particularly in labour use, at the level of the formula. Carrefour's hypermarket, for example, has some cost returns to scale but the main reason for larger stores is the benefits they provide to consumers by providing a larger range and lower costs of shopping.

The largest area of scale economies of organization is in sourcing and it is these particularly that have proved to be so important for the large European firms. These scale-related benefits from sourcing occur when firms source centrally through a coordinated system of buying centres (see Chapter 2). The search costs for suppliers are reduced and volume-related discounts can be procured. This is evident in the large increase in sourcing from East Asia that major European retailers have undertaken. The consolidation of buying power is further illustrated by the discount supermarket retailers who have focused their buying power on a limited number of items and so gain substantial sourcing benefits on these items.

Scale-related benefits in marketing are illustrated by the promotional activity of Ahold (see Chapter 7) and the pricing activity of Asda Wal-Mart. Ahold's multinational promotion was run in 23 countries at the same time with 60 brands in 6,000 stores for two weeks. Although there are heavy organizational costs in undertaking a promotion of this type and also difficulties in ensuring the store disciplines to implement the promotions, there are pricing benefits that can be passed to consumers from consolidation of the buying power in this way. The pricing policy in Asda Wal-Mart also reflects the advantages of large-scale operation. The large volumes purchased provide substantial volume-related discounts to the buying price and this is passed to consumers with the aim to have a general price level at 5–10 per cent below the main competitors. Profit results from the increases in volume not from higher margins. The increases in sales volume then drive purchase prices even lower. The policy of Every Day Low Prices emphasizes volume by reducing the fluctuations in purchasing volumes. The EDLP policy carries through to merchandising with the lowest price being displayed rather than a price point ending in 5 or 9 (typical of traditional price points in Europe) being used. The EDLP policy is supplemented by very limited promotional activity.

The large retailers have been exploiting economies of scale for a considerable time and this has proved to be an important factor of competitive advantage. A more recent source of competitive advantage is the increase in the exploitation of economies of scope. These previously were seen as a competitive advantage for smaller firms in which they could match closely, their total product and service offering, to the local market. The large firms have been able to take similar measures through the use of loyalty cards and customer information collected in other ways (see Chapter 4). In addition to the store-level scope economies associated with more competitive ranges there have also been scope economies obtained at organization level. These economies result from multi-format operation and sectoral diversification in which costs are shared across the different formats and across sectors, for example, Ahold's and Tesco's use of the information systems of stores to support the operation of their financial services initiatives.

Many of these economies of scale and of scope are transferable by the large European firms into foreign markets. The transferability is possible because the economies derive from managerial systems that can be transferred. Some of the economies of scale, for example, associated with logistics and advertising, can only be transferred when the retailer achieves a local critical mass in the foreign market rather than achieving scale in the firm overall. Nonetheless, scale economies are achievable in the foreign operations, irrespective of the culture realm. Similarly, there do not appear to be reasons why the economies of scope cannot also be obtained in foreign markets.

Faster operation of all processs

The final major success factor evidenced by the European firms in their domestic markets is the ability of the firms to have faster responses throughout all business processes. While there is argument over whether retailing has become more complex over the second half of the twentieth century there is little dispute over the view that response times have been reduced and competitive processes operate at a faster rate. The ability to accommodate the faster rate is a key factor in the competitive success of retailers.

The faster competitive responsiveness is seen in many ways, for example, in responding to price reductions or promotions in other firms, in taking time out of the supply chain and in the speed at which stores are developed. Products are developed more quickly to enter the retail brand ranges with the result that test marketing stages may be removed and items sent directly to stores such that all marketing is, in effect, test marketing (see Chapter 4).

This success factor of the speeding up of activity is transferable internationally but for many foreign markets it may be of different importance than it is within Europe. In many developing economies the retail structure is changing in different ways than in Europe and the speed of competitive processes is less rapid. But the requirement on foreign retailers to become established quickly in order to achieve critical mass or to establish a market presence, for example in China, means that the ability to have a fast response is important for different reasons. Given the levels of international activity in 2005, however, it is likely that before 2010 the importance of fast competitive response will be as great in these emerging markets as it is in Europe.

Considering the five identified dimensions of competitive advantage that European retailers have sought in their domestic markets all five are transferable to some degree to their operations in markets in different cultural realms. In summary:

A focus on innovation	Yes – fully transferable
Use of and control of the brand	Yes – the brand can be built, but control will come later
Adapting to new markets	Partially transferable but of even more importance
Exploiting scale and economies	Yes – fully transferable
Operating at a faster rate	Yes – but may not be for different reasons in short term

These factors are internal to the firms and depend upon knowledge that resides in the firms involved. The five factors that have generated competitive advantage do not operate in isolation of each other. There is a potential for them to be managed by the retailer as mutually supportive. The management of the interactions, however, is likely to be different in markets with different cultural values.

THE IMPACTS OF THE TRANSFER OF SUCCESS FACTORS

Given that the strategies and dimensions of competitive advantage that have proved successful in Europe can be transferred to other markets it is valuable to explore what the impact will be on the new host markets. Dawson (2003) considered a

Table 9.1 *Illustrative interconnections between transferred success factors and types of impact in the host market*

Type of impact	Transferred success factor				
	Innovation	Branding	Adaption	Scale and scope	Fast response
Inter-industry channel relationships	New ICT technologies introduced into channel New logistics channels introduced Product development alliances with suppliers	Local sourcing of retail brand items Competitive effects on local brand producers	Local practices adopted in negotiations with suppliers	Application of extra volume discounts to local producers	Delivery to central distribution centres Requirements on local suppliers to produce to continuous orders
Intra-industry retail competitive relationships	More efficient merchandising and display methods E-retailing introduced	Multi-positions of retail branded items	Adjustments to formulae to reflect local consumer demand	Foreign firms take market share from local firms through large stores	Price changes using new technologies Fast fashion introductions
Institutional and macro-economic relationships	Providing industry standards Higher productivity of the sector and suppliers to foreign firms	Increase in retailer power in the economy	Adapting to local labour practices	Competition policy with more consideration of retail issues	New technology introductions Faster stock-turns as industry norm

Consumer relationships	Customer relationship management methods Loyalty cards	New price–quality positions for retail brands	Product development for the market New types of store with customer orientation	Lower prices with large-scale procurement	New forms of store-based promotions 'Freshness' of ranges
Parent firm managerial relationships	Creation of specialist teams to implement foreign development	Local suppliers for branded products through firm	Transfer of knowledge from foreign operation back to domestic and to other countries Parent firm's awareness of different social values	Profit contribution from larger operation Increased volume for standard products giving extra volume discounts	
Relationship to wider society	Introduction of new products to the market	Raising awareness of brand	Erosion of traditional social values and replacement by foreign values		Expectations change on what is available and when it is available

framework for the impacts of retail internationalization but did not relate these to the managerial processes that are likely to generate impacts and reactions. This framework considered vertical channel relationships and horizontal sectoral competitive relationships, impacts on consumers and on the firm involved, responses from institutions, particularly government, and, finally, the effects on established social and cultural values in the host market (see Chapter 2).

Meyer (2004: 259), in a broad ranging review of multinational enterprises in emerging markets, suggests that 'Multinational enterprises play a pivotal role in linking rich and poor countries, and in transmitting capital, knowledge, ideas and value systems across borders'. He further points to both positive and negative 'spillovers'. The framework he suggests for reviewing the effects of multinational enterprises is similar to that of Dawson except that by considering multinational firms in a generic way the impacts on consumers, that are so important for retail multinational enterprises, become subsumed into a list of 'social issues'. Using these two similar frameworks it is possible to consider the relationship between the key success factors that may be transferred and the area of impact. Table 9.1 is provided to illustrate this interconnection.

In considering the impacts of international retailers it is important to remember some of the differences inherent in retailing compared with manufacturing (see Chapter 1). Of particular note is the potential difference in the reason for internationalization. Retailers, in moving international, are seeking to gain profits from providing services to the local market. Whether development is organic or by acquisition the aim is to gain a share of the spending of local consumers. This may not be the case in manufacturing where a foreign acquisition may be made to obtain access to resources used elsewhere in the firm. Thus, for example, an acquisition may provide lower-cost components for the assembly or manufacture of an item in the home country or in another country. This idea of accessing resources to support other functions is absent as a rationale for retailers having an operational presence in a country. International activity by retailers to obtain resources for further use is, in effect, international sourcing which is a very different function from international operations and has a very different managerial structure (see Chapter 1).

A further difference between retailers and manufacturers is also relevant to the transferability of retail success factors. When the retail multinational enterprise has difficulties in the home market there is a tendency to withdraw from international activities. This has been the case many times, most notably in recent years with Marks & Spencer and Boots (see Chapter 6). For the manufacturer the reverse is often the case with problems in domestic operations often addressed by moving production internationally or by increasing export sales. Thus, a domestic market problem is addressed in very different ways by retailers and manufacturers.

In transferring the key success factors in retailing to foreign markets the different form of assets that are generated is an important part of the transfer

Table 9.2 *Contrasts between knowledge assets and physical assets in transfer of success factors*

	Knowledge assets	Physical assets
Publicness	Use by a firm does not prevent use by another	Use by a firm precludes simultaneous use by another
Depreciation	Does not wear out but may depreciate rapidly if copied	Wears out. May depreciate rapidly or slowly. Needs refreshing
Transfer costs	Difficult to establish because of tacit elements	Easy to establish
Property rights	Limited and fuzzy. Difficult to enforce	Clearer and often protected and enforced

Source: based on Teece (2000)

process. In general, knowledge assets are transferred in order to generate physical assets. The distinction between these two types of asset is important. While brand values, for example, are a knowledge asset, the items that carry the retailer brand name are physical assets. The brand values of a retailer are a knowledge asset which, although specific to the firm, may be copied and thus are a public good. The items are specific physical assets and so part of the intellectual property of the firm. Similarly, the knowledge asset is the formula that a retailer generates as the adaption to the market. The physical asset is the store that makes the formula concept operational. The retail firm owns the store but the formula is transparent and may be copied. An aim of the retailer in these cases is to include some elements, in the brand values or in the formula, that carry specific tacit knowledge exclusive to the firm. In retailing this is difficult given that the nature of retailing involves transparency of the operation to the customer. This distinction between knowledge asset and physical asset is important as success factors are transferred to foreign markets. Table 9.2 illustrates the major differences between knowledge assets and physical assets.

CONCLUSIONS

The focus of this book has been on the way that European-based retailers have developed a European management model to extend their operations internationally. Many aspects of this model appear to transfer successfully to other market cultures. An interesting question that results from this conclusion is whether there is a comparable American or Japanese model that would be as successful in its transference. While a Japanese model may be suited to transfers in Asia would it transfer to Europe as successfully as the European model is transferring to Asia? The difficulty in resolving this question is bound up with the apparent considerable success of the European model when applied to emerging economies rather than to highly competitive and structured retail economies outside Europe. The opportunities for Japanese retailers, should they wish to test their model in emergent markets outside Asia, are limited with Russia being the only obvious candidate.

Retail internationalization, although gaining considerably in importance, is still at a relatively early stage as a managerial process. In the current state of the process most of the transfers of knowledge are from domestic to foreign markets although there is some, albeit limited, reverse flow of information, knowledge and expertise. There is presently even less flow between foreign operations but, again, the beginnings of this are starting to be seen. As the process becomes more established in the next decade we are likely to see a greater transfer of knowledge within the retail firm and between the various national operating units. This will introduce new ideas and concepts of transferability. As retail internationalization becomes more mature as a strategy and process so the patterns of knowledge transfer will become increasingly complex.

Since the early 1990s the number of retailers operating internationally has increased substantially. The number of countries they have moved to has increased. The market shares that they command in the host countries have increased. In parallel with this unprecedented increase in international retail activity, the retail market in Europe and North America has become increasingly concentrated. A small group, less than about 300 firms, dominates the market across Europe. The increasing level of concentration in domestic markets and the increasing amount of international activity are related because it is frequently the same firms that are involved in both processes. The criteria of success that have been used to grow in the home market are being transferred to foreign markets. Often it is the emerging markets that are proving most attractive to these large European-based firms. While firms in emerging markets, increasingly, are making the consumer goods bought by consumers in Western Europe with consequences for the structure of the European manufacturing sector, European retailers are the new exporters of knowledge to the emerging economies, with consequences for the structure of the host country retailing sector. North American and Japanese retail firms are following a similar strategy. Retailing is fast becoming an export industry.

REFERENCES

Augier, M. and Vendelø, M. T. (1999) Networks, cognition and the management of tacit knowledge. *Journal of Knowledge Management,* 3(4): 252–261

Bauman, W. (1956) *Das Selbstbedienungssystem in den Migros-Genossenschaften.* (Zürich: Migros)

Bennett, R. H. III (1998) The importance of tacit knowledge in strategic deliberations and decisions. *Management Decision*, 36(9): 589–597

Boggis, F. D. (1966) The European Economic Community. In: B. Yamey (ed.) *Resale price maintenance* (London: Weidenfeld & Nicolson)

Costa, C. Gerstenberger, W., Lachner, J., Nassau, T., Täger, U. and Weitzel, G. (1997) *Structures and trends in the distributive trades in the European Union.* (Munich: Ifo Institut)

Davies, B. K. (1998) Applying evolutionary models to the retail sector. *International Review of Retail, Distribution and Consumer Research*, 8(2): 165–181

Dawson, J. (1984) Structural-spatial relationships in the spread of hypermarket retailing. In: E. Kaynak and R. Savitt (eds) *Comparative marketing systems.* (New York: Praeger) pp. 156–182

Dawson, J. (1999) The evolution and future structure of retailing in Europe. In: K. Jones (ed.) *The internationalisation of retailing in Europe.* (Toronto: Centre for Study of Commercial Activity) pp. 1–13

Dawson, J. (2003) Towards a model of the impacts on retail internationalisation. In: J. Dawson, M.Mukoyama, S. Chul Choi and R. Larke (eds) *The internationalisation of retailing in Asia.* (London: RoutledgeCurzon) pp. 189–209

Dawson, J. (2005) New cultures, new strategies, new formats and new relationships in European retailing: some implications for Asia. *Journal of Global Marketing*, 18(1/2): 73–97

Dickinson, R. E. (1951) *The West European city.* (London: Routledge & Kegan Paul)

Eurostat (2000) *Commerce 99 – proceedings of the seminar on distributive trades in Europe.* (Luxembourg: Eurostat)

Eurostat (2002) *Distributive Trades in Europe 1995–1999.* Data CD (Luxembourg: Eurostat)

Henksmeier, K. H. (1960) *The economic performance of self service in Europe.* (Paris: OEEC)

Jefferys, J. B. and Knee, D. (1962) *Retailing in Europe.* (London: Macmillan)

LSA (2004) Oscars de l'innovation. *Libre Service Actualite*, 16 September, 1873: 55–85

Meyer, K. E. (2004) Perspectives on multinational enterprises in emerging economies. *Journal of International Business Studies*, 35: 259–276

Mintel (2003) Cross border retailing. *European Retail Briefing*, 44: 5–11

Nisbett, R. E. (2003) *The geography of thought.* (New York: Free Press)

Nooteboom, B. and Six, F. (2003) (eds) *The trust process in organizations.* (Cheltenham: Edward Elgar)

Reynolds, Howard E., Dragun, D., Rosewell, B. and Ormerod, P. (2005) Assessing the productivity of the UK retail sector. *International Review of Retail, Distribution and Consumer Research*, 15(3): 237–280

Teece, D. J. (2000) *Managing intellectual capital.* (Oxford: Oxford University Press)

Thygesen, J. (1951) *Om Selvebetjening.* (Copenhagen: FDB)

Index

Pages containing relevant figures and tables are indicated in *italic* type.

eBooks – at www.eBookstore.tandf.co.uk

A library at your fingertips!

eBooks are electronic versions of printed books. You can store them on your PC/laptop or browse them online.

They have advantages for anyone needing rapid access to a wide variety of published, copyright information.

eBooks can help your research by enabling you to bookmark chapters, annotate text and use instant searches to find specific words or phrases. Several eBook files would fit on even a small laptop or PDA.

NEW: Save money by eSubscribing: cheap, online access to any eBook for as long as you need it.

Annual subscription packages

We now offer special low-cost bulk subscriptions to packages of eBooks in certain subject areas. These are available to libraries or to individuals.

For more information please contact webmaster.ebooks@tandf.co.uk

We're continually developing the eBook concept, so keep up to date by visiting the website.

www.eBookstore.tandf.co.uk

8015